# UNCONSCIOUS INFLUENCE

# UNCONSCIOUS INFLUENCE

## AND OTHER SERMONS

### HORACE BUSHNELL

Unconscious Influence, A Sermon Preached by Rev. Horace Bushnell, D.D., of the United States, Preached at Fetter Lane Chapel, on Sunday, March 29, 1846

This text was originally published in the United Kingdom in the year 1846
The text is in the public domain.
Modern Edition © 2023
Historical Sermons

The publishers have made all reasonable efforts to ensure this book is indeed in the Public Domain in any and all territories it has been published.

# INTRODUCTORY

# HORACE BUSHNELL, THE CITIZEN.
## PUBLISHED 1900
### EDWIN DOAK MEAD

When the Twentieth Century Club of Boston was organized, half dozen years ago, the first general meeting of the club was a memorial to Phillips Brooks, who had been interested in the idea of such a club in Boston and had purposed to become a member. At this memorial meeting there were addresses by Edward Everett Hale and Dr. Donald, Brooks's successor as rector of Trinity Church. In the course of his address, which was a fine analysis of Brooks's genius and influence, Dr. Donald observed that that influence did not lie in the contribution of anything distinctly original to American religious thought; Phillips Brooks's theology, he said, was "simply the theology of Bushnell."

This is substantially the truth; and it could be said of great numbers of the most thoughtful and influential men in the American pulpit to-day. In the religious turmoil and confusion of a generation ago, Bushnell was a great light and a positive guide, mediating to many minds a rational theology and a noble and satisfying method. Washington Gladden undoubtedly spoke for hundreds when he recently wrote: "I could not have remained in the ministry, an honest man, if it had not been for him. The time came, long before I saw him, when the legal or forensic theories of the Atonement were not true for me; if I had not found his 'God in Christ' and 'Christ in Theology,' I must have stopped preaching. Dr. Bushnell gave me a moral theology, and helped me to believe in the justice of God. If I have had any gospel to preach during the last thirty-five years, it is because he led me into the light and joy of it."

Horace Bushnell was certainly the most original and influential theologian in New England in this last half of the nineteenth century, save Theodore Parker alone. It is interesting to know that the two great thinkers knew each other personally. In 1843 — in which year also it is pleasant to read that Bushnell walked arm in arm with George Ripley of Brook Farm to hear Webster's Bunker Hill oration — he spent an evening with Theodore Parker, when they "went over the whole ground of theology together"; and Dr. Munger, who mentions the fact in his new biography of Bushnell, observes that it is safe to say that neither appealed to the "standards." Greatly as the two men differed in intellectual nature, manner, emphasis and conclusions, their community was far more impressive and important; they were fellow-workers in liberating New England religion from the tyranny of tradition and authority, and in helping it to the method of reason and nature. Bushnell, as Dr. Munger truly says, "questioned the prevailing orthodoxy at all points, — inspiration, regeneration, trinity, atonement, miracles." The character of his appeal to a higher court than that of any current definitions is well illustrated by the following passage from one of his controversial treatises: "I do peremptorily refuse to justify myself, as regards this matter of trinity, before any New England standard. We have no standard better than the residuary tritheistic compost, such as may be left us after we have cast away that which alone made the old historic doctrine of trinity possible. I know not whether you design to make a standard for me of this decadent and dilapidated orthodoxy of ours; but if you do, then I appeal to Cæsar; I even undertake to arraign your standard itself before the tribunal of history."

"Christian Culture," "The Vicarious Sacrifice," "God in Christ," "Christ and his Salvation," — each of these works bore in it a revolution for American religious thought and life. Epoch-making above all was the work on "Nature and the Supernatural." Some chapters of this great work differ from others in value, and much of it has been left behind, so far as concerns much more than detail, by the advancing thought of the last generation; but it is and will remain a monument to Bushnell's comprehensive and philosophic mind; and appearing as it did in the early days of the controversies over Darwinism, evolution and German criticism, it performed a unique service in what has become the most important realm of theology. Bushnell, as Dr. Munger well defines it, "did not deny a certain antithesis between nature and the supernatural; but he so defined. the latter that the two could be embraced in the one category of nature when viewed as the ascertained order of God in creation. The supernatural is simply the realm of freedom, and it is as natural as the physical realm of necessity. Thus he not only got rid of the traditional antinomy between them, but led the way into that conception of the relation of God to his world which more and more is taking possession of modern thought." The power of Bushnell was not so much in the new doctrines which he taught, although he was a prolific, radical and sweeping teacher of new doctrines, as in the new and inspiring spirit, the spirit of nature and of freedom, which he brought to every question. "He was," as Dr. Munger says, "the first theologian in New England to admit fully into his thought the modern sense of nature, as it is found in the literature of the century, and notably in Wordsworth and Coleridge. The secret of this movement was a spiritual interpretation of nature. It was a step in the evolution of human thought; and appearing first in literature, its natural point of entrance, it was surely to reach all forms of thought, as in time it will reach all forms of social life."

WE HAVE SPOKEN of Bushnell as one of the two most original and influential New England theologians in recent time. A certain critic has said that "the designation of a theologian cannot, in any technical sense at all events, be applied to him." Dr. Munger, noticing the word, says, "Whatever truth there may be in this remark lies in the fact that he was preëminently a preacher, and a preacher is seldom a technical theologian." It would certainly be interesting to know what a theologian is, if the great works of Bushnell which we have enumerated are not the works of a theologian. It is also interesting. to remember that few "technical theologians" have had a tithe of the influence upon religious and distinctly theological thought in our time that has been exerted by such minds as Emerson and Browning and Tennyson. It is true, however, as Dr. Munger says, that Bushnell was preëminently a preacher, if not the "ablest preacher of his day," certainly one of the very ablest, and that in him "the preacher absorbed the theologian and supplanted his methods." Professor George Adam Smith has said that Bushnell is the preacher's preacher, as Spenser is the poet's poet. His early sermon on "Every Man's Life a Plan of God" has been spoken of by one enthusiast as "one of the three greatest sermons ever preached," the other two named by this classifier being Canon Mozley's on "The Reversal of Human Judgments" and Phillips Brooks's "Gold and the Calf." Dr. Munger's judgment is: "No sermons have a better claim to be ranked in 'the literature of power,' and it may be expected that they will live on in the world of literature along with those of Bishop Butler, Mozley and Newman, with hardly less weight of matter, and with even deeper insight into the ways of the spirit, both of God and man. They are universal; and yet they especially reflect the New England mind as a combination of ideality, conscience and practicality."

WE WISH to consider Bushnell here as a representative of the New England mind, as one of its greatest and truest representatives in this half century, and that upon the side not theological or distinctly religious. We are all rejoicing in the new Life of Bushnell which has just been given us by Dr. Munger. There is no other man so well qualified as he to write such a book, not only by reason of his unusual knowledge of Bushnell's work and the religious conditions under which his life was lived, but much more by reason of peculiar intellectual and spiritual affinity. The work is a welcome and necessary complement to the "Life and Letters of Horace Bushnell" prepared by his daughters not many years after his death. Of that admirable biography Dr. Munger truly says: "Nothing more in the way of personal history could be desired; but it made no attempt to deal with his theological treatises in a critical and thorough way." His own book "owes its existence to the fact that no full and connected account of Dr. Bushnell's work as a theologian has yet been made." His book is properly entitled "Horace Bushnell, Preacher and Theologian." The earlier biography might properly have been entitled "Horace Bushnell, the Man." A third book yet remains to be written, to accomplish the adequate presentation of Dr. Bushnell's broad interests and far-reaching influence; and that book should be entitled "Horace Bushnell, the Citizen." It is true that Bushnell the man and Bushnell the preacher could not be treated. without attention to Bushnell the citizen. The vital and varied activity of Dr. Bushnell in social and civic things constantly appears in the early biography by his daughters, and is emphasized by Dr. Parker in his supplementary chapter to that work. Dr. Munger also does not fail to glance at it again and again; but the brief chapter, "Essays and Addresses," devoted expressly to what may be called Bushnell's secular work, is quite inadequate, if the volume were to be viewed as a general biography and not primarily and essentially as an account of Dr. Bushnell's work as a theologian.

A man could not indeed be so great a theologian as Dr. Bushnell was without being much more than a theologian. One who was himself an eminent theologian has well said. that "a theologian must needs have. heard the voice of his own generation," and that "theology stagnates when it is cut off from present life." Dr. Bushnell himself, speaking of the true training and scholarship for the preacher, says that such scholarship "needs to be universal; to be out in God's universe; that is, to see and study and know everything, books and men and the whole work of God, from the stars downward; to have a sharp observation of war and peace and trade; of animals and trees and atoms; of the weather and the evanescent smells of the creations; to have bored into society in all its grades and meanings, its manners, passions, prejudices and times; so that, as the study goes on, the soul will be getting full of laws, images, analogies and facts, and drawing out all subtlest threads of import to be its interpreters when the preaching work requires. Of what use is it to know the German, when we do not know the human,— or Hebrew points, when we do not. know at all the points of our wonderfully punctuated humanity?" But one might say all this with fair fidelity of many a preacher, and yet not describe Dr. Bushnell in his varied capacities and creativeness. Dr. Bartol, who was Bushnell's dear friend for so many years, and whose correspondence with Bushnell fills some of the most interesting pages of Dr. Munger's book, wrote to Mrs. Bushnell after his death: "He had it in him to be an artist, architect, road-builder and city-builder, as well as scholar; and well is your Hartford park called by his name." Bishop Clark, who was the rector of a church in Hartford for several years during Bushnell's pastorate, wrote of the things of which one might have heard him chatting in the bookstore, with all sorts of people, — "the news of the day, the doings of public men, the affairs of the city, in which he took especial interest, politics, farming, mechanics, inventions, books." "Those who know him only by his theological writings," said Bishop Clark, "have no conception of the range of his mind and the variety of subjects that he had investigated. He was skilled in mechanics, and has given the world. some inventions of his own. The house in which I once lived was warmed by a furnace which he devised, when such domestic improvements were comparatively new. He could plan a house or lay out a park or drain a city better than many of our experts. He was as much at home in talking with the rough guides of the Adirondacks as he was in discussing metaphysics with theologians in council. If he had been a medical man, he would have struck at the roots of disease and discovered remedies as yet unknown. If he had gone into civil life, he would have taught our public men some lessons in political economy which they greatly need to know." Dr. Munger, speaking especially of Bushnell's political essays, says. "Many of these essays reveal Bushnell as a publicist of the first order. No man of his day handled those questions of state that involved the moral sense of the people with such breadth of view and such fidelity, both to the nation and to conscience, as are displayed in many a sermon and address from 1837 to the very end of his life."

WITH A POLITICAL OUTLOOK as broad always as the nation and the world, Dr. Bushnell's was emphatically a New England nature and a New England mind. He found himself in the right place when he welled up to consciousness in the New England country, when he went for his book learning to Yale College, and when as the place for his life-work he took a Hartford pulpit.

His youth was the best kind of a New England youth, which is the best. youth in the world, a genuine "age of homespun." He was born in precisely that part of Connecticut in which one would choose to be born if he is to be born in Connecticut, the neighborhood of Litchfield, with its beautiful landscapes and its strong traditions. In one place and another in this historic region he lived until he was twenty-one years of age, working on the farm and supplementing this work by wool-carding and cloth-dressing, after the manner of the time. "There was always something for the smallest to do, — errands to run, berries to pick, weeds to pull, earnings all for the common property, in which he thus begins to be a stockholder." "There is nothing in those early days," he tells us himself, "that I remember with more zest than that I did the full work of a man for at least five years before the manly age, — this, too, under no eight-hour law of protective delicacy, but holding fast the astronomic ordinance in a service of from thirteen to fourteen hours." It was a life well calculated to make a young man self-reliant, practical and "shifty"; and the hills and valleys, lakes and brooks, forests and fields, amid which his life was lived, were the best school for the lover of nature that he was. "The homestead was on the slope of a broad-backed hill that stretched away for a mile to the summit, on which stood the only church in the town. The house was one of those which marked the best period of rural architecture in New England, — roomy, cheerful and with an indefinable air of dignity, simplicity and comfort, — character, in brief, in the terms of architecture."

Through all was the atmosphere of a strong and beautiful religion, a religion far more catholic and genial than that common in many Connecticut households at the beginning of the century. The father had imbibed Arminian views, the mother had been reared in the Episcopal Church; and when both became members of the Congregational Church, it was with this background and with the strict Calvinism of the time and place tempered in them by these influences. There was music and love in that Litchfield county home, there was hard work and honest play, there was truth, — "I do not remember ever hearing any one of the children accused of untruth," — there was a noble mother with ambitions for a liberal education and life more abundant for the children. It was a household which, as the world counts, belonged to a higher class than that of Burna's cotter; yet as we read of its life and spirit, it is the words of Burns that well up to speak for the feeling of our hearts. From scenes like this, we feel, New England's grandeur springs!

IF THERE BE a prose counterpart to "The Cotter's Saturday Night" and "Snow Bound," it is "The Age of Homespun." This great address, given as a sermon at the centennial celebration of Litchfield county in 1851, and now one of our New England classics, Dr. Munger believes will "probably be longer remembered and oftener quoted than any other writing of Bushnell, because it is so true a picture of rural New England life in the early part of the century. [Note 1: "The Age of Homespun," was reprinted in the New England Magazine for January, 1898.] It is an outburst of grateful recollection of his early life, — pathetic, humorous, photographic in its accuracy, keen in its analysis, reverent and noble in its tone, revealing not more the period it describes than the man himself." There is not in our New England literature any other work which shows with such true sympathy and understanding, such sturdiness and tenderness and insight, the character of the people of the old New England country and the spirit which has created what is best and most enduring in New England and in the nation. It treats of the day before the factory day, the day when the cloth upon men's backs was made not by water and steam power, but by "mother and daughter power." this fine passage upon the village graveyard, he gives the eloquent and didactic census of the real forces which made New England:

"Here lie the sturdy kings of Homespun, who climbed among these hills, with their axes, to cut away room for their cabins and for family prayers, and so for the good future to come. Here lie their sons, who foddered their cattle on the snows and built stone fence, while the corn was sprouting in the hills, getting ready in that way to send a boy or two to college. Here lie the good housewives, that made coats every year, like Hannah, for their children's bodies, and lined their memory with catechism; here the millers that took honest toll of the rye; the smiths and coopers that superintended two hands and got a little revenue of honest bread and schooling from their joint stock of two-handed investment; here the district committees and schoolmistresses, society founders and church deacons, and withal a great many sensible, wise-headed men. who read the weekly newspaper, loved George Washington and their country, and had never a thought of going to the General Assembly. Who they are, by name, we cannot tell — no matter who they are — we should be none the wiser if we could name them, they themselves none the more honorable."

We do not know of any other tribute equal to that here to the home life in the New England country a century ago, — a life which continued to a far later time, and which in its main and noblest features is, thank God, not yet extinct upon our hills and in a hundred little towns. We do not know of any more memorable tribute to the district school, — "those little primitive universities of homespun, where your mind was born." We do not know of any other tribute so impressive to the stern old New England religion, nor any other picture so touching or so just of the Sab. bath assemblage and the men of the New England churches.

"True, there was a rigor in their piety, a want of gentle feeling; their Christian graces were cast-iron shapes, answering with a hard metallic ring. But they stood the rough wear of life none the less durably for the excessive hardness of their temperament, kept their families and communities none the less truly, though it may be less benignly, under the sense of God and religion. If we find something to modify or soften in their over-rigid notions of Christian living, it is yet something to know that what we are they have made us, and that when we have done better for the ages that come after us, we shall have a more certain right to blame their austerities."

Most noteworthy and most noble is his fine defence of these strong men and women of the New England country, forced as they were to their close economies, from the charge of meanness, which has so often and so carelessly been made against them. It is a defence throbbing with tender reverence for those whom his own life had touched so intimately.

"When the hard, wiry-looking patriarch of homespun, for example, sets off for Hartford, or Bridgeport, to exchange the little surplus of his year's production, carrying his provision with him and the fodder of his team, and taking his boy along to show him the great world, you may laugh at the simplicity, or pity, if you will, the sordid look of the picture; but, five or ten years hence, this boy will probably enough be found in college, digging out the cent's worths of his father's money in hard study; and some twenty years later he will be returning in his honors, as the celebrated judge, or governor, or senator and public orator, from some one of the great states of the republic, to bless the sight once more of that venerated pair who shaped his beginnings and planted the small seed of his future success. Small seeds, you may have thought, of meanness; but now they have grown up and blossomed into a large-minded life, a generous public devotion, and a free benevolence to mankind."

We have quoted thus largely from this noble address, because it reveals like nothing else the background and the shaping forces of this great New England life, and because it strikes again and again the real key-note of his gospel of citizenship. That gospel was a gospel of virtue, of morality, of self-reliance and of work, of simplicity, high-mindedness, fraternity and public spirit, of a politics commanded and surcharged with religion, a new Puritanism. There was no one of his political addresses in which the closing words of "The Age of Homespun" would not somewhere have found proper place.

"Your condition will hereafter be softened, and your comforts multiplied. Let your culture be as much advanced. But let no delicate spirit that despises work grow up in your sons and daughters. Make these rocky hills smooth their faces and smile under your industry. Let no absurd ambition tempt you to imitate the manners of the great world of fashion, and rob you thus of the respect and dignity that pertain to manners properly your own. Maintain, above all, your religious exactness. Think what is true, and then respect yourselves in living exactly what you think. Fear God and keep his commandments, as your godly fathers and mothers did before you, and found to be the beginning of wisdom."

As Bushnell was a warm lover of his own Litchfield county, so was he a supremely loyal son of his own state; and as "The Age of Homespun" is the most noteworthy literary tribute to the life and people of his boyhood home, so is his "Historical Estimate" of Connecticut, an address delivered before the legislature of the state, it may be observed, the same summer that the sermon was given at Litchfield, the most significant review which has ever been written of the noteworthy and noble things for which Connecticut has stood. In all the circles of his patriotism, Bushnell's heart beat strongly. He loved his native place, he loved his city of Hartford, he loved Connecticut, he loved America, and he loved the world; and his patriotism in each narrower circle was food and inspiration for that in the wider and the wider still. "The man who does not love and honor the state in which he and his children are born has no heart in his bosom," he says at the beginning of his "Historical Estimate;" and this eloquent survey of the history of Connecticut is indeed the tribute of a lover. It is the tribute of the most just and intelligent lover. Nothing perhaps reveals more truly Bushnell's splendid scholarship; and after we have followed him in his careful survey of the services of Hooker, Davenport, the younger Winthrop and the other founders of Connecticut, and the men of the period of the Revolution and the Constitutional Convention, we are not disposed in any way to temper his enthusiastic tributes. His study of the strong local independence of the little Connecticut towns has a peculiar value. We discussed in these pages some months ago the splendid opportunities which our American history offers to the American painter; and we spoke of several noteworthy hints and outlines of particular subjects given by various imaginative writers. Bushnell gives such a hint in his "Historical Estimate," and it is such a striking picture which he suggests that we must quote the passage. It is where he pictures the return of Mason with his little Puritan legion to Hartford, after the Pequot war, when the colony made him its general-in-chief, and Hooker, in presence of the people, delivered him his commission.

"Here is a scene for the painter of some future day — I see it even now before me. In the distance and behind the huts of Hartford waves the signal flag by which the town watch is to give notice of enemies. In the foreground stands the tall, swart form of the soldier in his armor; and before him, in sacred, apostolic majesty, the manly Hooker. Haynes and Hopkins, with the legislature and the hardy, toilworn settlers and their wives and daughters, are gathered round them in close order, gazing with moistened eyes at the hand which lifts the open commission to God, and listening to the fervent prayer that the God of Israel will endue his servant, as heretofore, with courage and counsel to lead them in the days of their future peril. True there is nothing classic in this scene; this is no crown bestowed at the Olympic games, or at a Roman triumph; and yet there is a severe, primitive sublimity in the picture, that will sometime be invested with feelings of the deepest reverence."

The Massachusetts man may feel that the space which Bushnell gives to arguing that Putnam and not Prescott was the commander at Bunker Hill is disproportionate; but he does not grudge any word of praise for Putnam any more than he grudges the warm words to Wooster, Wolcott, Ledyard and Brother Jonathan. It is not with Connecticut statesmen and warriors only that this "Historical Estimate" concerns itself; the Connecticut clergy and poets, inventors and educators, have due honor, — and the names of these are many and great. The occasion of the address was the inauguration of the State Normal School at New Britain, and therefore, as was fitting, the educational institutions of Connecticut, from Yale College to the district schools of "a little obscure parish in Litchfield county," whose remarkable contributions to the intellectual life of the nation he enumerated with joy and pride, were given special prominence.

Connecticut, he said, "is to find her first and noblest interest, apart from religion, in the full and perfect education of her sons and daughters." No other New England state can point to such a historical estimate as Dr. Bushnell has made of Connecticut in this glowing essay; and the history as it rises to view under his loving pen is seen to be what he pronounces it, — "a history of practical greatness and true honor; illustrious in its beginning; serious and thoughtful in its progress; dispensing intelligence, without the rewards of fame; heroic for the right, instigated by no hope of applause; independent, as not knowing how to be otherwise; adorned with names of wisdom and greatness, fit to be revered as long as true excellence may have a place in the reverence of mankind."

IT WAS MOST fitting that Connecticut should call Dr. Bushnell to give the address before her legislature upon the occasion of the opening of her State Normal School. His services for the cause of education altogether were very great. It would be interesting to dwell upon his relations to Yale College, from his student days there to the day of his death. It was before the alumni of Yale College that he delivered, in 1843, his oration upon "The Growth of Law," to which we shall presently refer in speaking of his conspicuous services for the cause of internationalism and the organization of the world. It was before the alumni of Yale College that he delivered, in 1865, at the commemorative celebration in honor of those of the alumni who fell in the war of the rebellion his great oration upon "Our Obligations to the Dead." He led his class at Yale, we read, in athletic sports, as well as on the intellectual side; and he left in the college an enduring monument in the Beethoven Society, which he organized in order to lift the standard of the music in the chapel. Bushnell, someone has written, was "musically organized;" and his discourse on "Religious Music," which was delivered before this Beethoven Society at the opening of a new organ — the first used in the college — is a discourse which should be read and honored in every school of music, as its author's luminous and inspiring essay upon "Building Eras in Religion" should be read by every student and teacher of architecture. As we turn the pages of his volumes, we note that it was before various Yale bodies that many of his addresses were delivered; and there were addresses there delivered which have not been reprinted. As a frequent preacher in the college chapel, he was a perennial influence at Yale; and as we write the word, an old Yale student, now the head of one of our great educational institutions, enters our room to tell us how for him, as for so many others, those sermons were the beginning of the real life of thought.

It was at New Haven, before the Sheffield Scientific School, at Commencement in 1870, that Bushnell gave his address upon "The New Education," which is one of the warmest and wisest welcomes of the new scientific tendencies in our schools and universities which can be found in the books. Like every word of Bushnell's, this word is strong and satisfying because it is comprehensive and proportionate. Nowhere are the defects of the old academic method more frankly pointed out; nowhere are the usefulness and need of scientific training more enthusiastically emphasized. So far from sharing the jealousies of the new scientific movement in education, which was so common in religious circles thirty years ago, Bushnell took "a most particular pleasure in the advocacy of a way of education specially devoted to the applications of science, because of the conviction I feel that our schools of application will be the best and most certain rectifiers possible of the unbelieving tendencies of science itself." So far from sharing the apprehension which was then common among academic folk, that the new scientific enthusiasm was a menace to literary and humanistic culture, he confidently prophesied precisely the results which have followed. Replying to the general charge that in his criticism of the old and his hospitality to the new he was willing to take down the honors of the fuller and more fertilizing courses, he exclaimed:

"Far from it. I accept no such construction as that. I can think of it only as absurd. No, a true classic culture can never be antiquated; and if I seem to raise a crusade for the shorter methods of applied science, I do it in the clear understanding that such shorter methods are wanted, and that I am doing nothing against, but everything for the advancement of the old methods. For if we push the new education to its utmost efficiency and far enough to practically fill the whole tier of life for which it is organized, making every walk of industry and enterprise, every farmhouse, factory, mine, trade, road, every shop of handicraft, every humblest toil, even down to the knife-grinder's lathe and fisherman's barrow, to feel its quickening touch of intelligence, the classic culture will only be as much more largely sought, and its courses as much more frequented, as the general under-lift of mind is higher than it was before."

IT WAS NOT, however, solely nor indeed chiefly to the university that Bushnell addressed his interest and effort as an educational thinker. We know of no words of his upon the higher education — and we think of many earnest ones — so earnest or so pregnant as those upon the common school. If we were to commend one of his educational addresses above all others to the American people today, it would be that upon "Common Schools." He insists upon the fundamental importance of the common school as "a great American institution; one that has its beginnings with our history itself; one that is inseparably joined to the fortunes of the republic; and one that can never wax old or be discontinued in its rights and reasons till the pillars of the State are themselves cloven down forever." He sees clearly the inseparableness of democracy and public education. He would have said, as we said last month in these pages, that *education* is simply another way of spelling *democracy*. The common school, he said, "is an integral part of the civil order." "An application against common schools is an application for the dismemberment and reorganization of the civil order of the State." The true schools for our American democracy, the schools which alone can make for the perpetuity and integrity of a really democratic society and democratic institutions, he emphasizes most strongly and with impressive detail, must be public and common, "in just the same sense that all the laws are common; so that the experience of families and of children under them shall be an experience of the great republican rule of majorities; an exercise for majorities of obedience to fixed statutes, and of moderation and impartial respect to the rights and feelings of minorities; an exercise for minorities of patience and of loyal assent to the will of majorities; a schooling, in that manner, which begins at the earliest moment possible, in the rules of American law and the duties of an American citizen." In all the discussions of the parochial school question which have followed in the half century, few really important principles have been laid down which are not clearly outlined in this address by Bushnell, in 1853. He points out with careful kindness what the ways and places are for toleration and for generous hospitality; but he shows with a firmness and common sense equally great what the imperatives of a republic are upon all citizens alike, whatever their religion. The danger to the American public school from religious parochialism of any kind is perhaps passing by. The danger from social parochialisms of many kinds is today greater; and Bushnell's words upon this point are so serious and important that we quote the passage in its entirety, as something upon which many men and women of wealth and high social position in our American. cities should solemnly ponder. We do not remember any word upon this subject so impressive as this, save one, the word of Phillips Brooks in his great address before the Boston Latin School.

"This great institution of common schools is not only a part of the state, but is imperiously wanted as such, for the common training of so many classes and conditions of people. There needs to be some place where, in early childhood, they may be brought together and made acquainted with each other; thus to wear away the sense of distance, otherwise certain to become an established animosity of orders; to form friendships; to be exercised together on a common footing of ingenuous rivalry; the children of the rich to feel the power and do honor to the struggles of merit in the lowly, when it rises above them; the children of the poor to learn the force of merit and feel the benign encouragement yielded by its blameless victories. Indeed, no child can be said to be well trained, especially no male child, who has not met the people as they are, above him or below, in the seatings, plays and studies of the common school. Without this he can never be a fully qualified citizen, or prepared to act his part wisely as a citizen. Confined to a select school, where only the children of wealth and distinction are gathered, he will not know the merit there is in the real virtues of the poor, or the power that slumbers in their talent. He will take his better dress as a token of his better quality, look down upon the children of the lowly with an educated contempt, prepare to take on lofty airs of confidence and presumption afterward; finally, to make the discovery when it is too late that poverty has been the sturdy nurse of talent in some unhonored youth who comes up to affront him by an equal, or mortify and crush him by an overmastering, force. So also the children of the poor and lowly, if they should be privately educated in some inferior degree by the honest and faithful exertion of their parents, secreted, as it were, in some back alley or obscure corner of the town, will either grow up in a fierce, inbred hatred of the wealthier classes, or else in a mind cowed by undue modesty, as being of another and inferior quality, unable therefore to fight the great battle of life hopefully, and counting it a kind of presumption to think that they can force their way upward, even by merit itself. Without common schools, the disadvantage falls both ways in about equal degrees, and the disadvantage that accrues to the state, in the loss of so much character and so many cross ties of mutual respect and generous appreciation, e embittering so fatally of all outward distinctions, and the propagation of so many misunderstandings, righted only by the immense public mischiefs that follow. — this, I say, is greater even than the disadvantages accruing to the classes themselves; a disadvantage that weakens immensely the security of the state and even of its liberties. Indeed, I seriously doubt whether any system of popular government can stand the shock, for any length of time, of that fierce animosity that is certain to be gendered where the children are trained up wholly in their classes, and never brought together to feel, understand, appreciate and respect each other, on the common footing of merit and of native talent, in a common school. Falling back thus on the test of merit and of native force, at an early period of life, moderates immensely their valuation of mere conventionalities and of the accidents of fortune, and puts them in a way of deference that is genuine as well as necessary to their common peace in the state. Common schools are nurseries thus of a free republic; private schools, of factions, cabals, agrarian laws and contests of force. Therefore, I say, we must have common schools; they are American, indispensable to our American institutions, and must not be yielded for any consideration smaller than the price of our liberties."

IN CONNECTION with the subject of Dr. Bushnell's interest in education, his year in California constituted one of the most significant chapters of his life. Here he appears preeminently as the great citizen and as a distinct and shaping force in American education. This California episode receives but passing mention in Dr. Munger's book. The earlier biography devotes a chapter to it, occupied almost entirely by Bushnell's letters describing his California life; but the great purport of that life to the new Pacific state and its intellectual interests has no adequate statement. We have said that a special book is needed in America upon "Horace Bushnell, the Citizen." We commend to some bright and reverent historical student in the University of California the preparation of a special monograph upon "Horace Bushnell in California." In such a volume should be reprinted the three California addresses which have not been collected in any of the volumes of Bushnell's works, but exist, almost inaccessible, only in pamphlet form: "Society and Religion: a Sermon for California," delivered at the installation of the pastor of the First Congregational Church of San Francisco, in 1856, a sermon which may be compared, in its service for California, with John Cotton's "God's Promise to His Plantation," in its service for the colony of Massachusetts Bay; the appeal for an endowment for the new University of California, issued by Bushnell in 1857; and the article upon "The Characteristics and Prospects of California," published originally in the *New Englander* and then circulated in pamphlet form in 1858. We know of no other description of California and no forecast of its future in that early day so interesting or so valuable as this. It ranks with Manasseh Cutler's "Description of Ohio" in 1787. Horace Bushnell was indeed California's Manasseh Cutler; and like Manasseh Cutler his chief interests for the new world with whose opening he was concerned were not material, but political, religious and educational. His effort was to make California know at the beginning that "more to her than gold or grain" should be "the cunning hand and cultured brain." "The doing world of California," he said in his appeal for an endowment for the new university, "will be right when there is a right thinking world of California prepared, before the doing, to shape it." "It is not," he said, "in the gold, nor the wheat, nor the cattle on a thousand hills, that California is to find, after all, its richest wealth and its noblest honors; but it is in the sons she trains up and consecrates to religion, as the anointed prophets and preachers of God's truth, her great orators of every name and field, her statesmen, her works of art and genius, the voices of song that pour out their eternal music from her hills. Her pride is not that wanting a Shakespeare or a Bacon or an Edwards, she sent for him; but that having begotten and made him, he is hers."

It is indeed a memorable thing that it should have been this great New England Puritan who was the animating spirit in so high degree in the founding of the great university which looks forth through the Golden Gate; that he should have selected its unrivalled site and should have been invited to become its first president. "If I can get a university on its feet, or only the nest egg laid, before I return," he wrote from San Francisco to his Hartford friends, just before he went back to them, "I shall not have come to this new world in vain." Of all the interesting things in his letters from California, there are none so interesting as those in which he tells of his explorations for the best site for the university and discusses the considerations for and against his acceptance of the presidency. His sense of obligation to his faithful Hartford flock was the motive which finally determined him, and in New England, where his life began, it ended; but surely no memory should be held in higher honor in California and in its university than that of Bushnell.

When the trustees of the new university asked themselves by what name they should call the place where it was to be seated, their president, Frederick Billings, from Vermont, with that splendid idealism which often marks the businessman, said:

"Call it Berkeley. A century ago the great English philosopher published his famous verses upon the planting of the arts and sciences in America. He entertained high hopes of the future of learning and culture here. So deeply did he feel the importance of making the spiritualities instead of the materialities control this great new world, that he came here to give his own life to the work. He went home thwarted and disappointed. Let us here, on the shore of the Pacific, help to realize his dream. The course of the empire of knowledge can take its way no farther westward on the continent than this place. Let the place be given gratefully and reverently his name."

And Berkely is its name. In the splendid plans for the rebuilding and extension of the great university, of which just now we hear so much, some place should certainly be found, and that a central and impressive place, for a statue of the great bishop; and beside it should rise a statue of Horace Bushnell. They would be joined fittingly, not only because of the relation of their names and influences to this great seat of learning, but because they stand alike for that public spirit, that devotion to truth. and to humanity, and that high idealism, which we trust will ever there be native. Could the mouths of both men be opened there, they would unite in one prophecy and one prayer:

"In happy climes, the seat of innocence,
   Where nature guides and virtue rules;
Where men shall not impose for truth and sense
   The pedantry of courts and schools;—
"There shall be sung another golden age,
   The rise of empire and of arts,
The good and great inspiring epic page,
   The wisest heads and noblest hearts."

If the thought and learning of America command such an outlook through the Golden Gate upon the great new life and new duties that confront and invite the republic in the Pacific as would satisfy the eye and conscience of Berkeley and of Bushnell, then indeed will that life be secure and true; then will the nation be safe from every infidelity and every shame.

IN SELECTING the site and planning the grounds for a new university, Bushnell was exercising one of his most conspicuous and characteristic talents and indulging one of his dearest enthusiasms. As Dr. Munger says, "he was a born engineer, always laying out roads and building parks and finding the best paths for railways among the hills." "It is characteristic of him," says Dr. Munger in another place, speaking of his religious thought, "that all his leading contentions had their genesis early in his career and were almost never absent from his thoughts." What was true of him as a theologian was true of him as an engineer and landscape architect; he was these from his very boyhood. His daughter writes: "He saw twice as much as most people do out of doors, took a mental survey of all land surfaces, and kept in his head a complete map of the physical geography of every place with which he was acquainted. He knew the leaf and bark of every tree and shrub that grows in New England; estimated the water power of every stream he crossed; knew where all the springs were, and how they could be made available; engineered roads and railroads; laid out, in imagination, parks, cemeteries and private places; noted the laying of every bit of stone wall." Referring to his own boasted piece of stone wall at the old home in Litchfield county, as firm after fifty. years as when he laid it, she remarks that it is doubtful whether he was ever as well satisfied with any of his writings as he was with that stone wall. Dr. Bartol writes: "In our many walks in Boston, nothing in streets or buildings, Common or Public Garden, but was caught by his eye and had improvements suggested from his thought;" and Dr. Gladden, writing of his visit to North Adams, says: "He was up early in the summer mornings and out for a walk; once when he came in he said, 'I have found the place for your park,' and exhorted me to go to work at once and get the town to secure the site. It was indeed the very place for a park, and if the thriving city of North Adams could have it now, it would be a boon to her people; but my faith was not strong enough, and North Adams lacks its Bushnell Park." His house at Hartford was built from his own plans. "In selecting the lot he provided for two things, a garden and an open view of the country, ending in distant hills. Each was a necessity to him, — the manifold life of growing things and the distant horizon."

This engineering enthusiasm of his had large scope in California. In the section devoted to his California life, Dr. Munger says: "The variety of his studies and interests, especially in engineering and topography, reminds one of Da Vinci. If Bushnell had a passion outside of theology, it was for roads, and he closely connected the two; the new country afforded him a wide field for each. He was a critic of all he saw with the eye, and a builder in imagination of such as were needed or were possible. He foresaw a railroad across the continent — hardly dreamed of as yet — and, having examined all possible routes of entrance into San Francisco, named the one that was finally chosen." In this connection there is a passage in his remarkable essay upon "City Plans" which should be remembered. After showing how Sacramento and Marysville, which are actually set below high-water mark, could both at the distance of hardly a mile have secured ample high ground, equally convenient, he, notices the remarkable combination of disadvantages in San Francisco itself, which might all have been avoided by choosing another site.

"There was just over the bay, a few miles to the north, at a little hamlet called San Pablo, a grand natural city plat about five miles square, graded handsomely down to the bay, supplied on its upper edge with the very best water breaking out of a gorge in the hills, having straight path out to sea for ships, among islands of rock easily defended, and a fair open sweep for railroad connections, north, east and south; and behind the rock summit on its mid-front a natural dock-ground two miles long, partly covered by the tides even now, and open to the deep water at both ends. In short, there was never in the world such a site for a magnificent commercial city; but, alas, the city is fixed elsewhere by the mere chance landing of adventure, and a change is forever impossible! What an illustration of the immense or even literally unspeakable importance of the results that are sometimes pending on the right location of a city!"

It is a fair thing for San Francisco to consider, even at this late day, in view of the fact that she is likely to become one of the great cities of the world, whether it would not be profitable for her now boldly to act upon Bushnell's wisdom, and prove that to men of adequate vision and adequate energy no change which is commendable is too great to be impossible.

IT WAS JUST before his visit to California that Bushnell threw himself into the work of securing a public park in his own city of Hartford. This park, which bears his name, was, as we have shown, the fruit of a lifelong passion. He early noticed, in the very centre of the city, a great tract that had never been put to use and was really a deformity; and after years of effort he carried ut his plan of transforming this into the beautiful Hartford park which we know, crowned by the State Capitol. The action of the city government, recognizing that this public park was due to his foresight and persistence and naming it by his name, was announced to him on his last day of conscious life. Speaking of this park, upon whose border stands Bushnell's own church, Dr. Parker, his fellow Hartford minister, has well written: "The entire scene, one of the fairest in our land, — the park, the church, the capitol, — is Dr. Bushnell's lasting memorial. *Si quaeris monumentum, circumspice.*" Rev. Joseph Twichell, another Hartford friend and companion, has said that "Bushnell lies back of all that is best in the city. He quickened the men who have made Hartford what it is." And yet another, Rev. N. H. Egleston, writes:

"What interest of Hartford is not today indebted to him? Do we speak of schools? The fathers of those who are now enjoying our unsurpassed appliances for education know well that the city is indebted to no one more than to Dr. Bushnell for the new impulse which lifted its schools to their present grade of excellence. Do we speak of taste and culture? Who has been a nobler example and illustration of both, or who has by his just criticism and various instructions so aided in their development? If we turn to the business interests of the city, who of its older residents does not remember how, years ago, at a time when the impression had become prevalent that Hartford had reached its growth, that it was declining, while other cities were outstripping it, Dr. Bushnell lifted himself up in that crisis and asserted not only the ability but the duty of the city to prosper, and how he woke the city to new life, and gave an impulse which has been felt to this day? Hartford feels him to-day everywhere. It may be doubted whether another instance in our own history is to be found of a man impressing himself in so many ways and with such force upon a place of such size and importance as this, Hartford is largely what he has made it."

The reference to Bushnell's word in Hartford's business crisis is to his sermon, "Prosperity our Duty," preached in 1847, a sermon not included, we think, in any of Bushnell's volumes, but which shall be included in the monograph upon "Horace Bushnell and Hartford," which some young Hartford scholar will someday, we trust, place in the library. In that volume will also be reprinted Bushnell's "History of the Hartford Park," published in 1869 in *Hearth and Home*.

Most comprehensive and most valuable of Bushnell's writings as an engineer is the essay, "City Plans," prepared for the Public Improvement Society of Hartford, but for reasons of health never delivered. In our own time there are many men alive to the great question of public beauty, to the idea of a city as a unit and a true work of art, to the principles of a good city plan, the utilizing of historical association, the conditions of health, the requisites to fine effect; but when Bushnell wrote his essay upon "City Plans," there were few such men. In this field, as in so many others, Bushnell was a prophet.

"There is wanted in this field," he wrote, "a new profession, specially prepared by studies that belong to the special subject matter. If a city as a mere property concern is to involve amounts of capital greater than a dozen or even a hundred railroads, why, as a mere question of interest, should it be left to the misbegotten planning of some operator totally disqualified? We want a city-planning profession, as truly as an architectural, house-planning profession. Every new village, town, city, ought to be contrived as a work of art, and prepared for the new age of ornament to come."

Of interest as an illustration of this engineering eye of his, as well as of his sense of the new life dawning for the world through the wonderful new opportunities of travel and communication, is his striking address upon "The Day of Roads;" and not remote in its interest is that great essay on "Building Eras in Religion," which gives its name to one of his volumes. Few of his essays have greater sweep than this, or illustrate more impressively his æsthetic mind and his constructive imagination. His interpretation of the spirit which reared the Jewish Temple and the spirit of the cathedral age is full of fine insight; but more stimulating is his forward glance to the building era which will come when the intellectual synthesis to which the world is now advancing is complete. The moral and spiritual regeneration of the world which he foresees "is going to require a great building age for its uses;" and he even ventures upon a program in large outline of this architecture of the new dispensation. "I know not anything that will fire us with higher thoughts and tone our energies for a loftier key than to see just what our prophets saw with so great triumph, glorious ages of building for God, such as never were beheld before; a city of God, or it may be many, complete in all grandeur and beauty, and representing fitly the great ideas and glorious populations and high creative powers of a universal Christian age." It is an essay for the American architect as well as for the religious man to study. What might we not hope, could we have an architectural genius fertilized by Bushnell's religious vision in as high degree as Bushnell's religious mind was enriched by his architectural taste and talent!

THE VOLUME ENTITLED "Moral Uses of Dark Things" contains two essays, that upon "Bad Government" and that upon "The Conditions of Solidarity," which must not be neglected by the student of Bushnell as a citizen, the latter being a noteworthy consideration of the organic nature of human society, upon which the whole tendency of thought since Bushnell's time has led us to lay even greater emphasis. In the volume of "Sermons on Living Subjects" is a noble sermon on "How to be a Christian in Trade," which touches many vital considerations in our present business and social life. But for the most part the writings which represent Bushnell the citizen are collected in the two volumes, "Building Eras in Religion" and "Work and Play." These volumes should lie upon the table in every American home. They should have place especially in the library of every young American student who is about to go out as an influence in our political and intellectual life, charged with the duty of keeping the republic true to the great ideals of its founders and to the moral imperative listened to so reverently and proclaimed with such power by the author of these pulsating pages. Few men in America have insisted more strenuously upon lifting political questions out of the region of temporary expediency into that of morals. The conflict with slavery gave him occasion enough to emphasize this principle. His article in the *Christian Freeman* in 1844, an answer to Dr. Taylor, not republished in his volumes, is a noble expression of it. "He taught the people that the only way to secure the greatest good was along the path of absolute righteousness and not in vain attempts to measure consequences. Dr. Taylor maintained that consequences created duty, a principle that determined political action in the country for twenty years. Bushnell contended that righteousness secures the only consequence worth having. It was this principle that carried the nation through the war and brought slavery to an end."

The Congregational Library in Boston is very rich in Bushnell material. It has in its collection many sermons and addresses which do not appear in Bushnell's collected works. Among them we have found a sermon preached in 1844, upon "Politics under the Law of God." It will be noted that this is the same year as that of the article in the *Christian Freeman* to which Mr. Munger refers. In the preface to this public discourse Bushnell says that it is offered to the public "because it has been so unfortunate as to be denounced for qualities positively mischievous and dishonorable to a minister." "My ideal in the discourse," he says, "was to make a bold push for principle as the test of public men and measures, and let the lines when drawn cut where they would. I think I saw clearly that, if we are ever to have any principle in politics, it must be enforced when there is a question on hand and results of consequence are to be effected." The discourse itself is the expression of a spirit which America in this time has sadly needed to find in all her pulpits, but has found in too few. Before coming directly to the slavery question he surveys the various evils in the nation at the time, which it was the duty of men who stood for morality in politics to denounce.

"In the great Missouri question, on which the personal freedom, character and happiness of so many families of human beings, the honor and security of our liberties and the moral well-being of a great section of our territory were pending, what were the considerations that weighed in the deliberation and determined the final vote? Was it the immutable principles of justice and humanity, those principles which God asserts and will forever vindicate? No, it was the balance of power between the slave-holding and non-slave-holding states." "In the Indian question, what did we do but lend the power of the civil arm to crush a defenceless people and their rights? We violated our most solemn treaties and pledges. If there was a just God in heaven, he could not be with us. It was policy — a composition with fraud and wickedness. An honored chieftain at the head of the nation recommended the measure, the nation decreed it, and the military enacted it with their bayonets!" "The Florida war was a transaction rooted in unmitigated iniquity and oppression." At the close of his survey, which covers other points, he declares: "We are guilty as a nation of the most daring wrongs, and if there be a just God we have reason to tremble for his judgments. We are ceasing as a nation to have any conscience about public matters. Good men and Christians are suffering an allegiance to party rule, which demolishes their personality, learning quietly to approve and passively to follow in whatever path their party leads." He considers some of the causes which operated to produce this result; and declares among other things that the neglect of the pulpit to assert the dominion of moral principles over what we do as citizens has hastened and aggravated the evil — and adds: "It is the solemn duty of the ministers of religion to make their people feel the presence of God's law everywhere, and especially where the dearest interests of life, the interests of virtue and religion, are themselves at stake. This is the manner of the Bible. There is no one subject on which it is more full than it is in reference to the moral duties of rulers and citizens." Following his survey of causes, he speaks of consequences; and after noticing two or three of these observes: "Take away conscience, let party strife and discipline clear off the constraint of principle, and your constitutions have no value and no avenger; your civil order is shivered to fragments. Nor is it possible that public life or any warm sentiment of patriotism should survive the destruction of moral and religious influences in the state. Who will love his country when his country ceases from equity and protection? The divorce of politics from conscience and religion must infallibly end in the total wreck of our institutions and liberties." He then asks what shall be done, and answers: "First of all, we must open our eyes to what we have done. We must see our sin as a people and repent of it." And again, "Require it of your rulers to cease from the prostitution of their office to effect the reign of their party. Require them to say what is true, and do what is right; and the moment they falter, forsake them." The sermon, which is one of the most impassioned which Bushnell ever preached, ends with a scathing denunciation of slavery, which was then the great source of our political corruption and infidelity: "Slavery is the great curse of this nation. I blush to think how tamely we have suffered its encroachments. The time has come to renounce our pusillanimity. We have made a farce of American liberty long enough. God's frown is upon us, and the scorn of the world is settling on our name in the earth. God I know is gracious, and how much he will bear I cannot tell. He is also just, and how long his justice can suffer is past human foresight. Our politics are now our greatest immorality, and what is most of all fearful, the immorality sweeps through the Church of God."

Bushnell's first public public sermon, "The Crisis of the Church," was occasioned by the mobbing of Garrison in the streets of Boston in 1835. This was a time when in many pulpits the subject of slavery was a tabooed subject, and churches were divided upon it. But Bushnell, as Dr. Munger says, "held to the Puritan conception of the state as moral, and did not hesitate to use his pulpit to enforce this conception and to denounce any departure from it. The antislavery movement was so distinctly Christian that he would not keep it out of his pulpit, even if his sermons were regarded and used as campaign documents." Of the fugitive slave law he prayed that God would grant him grace never to "do the damning sin" of obedience to it. "The first duty that I owe to civil government," he said, "is to violate and spurn such a law." Of the spoils system he spoke in a notable sermon on "American Politics," in 1840, as the civil service. reformer speaks today. "In all matters pertaining to our national welfare," wrote his daughter, "his patriotism was ever on the alert." His constant refuge was in the Puritan spirit and in the companionship of the founders of New England and of the republic. Few addresses have been given upon the Pilgrim Fathers worthier or weightier than his "The Founders Great in their Unconsciousness," before the New England Society of New York on Forefathers Day, 1849, just fifty years ago. "The way of greatness is the way of duty," — to learn this principle from them and take it to our hearts, this, he said, is the most fitting monument we can erect to the fathers. His profound address on "Popular Government by Divine Right," delivered as a sermon on the day of the national thanksgiving in 1864, in the very midst of the civil war, is a luminous study of the development of our nationality and, still more important, a searching criticism of the dictum that the "consent of the governed" is the real and sufficient basis of just government. Ultimate and true sovereignty resides not in any majority of men, but in the law of God, which nations, through whatever painful processes, must discover and conform to. Political inquiry becomes a search for right, for moral relations; and in closing his essay, Bushnell says these remarkable words, — speaking of government, of course, in its limiting and controlling, and not in its constructive and coöperative aspects: "There will be less and less need of government, because the moral right of what we have is felt; and as what we do as right is always free, we shall grow more free as the centuries pass, till perhaps even government itself may lapse in the freedom of a righteousness consummated in God."

THE NEXT YEAR Bushnell was the orator at the commemoration by Yale College of her alumni who had fallen in the war, giving his great oration, "Our Obligations to the Dead." We have spoken of "The Age of Homespun" as the prose counterpart of Burns's "Cotter's Saturday Night." The oration on "Our Obligations to the Dead" is the prose counterpart of Lowell's "Commemoration Ode," which was read at Harvard just five days before, in that midsummer of 1865. It would be useful to compare the oration and the poem and see how many of the same great thoughts were developed independently, in the different ways. This word of the orator is of interest in remembrance of the poet's word on Lincoln: "In the place of politicians we are going to have at least some statesmen; for we have gotten the pitch of a grand new Abrahamic statesmanship, unsophisticated, honest and real, — no cringing sycophancy or cunning art of demagogy." Of interest in this connection, too, is Bushnell's application in another essay, that on "The True Wealth of Nations," of the term "the first American" to one daring to renounce a state of cliency upon Europe and stand upon his own national feet. This word of Bushnell's antedates Lowell's ode by thirty years. An echo, or an anticipation — we do not remember which — of a striking word in Lowell's Lessing essay is this word of Bushnell's in his Commemoration address: "Great action is the highest kind of writing, and he that makes a noble character writes the finest kind of book." It would be inspiring to quote many of the eloquent passages from this great address; we shall instead quote one practical suggestion, the deliverance of a far-seeing statesmanship, which, could it have been acted on, would have saved the nation how much trouble and have been the source of how great order and strength today:

"Do simply this, which we have a perfect constitutional right to do, — pass this very simple amendment, that the basis of representation in Congress shall hereafter be the number, in all the states alike, of the free male voters therein. Then the work is done; a general free suffrage follows by consent, and as soon as it probably ought. For these returning states will not be long content with half the offices they want and half the power allowed them in the republic. Negro suffrage is thus carried without even naming the word."

BUSHNELL'S ADDRESS upon "The True Wealth or Weal of Nations" was given in 1837, eight years before Charles Sumner's great oration on "The True Grandeur of Nations." The latter address was a war upon militarism; the former was chiefly a war upon mammonism. It was an effort to arouse America to an understanding of how much more man is than money. Bushnell already saw the broad and hostile distinctions beginning to display themselves in New England, "sad omens, which leave us no time to squander in merely economical policies." He arraigned the great wastes of our life. "It can be shown from unquestionable data that fashionable extravagance in our people such as really transcends their means to a degree that is not respectable, theatrical amusements known to be only corrupt and vulgar in character, together with intemperate drinking and all the idleness, crime and pauperism consequent, have annihilated since we began our history not less than three or four times the total wealth of the nation." Elsewhere he dwells upon the immense social improvement which will come, especially in the condition of the laboring classes, when the enormous expenditures of war and vice are discontinued, and our substance and forces are properly utilized. He arraigned the disproportion in men's expenditures. "I found that a man who would give a cheap sort of lawyer from ten to twenty dollars for a few hours' service is giving the professor of education from one to two dollars for a whole winter's work on the mind of his son." He closed with a great plea for a true education, for devotion to "the noble purpose of making our whole people, since they are called to rule, fit to rule.:

BUT THE WORDS which we would leave in the minds of our readers, as we take leave here of this great citizen, are those of his prophetic oration upon "The Growth of Law." It is, in the first place, a survey of history, to trace the development of law, to show what Greece did for the world and what Rome did; but the most significant pages of the essay are those in which he looks forward to the triumph of the true international spirit, and sees the end of wars in a rational and organized world. His tribute to Hugo Grotius, the first great international man, is one of the most eloquent passages in all his works. Summing up the achievements already of international law, he adds:

"A day will come when the dominion of ignorance and physical force, when distinctions of blood and the accidents of fortune will cease to rule the world. Beauty, reason, science, personal worth and religion will come into their rightful supremacy, and moral forces will preside over physical as mind over the body. Liberty and equality will be so far established that every man will have a right to his existence and, if he can make it so, to an honorable, powerful and happy existence. Policy will cease to be the same as cunning, and become a study of equity and reason. It is impossible that wars should not be discontinued. if not by the progress of the international code, as we have hinted, yet by the progress of liberty and intelligence; for the masses who have hitherto composed the soldiery must sometime discover the folly of dying, as an ignoble herd, to serve the passions of a few reckless politicians, or to give a name for prowess to leaders whose bravery consists in marching *them* into danger. The arbitrament of arms is not a whit less absurd than the old English trial by battle, and before the world has done rolling they will both be classed together."

"Who shall think it incredible that this same progress of moral legislation, which has gone thus far in the international code, may ultimately be so far extended as to systematize and establish rules of arbitrament, by which all national disputes shall be definitely settled, without an appeal to arms! And so it shall result that, as the moral code is one, all law shall come into unity, and a kind of virtual oneness embrace all nations. We shall flow tog ther in the annihilation of distances and become brothers in the terms of justice."

True citizen of the little Litchfield county town, true citizen of Connecticut, true citizen of America, true citizen of the world, true citizen, in each and all of these earthly circles, of the divine commonwealth, the kingdom of God, — such was Horace Bushnell.

# ABOUT THE AUTHOR

Horace Bushnell (1802-1876) was an American Congregational minister and theologian.

Bushnell was born in the village of Bantam, township of Litchfield, Connecticut. He attended Yale College where he roomed with future magazinist Nathaniel Parker Willis. After graduating in 1827, he was literary editor of the *New York Journal of Commerce* from 1828-1829, and in 1829 became a tutor at Yale. Here he initially studied law, but in 1831 he entered the theology department of Yale College. In May, 1833 Bushnell was ordained pastor of the North Congregational church in Hartford, Connecticut. He married Mary Apthorp in 1833 and the couple had three children. Bushnell remained in Hartford until 1859 when, due to extended poor health he resigned his pastorate. Thereafter he held no appointed office, but, until his death at Hartford in 1876, he was a prolific author and occasionally preached.

While in California in 1856, for the restoration of his health, he took an active interest in the organization, at Oakland, of the College of California (chartered in 1855 and merged with the University of California in 1869), the presidency of which he declined. As a preacher, Dr Bushnell was very effective. Though not a dramatic orator, he was original, thoughtful and impressive in the pulpit. His theological position may be said to have been one of qualified revolt against the Calvinistic orthodoxy of his day. He criticized prevailing conceptions of the Trinity, the atonement, conversion, and the relations of the natural and the supernatural. Above all, he broke with the prevalent view which regarded theology as essentially intellectual in its appeal and demonstrable by processes of exact logical deduction. To his thinking its proper basis is to be found in the feelings and intuitions of humankind's spiritual nature. He had a marked influence upon theology in America, an influence not so much, possibly, in the direction of the modification of specific doctrines as in the impulse and tendency and general spirit which he imparted to theological thought. Dr Munger's estimate was that "He was a theologian as Copernicus was an astronomer; he changed the point of view, and thus not only changed everything, but pointed the way toward unity in theological thought. He was not exact, but he put God and humanity and the world into a relation that thought can accept while it goes on to state it more fully with ever growing knowledge. Other thinkers were moving in the same direction; he led the movement in New England, and wrought out a great deliverance. It was a work of superb courage. Hardly a theologian in his denomination stood by him, and nearly all pronounced against him."

Four of his books were of particular importance: *Christian Nurture* (1847), in which he virtually opposed revivalism and effectively turned the current of Christian thought toward the young ; *Nature and the Supernatural* (1858), in which he discussed miracles and endeavoured to lift the natural into the supernatural by emphasizing the supernatural nature of man; *The Vicarious Sacrifice* (1866), in which he contended for what has come to be known as the moral view of the atonement in distinction from the governmental and the penal or satisfaction theories; and *God in Christ* (1849) (with an introductory Dissertation on Language as related to Thought and Spirit), in which he expressed, it was charged, heretical views as to the Trinity, holding, among other things, that the Godhead is "instrumentally three—three simply as related to our finite apprehension, and the communication of God's incommunicable nature." Attempts were made to bring him to trial, but they were unsuccessful, and in 1852 his church unanimously withdrew from the local consociation, thus removing any possibility of further action against him. To his critics Bushnell formally replied by writing *Christ in Theology* (1851), in which he employs the important argument that spiritual truth can be expressed only in approximate and poetical language, and concludes that an adequate dogmatic theology cannot exist. That he did not deny the divinity of Christ he proved in *The Character of Jesus, forbidding his possible Classification within Men* (1861). He also published *Sermons for the New Life* (1858); *Christ and his Salvation* (1864); *Work and Play* (1864); *Moral Uses of Dark Things* (1868); *Women's Suffrage; The Reform Against Nature* (1869); *Sermons on Living Subjects* (1872); and *Forgiveness and Law* (1874).

An edition of his works, in eleven volumes, appeared in 1876; and a further volume, gathered from his unpublished papers, as *The Spirit in Man: Sermons and Selections*, in 1903. New editions of his *Nature and the Supernatural, Sermons for this New Life, and Work and Play*, were published the same year.

Bushnell was greatly interested in the civic interests of Hartford, and was the chief agent in procuring the establishment of the first public park in the United States. It was named Bushnell Park in his honor by that city. The Bushnell Center for the Performing Arts, and a residence hall at the University of Hartford are also named for him.

# PART I
## UNCONSCIOUS INFLUENCE

A Sermon Preached by Rev. Horace Bushnell, D.D., of the United States, Preached at Fetter Lane Chapel, on Sunday, March 29, 1846.

# SERMON

*"Then went in also that other disciple."*

— JOHN 20:8.

IN THIS slight touch or turn of history, is opened to us, if we can scan it closely, one of the most serious and fruitful chapters of Christian doctrine. Thus it is that men are ever touching unconsciously the springs of motion in each other; thus it is that one man, without thought or intention, or even a consciousness of the fact, is ever leading some other after him. Little does Peter think, as he comes up where his doubting brother is looking into the sepulcher, and goes straight in, after his peculiar manner, that he is drawing in his brother apostle after him. As little does John think, when he loses his misgivings, and goes into the sepulcher after Peter, that he is following his brother. And just so, unawares to himself, is every man, the whole race through, laying hold of his fellowman, to lead him where otherwise he would not go. We overrun the boundaries of our personality—we flow together. A Peter leads a John, a John goes after a Peter, both of them unconscious of any influence exercised or received. And thus our life and conduct are ever propagating themselves, by a law of social contagion, throughout the circles and time in which we live.

There are, then, you will perceive, two sorts of influence belonging to man; that which is active or voluntary, and that which is unconscious; — that which we exert purposely, or in the endeavor to sway another, as by teaching, by argument, by persuasion, by threatenings, by offers, and promises,—and that which flows out from us unawares to ourselves, the same which Peter had over John when he led him into the sepulcher. The importance of our efforts to do good, that is our voluntary influence; and the sacred obligation we are under to exert ourselves in this way, are often and seriously insisted on. It is thus that Christianity has become, in the present age, a principle of so much greater activity than it has been for many centuries before; and we fervently hope, that it will yet become far more active than it now is, nor cease to multiply its industry, till it is seen by all mankind to embody the beneficence and the living energy of Christ himself.

But there needs to be produced, at the same time, and partly for this object, a more thorough appreciation of the relative importance of that kind of influence or beneficence which is insensibly exerted. The tremendous weight and efficacy of this, compared with the other, and the sacred responsibility laid upon us in regard to this, are felt in no such degree or proportion as they should be; and the consequent loss we suffer in character, as well as that which the church suffers in beauty and strength, is incalculable. The more stress, too, needs to be laid on this subject of insensible influence, because it is insensible, because it is out of mind, and, when we seek to trace it, it is not easily discovered.

If the doubt occur to any of you, in the announcement of this subject, whether we are properly responsible for an influence which we exert insensibly; we are not, I reply, except so far as this influence flows directly from our character and conduct. And this it does, even much more uniformly than our active influence. In the latter, we may fail of our end by a want of wisdom or skill; in which case we are still as meritorious, in God's sight, as if we succeeded. So, again, we may really succeed, and do great good by our active endeavors, from motives altogether base and hypocritical, in which case we are as evil in God's sight as if we had failed. But the influences we exert unconsciously will scarcely ever disagree with our real character. They are honest influences, following our character as the shadow follows the sun; and, therefore, we are much more certainly responsible for them and their effects on the world. They go streaming from us in all directions, though in channels that we do not see, poisoning or healing around the roots of society and among the hidden wells of character. If good ourselves, they are good; if bad, they are bad. And, since they reflect so exactly our character, it is impossible to doubt our responsibility for their effects on the world. We must answer not only for what we do with a purpose, but for the influence we exert insensibly. To give you any just impressions of the breadth and seriousness of such a reckoning I know to be impossible. No mind can trace it. But it will be something gained, if I am able to awaken only a suspicion of the vast extent and moment of those influences which are ever flowing out unbidden upon society, from your life and character.

In the prosecution of my design, let me ask of you, first of all, to expel the common prejudice that there can be nothing of consequence in unconscious influences, because they make no report and fall on the world unobserved. Histories and biographies make little account of the power men exert insensibly over each other. They tell how men have led armies, established empires, enacted laws, gained causes, sung, reasoned, and taught; — always occupied in setting forth what they do with a purpose. But what they do without a purpose, the streams of influence that flow out from their persons unbidden on the world, they cannot trace or compute, and seldom even mention. So also the public laws make men responsible only for what they do with a positive purpose, and take no account of the mischiefs or benefits that are communicated by their noxious or healthful example. The same is true in the discipline of families, churches, and schools; they make no account of the things we do except we will them. What we do insensibly passes for nothing, because no human government can trace such influences with sufficient certainty to make authors responsible.

But you must not conclude that influences of this kind are insignificant, because they are unnoticed or noiseless. How is it in the natural world? Behind the mere show, the outward noise and stir of the world, nature always conceals her hand of controul, and the laws by which she rules. Who ever saw with the eye, for example, or heard with the ear, the exertions of that tremendous astronomic force, which every moment holds the compact of the physical universe together? The lightning is, in fact, but a mere fire-fly spark in comparison; but because it glares on the cloud, and thunders so terribly in the ear, and rives the tree or the rock where it falls, many will be ready to think that it is a vastly more potent agent than gravity.

The bible calls the good man's life a light, and it is the nature of light to flow out spontaneously in all directions, and fill the world unconsciously with its beams. So the Christian shines, I would say, not so much because he will, as because he is a luminous object. Not that the active influence of Christians is made of no account in the figure, but only that this symbol of light has its propriety, in the fact that their unconscious influence is the chief influence, and has the precedence in its power over the world. And yet there are many who will be ready to think that light is a very tame and feeble instrument because it is noiseless. An earthquake, for example, is to them a much more vigorous and effective agency. Hear how it comes thundering through the solid foundations of nature. It rocks a whole continent. The noblest works of man, cities, monuments and temples, are in a moment levelled to the ground, or swallowed down the opening gulfs of fire. Little do they think that the light of every morning, the soft and genial and silent light is an agent many times more powerful. But let the light of morning cease and return no more; let the hour of morning come and bring with it no dawn;

the outcries of a horror-stricken world fill the air, and make, as it were, the darkness audible. The beasts go wild and frantic at the loss of the sun. The vegetable growths turn pale and die. A chill creeps on, and frosty winds begin to howl across the freezing earth. Colder, and yet colder, is the night. The vital blood, at length, of all creatures stops congealed. Down goes the frost towards the earth's centre. The heart of the sea is frozen; nay, the earthquakes are themselves frozen in under their fiery caverns. The very globe itself, too, and all the fellow planets that have lost their sun are become mere balls of ice, swinging silent in the darkness. Such is the light which revisits us in the silence of the morning. It makes no shock or scar. It would not wake an infant in his cradle. And yet it perpetually new creates the world, rescuing it, each morning, as a prey from night and chaos. So the Christian is a light, even "the light of the world," and we must not think that because he shines insensibly or silently, as a mere luminous object, he is therefore powerless. The greatest powers are ever those which lie back of the little stirs and commotions of nature; and I verily believe, that the insensible influences of good men are as much more potent than what I have called their voluntary or active, as the great silent powers of nature are of greater consequence than her little disturbances and tumults. The law of human influence is deeper than many suspect, and they lose sight of it altogether. The outward endeavors made by good men or bad to sway others, they call their influence; whereas it is, in fact, but a fraction, and, in most cases, but a very small fraction of the good or evil that flows out of their lives. Nay, I will even go farther. How many persons do you meet, the insensible influences of whose manners and characters is so decided, as often to thwart their voluntary influence; so that whatever they attempt to do, in the way of controlling others, they are sure to carry the exact opposite of what they intend! And it will generally be found, that where men undertake by argument or persuasion to exert a power, in the face of qualities that make them odious or detestable, or only not entitled to respect, their insensible influence will be too strong for them. In all such cases the voluntary influence of men will not even compose a fraction, however small, of what they do.

I call your attention, next, to the twofold powers of effect and expression by which man is connected with his fellowman. If we distinguish man as a creature of language, and thus qualified to communicate himself to others, there are in him two sets or kinds of language; one which is voluntary in the use, and one that is involuntary—that of speech in the literal sense; and that expression of the eye, the face, the look, the gait, the motion, the tone or cadence, which is sometimes called the natural language of the sentiments. This natural language, too, is greatly enlarged by the conduct of life, that which, in business and society, reveals the principles and spirit of men. Speech, or voluntary language, is a door to the soul that we may open or shut at will; the other is a door that stands open evermore, and reveals to others constantly, and often very clearly, the tempers, tastes, and wishes of their hearts. Within, as we may represent, is character, charging the common reservoir of influence, and through these twofold gates of the soul pouring itself out on the world. Out of one it flows at choice, and whensoever we purpose to do good or evil to men. Out of the other it flows each moment, as light from the sun, and propagates itself in all beholders.

Then if we go over to others, that is, to the subjects of influence, we find every man endowed with two inlets of impression; the ear and the understanding for the reception of speech, and the sympathetic powers, the sensibilities or affections, for tinder to those sparks of emotion revealed by looks, tones, manners, and general conduct. And these sympathetic powers, though not immediately rational, are yet inlets, open on all sides to the understanding and character. They have a certain wonderful capacity to receive impressions, and catch the meaning of signs, and propagate in us whatsoever falls into their passive moulds from others. The impressions they receive do not come through verbal propositions, and are never received into verbal proposition, it may be, in the mind, and therefore many think nothing of them. But precisely on this account are they the more powerful, because it is as if one heart were thus going directly into another, and carrying in its feelings with it. Beholding, as in a glass, the feelings of our neighbour, we are changed into the same image by the assimilating power of sensibility and fellow feeling. Many have gone so far, and not without show, at least, of reason, as to maintain that the look or expression, and even the very features of children, are often changed by exclusive intercourse with nurses and attendants. Furthermore, if we carefully consider we shall find it scarcely possible to doubt, that simply to look on bad and malignant faces, or those whose expression has become infected by vice, to be with them and become familiarized to them, is enough permanently to affect the character of persons of mature age. I do not say that it must of necessity subvert their character, for tlje evil looked upon may never be loved or welcomed in practice; but it is something to have these bad images in the soul, giving out their expression there, and diffusing their odour among the thoughts as long as we live. How dangerous a thing is it, for example, for a man to become accustomed to sights of cruelties! What man, valuing the honour of his soul, would not shrink from yielding himself to such an influence? No more is it a thing of indifference to become accustomed to look on the manners, and receive the guilty expression of any kind of sin.

The door of involuntary communication, I have said, is always open. Of course we are communicating ourselves in this way to others, at every moment of our intercourse or presence with them. But how very seldom, in comparison, do we undertake, by means of speech, to influence others! Even the best Christian, one who most improves his opportunities to do good, attempts but seldom to sway another by voluntary influence, whereas he is all the while shining as a luminous object, unawares, and communicating of his heart to the world.

But there is yet another view of this double line of communication which man has with his fellowmen, which is more general, and displays the import of the truth yet more convincingly. It is by one of these modes of communication that we are constituted members of voluntary society; and, by the others, parts of a general mass, or members of voluntary society. You are all, in a certain view, individuals, and separate as persons from each other. You are also, in a certain other view, parts of a common body, as truly as the parts of a stone. Thus, if you ask how it is that you and all men came, without your consent, to exist in society, to be within its power, to be under its laws; the answer is, that while you are a man you are also a fractional element of a larger and more comprehensive being, called society—be it the family, the church, the state. In a certain department of your nature it is open; its sympathies and feelings are open. On this open side you all adhere together as parts of a larger nature, in which there is a common circulation of want, impulse, and law. Being thus made common to each other involuntary, you become one mass, one consolidated social body, animated by one life. And observe how far this involuntary communication and sympathy, between the members of a state or family, is sovereign over their character. It always results in what men call the national or family spirit; for there is a spirit peculiar to every state and family in the world. Sometimes, too, this national or family spirit takes a religious or an irreligious character, and appears to absorb the religious self-government of the individual. What was the national spirit of France, for example, at a certain time, but a spirit of infidelity. What is the religious spirit of Spain, at this moment but a spirit of bigotry, quite as wide of Christianity and destructive to character as the spirit of falsehood? What is the family spirit, in many a house, but the spirit of gain, or pleasure, or appetite, in which everything that is warm, genial, dignified, and good in religion, is visibly absent? Sometimes you will almost fancy that you see the shapes of money in the eyes of the children. So it is that we are led on by nations, as it were, to a good or bad immorality. Far down, in the secret foundations of life and society, there lie concealed great laws and channels of influence, which make the race common to each other in all the main departments or divisions of the social mass—laws which often escape our notice altogether, but which are to society as gravity to the general system of God's works.

But these are general considerations, and more fit, perhaps, to give you a rational conception of the modes of influence and their relative power, than to verify that conception, or establish its truth. I now proceed to add, therefore, some miscellaneous proofs of a more particular nature.

And I mention, first of all, the instinct of imitation in children. We begin our mortal experience, not with acts grounded in judgment or reason, or with ideas received through language, but by simple imitation; and, under the guidance of this, we lay our foundations. The child looks and listens, and whatsoever tone of feeling or manner of conduct is displayed around him, sinks into his plastic, passive soul, and becomes a mould of his being ever after. The very handling of the nursery is significant, and the petulance, the passion, the gentleness, the tranquility indicated by it, are all produced in the child. His soul is of a purely receptive nature, and that, for a considerable period, without choice or selection. A little further on he begins voluntarily to copy everything he sees. Voice, manner, gait, everything which the eye sees, the mimic instinct delights to act over. And thus we have a whole generation of future men, receiving from us their very beginnings and the deepest impulses of their life and immortality. They watch us every moment, in the family, before the hearth, and at the table; and when we are meaning them no good or evil, when we are conscious of exerting no influence over them, they are drawing from us impressions and moulds of habit, which, if wrong, no patience of discipline can wholly remove; or, if right, no future exposure utterly dissipate. Now, it may be doubted, I think, whether, in all the active influence of our lives, we do as much to shape the destiny of our fellowmen, as we do in this single article of unconscious influence over children.

Still further on, respect for others takes the place of imitation. We naturally desire the approbation or good opinion of others. You see the strength of this feeling in the article of fashion. How few persons have the nerve to resist a fashion! We have fashions, too, in literature, and in worship, and in moral and religious doctrine almost equally powerful. How many will violate the best rules of society, because it is the practice of their circle! How many reject Christ, because of friends or acquaintance, who have no suspicion of the influence they exert, and will not have, till the last day shows them what they have done! Every good man has thus a power in his person, more mighty than his words and arguments, and which others feel when little he suspects it. Every bad man has a fund of poison in his character which is tainting those around him, when it is not in his thoughts to do them an injury. He is read and understood. His sensual tastes and habits, his unbelieving spirit, his suppressed jeer at religion, have all a power, and take hold of the hearts of others, whether he will have it so or not.

Again, how well understood is it that the most active feelings and impulses of mankind are contagious! How quick enthusiasm of any sort is to kindle, and how rapidly it catches from one to another till a nation blazes with the flame! In the case of the crusades you have an example, where the personal enthusiasm of one man put all the states of Europe in motion. Fanaticism is almost equally contagious. Fear and superstition always infect the mind of the circle in which they are manifested. The spirit of war generally becomes an epidemic of madness, when once it has got possession of a few minds. The spirit of party is propagated in a similar manner. How any slight operation in the market may spread, like a fire, if successful, till trade runs wild in a general infatuation, is well known. Now, in all these examples, the effect is produced, not by active endeavor to carry influence, but mostly by that insensible propagation which follows, when a flame of any kind is once kindled.

Is it also true, you may ask, that the religious spirit propagates itself, or tends to propagate itself in the same way? I see no reason to question that it does. Nor does anything in the doctrine of spiritual influences, when rightly understood, forbid the supposition; for spiritual influences are never separated from the laws of thought in the individual, and the laws of feeling and influence in society. If, too, every disciple is to be an "epistle known and read of all men," what shall we expect, but that all men will be somehow affected by the reading? Or, if he is to be a light in the world, what shall we look for, but that others, seeing his good works, shall glorify God on his account? How often is seen, too, as a fact of observation, that one or a few good men kindle at length a holy fire in the community in which they live, and become the leaven of a general reformation! Such men give a more vivid proof in their persons of the reality of religious faith, than any words or arguments could yield. They are active; they endeavor, of course, to exert a good voluntary influence; but still their chief power lies in their holiness, and the sense they produce in others of their close relation to God.

It now remains to exhibit the very important fact, that where the direct or active influence of men is supposed to be great, even this is due in a principal degree to that insensible influence by which their arguments, reproofs, and persuasions are secretly invigorated. It is not mere words that turn men; it is the heart mounting uncalled into the expression of the features; it is the eye illuminated by reason, the look beaming with goodness. It is the tone of the voice—that instrument of the soul—which changes quality with such amazing facility, and gives out, in the soft, the tender, the tremulous, the firm, every shade of emotion and character: and so much is there in this, that the moral stature and character of the man that speaks, are likely to be well represented in his manner. If he is a stranger, his way will inspire confidence and attract goodwill. His virtues will be seen, as it were, gathering round him, to minister words and forms of thought; and their voices will be heard in the fall of his cadence. And the same is true of bad men, or men who have nothing in their character corresponding to what they attempt to do. If without heart or interest you attempt to move another, the involuntary man tells what you are doing, in a hundred ways at once. A hypocrite endeavoring to exert a great influence, only tries to convey by words what the lying look, and the faithless affectation, and a dry exaggeration of his manner, perpetually resist. We have it for a fashion, to attribute great or even prodigious results to the voluntary efforts and labors of men. Whatever they effect, is commonly referred to nothing but the immediate power of what they do. Let us take an example, like that of Paul, and analyze it. Paul was a man of great fervor and enthusiasm. He combined, withal, more of what is lofty and morally commanding in his character, than most of the very distinguished men in the world. Having this for his natural character, and his natural character exalted and made luminous by Christian faith and the manifest indwelling of God, he had of course an almost superhuman sway over others. Doubtless he was intelligent, strong in argument, eloquent, active, to the very utmost of his powers; but still he moved the world more by what he was than by what he did. The grandeur and spiritual splendor of his character were ever adding to his active efforts an element of silent power, which was the real and chief cause of their efficacy. He convinced, subdued, inspired, and led, because of the half divine authority which appeared in his conduct and his glowing spirit. He "fought the good fight," because "he kept the faith," and filled his powerful nature with influences drawn from higher worlds.

And here I must conduct you to a yet higher example, even that of the Son of God, "the light of the world." Men dislike to be swayed by direct voluntary influence. They are jealous of such control, and are therefore best approached by conduct and feeling, and the authority of simple worth, which seem to make no purposed onset. If goodness appears, they welcome its celestial smile; if heaven descends to encircle them, they yield to its sweetness; if truth appears in the life, they honor it with a secret homage; if personal majesty and glory appear, they bow with reverence, and acknowledge with shame their own vileness. Now, it is on this side of human nature that Christ visits us, preparing just that kind of influence which the Spirit of Truth may wield with the most persuasive and subduing effect. It is the grandeur of his character which constitutes the chief power of his ministry, not his miracles or teachings apart from his character. Miracles were useful at the time to arrest attention; and his doctrine is useful at all times as the highest revelation of truth possible in speech: but the greatest truth of the Gospel, notwithstanding, is Christ himself—a human body became the organ of the Divine nature, and revealing, under the conditions of an earthly life, the glory of God! The scripture writers have much to say in this connexion of the *image* of God; and an image, you know, is that which simply represents, not that which acts, or reasons, or persuades. Now it is this image of God which makes the centre—the sun itself— of the Gospel. The journeyings, teachings, miracles, and sufferings of Christ, all had their use in bringing out this image, or, what is the same, in making conspicuous the character and feelings of God, both towards sinners and towards sin. And here is the power of Christ. It is what of God's beauty, love, truth, and justice shines through him. It is the influence which flows unconsciously and spontaneously out of Christ, as the friend of man, "the light of the world," "the glory of the Father" made visible. And some have gone so far as to conjecture that God made the human person originally with a view to its becoming the organ or vehicle by which he might reveal his communicable attributes to other worlds. Christ, they believe, came to inhabit this organ, that he might execute a purpose so sublime. The human person is constituted, they say, to be a mirror of God; and God, being imaged in that mirror, as in Christ, is held up to the view of this and other worlds. It certainly is to the view of this; and if the divine nature can use this organ so effectively to express itself unto us—if it can bring itself through the looks, tones, motions, and conduct of a human person, more close to our sympathies than by any other means, how can we think that an organ so communicative, inhabited by us, is not always breathing our spirit and transferring our image insensibly to others?

I have protracted the argument on this subject beyond what I could have wished, but I cannot dismiss it without suggesting a few thoughts necessary to its complete practical effect.

One very obvious and serious inference from it, and the first which I will name, is that it is impossible to live in this world and escape responsibility. It is not they alone (as you have seen) who are trying purposely to convert or corrupt others, who exert an influence. You cannot live without exerting influence. The doors of your soul are open on others, and theirs on you. You inhabit a house which is well-nigh transparent; and what you are within you are ever showing yourself to be without, by signs that have no ambiguous expression. If you had the seeds of a pestilence in your body, you would not have a more active contagion than you have in your tempers, tastes, and principles. Simply to be, in this world, whatever you are, is to exert an influence—an influence, too, compared with which mere language and persuasion are feeble. You say that you mean well; at least you think you mean to injure no one. Do you injure no one? Is your example harmless? Is it ever on the side of God and duty? You cannot reasonably doubt that others are continually receiving impressions from your character. As little can you doubt that you must answer for these impressions. If the influence you exert is unconsciously exerted, then is it only the most sincere, the truest impression of your character. And for what can you be held responsible, if not for this? Do not deceive yourselves in the thought that you are, at least, doing no injury, and are therefore living without responsibility; first make it sure that you are not every hour infusing moral death insensibly into your children, wives, husbands, friends, and acquaintances. By a mere look or glance, not unlikely, you are conveying the influence that shall turn the scale of some one's immortality. Dismiss, therefore, the thought that you are living without responsibility; that is impossible. Better is it frankly to admit the truth; and, if you will risk the influence of a character unsanctified by duty and religion, prepare to meet your reckoning manfully, and "receive the just recompense of reward."

The true philosophy or method of doing good is also here explained. It is, first of all and principally, to be good—to have a character that will of itself communicate good. There must and will be active effort where there is goodness of principle; but the latter we should hold to be the principal thing, the root and life of all. Whether it is a mistake more sad or more ridiculous, to make mere stir synonymous with doing good, we need not inquire; enough to be sure that one who has taken up such a notion of doing good, is, for that reason, a nuisance to the Church. The Christian is called a "light," not lightning. In order to act with effect on others he must walk in the Spirit, and thus become the image of goodness: he must be so akin to God, and so filled with his dispositions, that he shall seem to surround himself with a hallowed atmosphere. It is folly to endeavor to make ourselves shine before we are luminous. If the sun without his beams should talk to the planets, and argue with them till the final day; it would not make them shine; there must be light in the sun itself, and then they will shine of course. And this, my brethren, is what God intends for you all. It is the great idea of his Gospel, and the work of his Spirit, to make you "lights in the world." His greatest joy is to give you character, to beautify your example, to exalt your principles, and make you each the depositary of his own almighty grace. But in order to this, something is necessary on your part—a full surrender of your mind to duty and to God, and a perpetual desire of this spiritual intimacy: having this, having a participation thus of the goodness of God, you will as naturally communicate good as the sun communicates his beams.

Our doctrine of unconscious and undesigning influence shows how it is, also, that the preaching of Christ is often so unfruitful, and especially in times of spiritual coldness. It is not because truth ceases to be truth, nor, of necessity, because it is preached in a less vivid manner; but it is because there are so many influences preaching against the preacher. He is one, the people are many; his attempts to convince and persuade are a voluntary influence; their lives on the other hand, and especially the lives of those who profess what is better, are so many unconscious influences, ever streaming forth upon the people, and back and forth between each other. He preaches the truth, and they, with one consent, are preaching the truth down; and how can he prevail against so many, and by a kind of influence so unequal? When the people of God are glowing with spiritual devotion to him, and love to men, the case is different; then they are all preaching with the preacher, and making an atmosphere of warmth for his words to fall into. "Great is the company of them that publish" the truth, and proportionably great its power. Shall I say more? Have you not already felt, my brethren, the application to which I would bring you? We do not exonerate ourselves; we do not claim to be nearer to God, or holier than you; but, ah! you know not how easy it is to make a winter about us, or how cold it feels! Our endeavor is to preach the truth of Christ and his cross as clearly and as forcibly as we can. Sometimes it has a visible effect, and we are filled with joy; sometimes it has no effect, and then we struggle on, as we must, but under great oppression. Have we none among you, that preach against us in your lives? If we show you the light of God's truth, does it never fall upon banks of ice, which if the light shines through the crystal masses are yet as cold as before? We do not accuse you— that we leave to God, and to those who may rise up in the last day to testify against you. If they shall come out of your own families; if they are the children that wear your names, the husband or wife of your affections; if they declare that you, by your example, kept them away from Christ's truth and mercy, we may have accusations to meet of our own, and we leave you to acquit yourselves as best you may. I only warn you here of the guilt which our Lord Jesus Christ will impute to them that hinder his gospel.

## PART II

# PROSPERITY OUR DUTY

A Discourse Delivered at the North Church, Hartford, Sabbath Evening, January 31, 1847

# SERMON

*This same Hezekiah also stopped the upper watercourse of Gibon, and brought it straight down to the west side of the city of David. And Hezekiah prospered in all his works.*

— 2 CHRONICLES 32:30.

Any community or city will prosper that will do its duty. Having the prudence necessary to a right husbandry of its resources, the industry to improve its advantages, and the spirit to seize on whatever opportunities are placed within its reach, the increase of substance and of numbers is a necessary consequence. It may not always come by damming water-courses, and opening sluices or canals, to bring in supplies of water. There are other sluices of prosperity besides water-sluices, and a wise people will make their election.

I ought therefore to say, first of all, that I have no design to offer a discourse, this evening, on the scheme just proposed for advancing the growth of our city. I have cited the former clause of my text only as an introduction to the latter and more general clause, that which sets forth the prosperity of a good ruler's works.

It is not for me to say that the scheme just proposed has any solid merits to commend it to confidence. And if I were sure that it had, it is not my office to advocate works of public improvement, or to meddle, in any respect, with schemes which are purely secular and belong only to the province of business men. I shall only speak of prosperity in general, and of the moral causes and consequences connected with it. Could I realize all that I wish, it would be to set you in the best possible attitude for the exercise of your own wisdom, and the prompt fulfilment of any responsibilities, that now or at any future time, may be laid upon you; to invigorate confidence, to consolidate public spirit, and prepare you to all works of sacrifice and industry that may be needed to sustain your growth, or advance your prosperity. Then, whatever you may undertake or decline, you will undertake or decline for yourselves—it will only be more sure that you will not be false to any just enterprise or call of duty that comes before you. It will not be amiss for you to notice the fact that revelation records it as one of the works of a good ruler's administration, that he raised a dam at Gihon and brought down the water to Jerusalem; also that he added prosperity to his realm by these and other like enterprises. Nor will it be amiss that the future generations should record the like of you, connected with a like result. But the probability of any such result rests wholly with you.

Most of you may be accustomed to look at this question of public prosperity as one that has a purely secular interest. Contrary to this, I regard it as a question that involves, in all coming time, the dearest interests of character and religion. For, on the one hand, it will be found that a state of prosperity is itself one of the truest evidences of character and public virtue,—a reward and honor which God delights to bestow upon an upright people,—and, on the other, it will be found that a want of prosperity, followed by decline and decay, discourages everything good, and works a moral prostration every way correspondent. And it is in this view that every Christian, and especially every Christian minister dreads the possibility of decline. For, while others are occupied chiefly with the mere outward loss, he is compelled to anticipate another kind of mischief, which, to him, is far more afflictive and depressing.

I do not know that we have any such result to fear. I cannot ascertain that we have suffered or begun to suffer any real diminution of numbers or of resources. But the opening of new avenues of trade and travel on every side of us has compelled the business of our city to change its form. Some kinds of trade have been partially destroyed, but others have been and are being created. And it is natural, while these changes are going on, that we should all suffer a degree of anxiety. Some may be unduly anxious. Others too, may be over confident. This at least is certain, that we have come now to a great and final crisis. The causes that are going to affect the interests of our city, as a place of business, in all future time, are now displayed and coming into action. Hereafter no great change is to be anticipated. It is not as when we lost our West India commerce. We have come to the last trial—the final crisis. And now it is to be decided, within the next five or ten years, whether we are to go on maintaining our growth and numbers, or to sink into decline. Up to this time, our city has maintained an even, healthy and generally constant growth, from the very first day of the settlement. The river has been its life. Now, at last, there are opening rivers of trade and motion above us and back of us on every side, and it is very soon to be seen whether we can turn the resources left us in such a way as to escape injury. If we can,—if we prove ourselves equal to the crisis that has now come, our foundation is sure for all future time,—we shall go on to increase in wealth and numbers indefinitely, though perhaps not rapidly. This it becomes every man of us to understand. Be it also remembered that the crisis we have reached is one that concerns not our business only, and our wealth, but quite as truly all the higher interests of character and religion. Indeed, there is nothing that I can think of as a heavier judgment, than to be doomed to spend one's declining days in bearing up the ark of God and his truth among a declining people.

We are often required as ministers of truth, to speak of the dangers of prosperity. Prosperity has its dangers. They are many and great. You cannot too often be apprised of them, or by any possible warnings be made to watch too carefully against them. But there is yet another kind of danger, quite as real and quite as hard to conquer, viz. the danger that springs from wasting and decline. And if such wasting or decline is caused by a man's own fault, as by a want of industry or attention to business, by a loose economy, by a self-indulgent or spendthrift habit, by any fault of application or manly effort to improve his condition, then are we to speak not of his danger, but of something worse—a downfall of character already half completed. For it is the duty of every man to be a prosperous man, if by any reasonable effort he may. God calls us to industry, and tempts us to it by all manner of promises. He lays it upon us as a duty to be diligent in business, to seek out ways of productive exertion, to make our five talents ten, and our ten talents twenty. He is pleased with thrift and makes it the sister of virtue. Every shiftless character, therefore, is a character so far lost to virtue. Give me then, as a minister of God's truth, a worldly, money-loving, prosperous, but strenuous and diligent hearer, and deliver me from one who has run down all his vigor, and debauched every earnest capacity, by his indolence or improvidence. What power can the stern arguments of religion, and the earnest appeals of duty have to him, who has given up the effort to care for himself—the man to whom every thing earnest is a burden, who is incapable of enterprise, rusting in his own indolence, lost to every manly purpose and responsibility.

And what is true of the individual man, is true, even more emphatically, of a community. An industrious, enterprising, hopeful, prosperous community, is far more easily moved by the demands of duty and religion than one that is drooping and running down. If prosperity is dangerous, decline is well nigh fatal. The moment any people begin to decline and give themselves up to decay, religion droops, good morals decline, hope, which is the nurse of character, yields to desperation, low and sordid passions grow rank in the mold of decay, one blames another, society rots into fragments, and every good interest is blasted. Let our city, for example, drop into a decline, let business of every kind become unprofitable, let capital withdraw itself, and the young men of enterprise go abroad to seek their fortune in other places, let those ominous words *"to let"* be hung on many tenements, let the paint begin to wear off, and a dingy look of decay to appear on the shops and dwellings, then too it will be found that religion and every good influence withers. The churches will begin also to wear a look of neglect and discouragement, and the ministers of religion will themselves droop at the altar. They will speak to a discouraged people, whose life is dying out for want of hope. They cannot be as acceptable as before, for nothing is acceptable. They cannot but flag themselves, for every thing flags. Hope is one of the strongest supports of character; when hope, therefore, dies, all efforts made to sustain the upward aim and the elevating influences of religion are made at the worst disadvantage. An old decayed town, one that is forsaken of business and business men, becomes too a hive for all shiftless characters. The dilapidated tenements, cheapened in price, invite the thriftless and desperate of every sort, to come in and try the last ends of fortune,—broken down mechanics, bankrupt tradesmen, political hacks, panderers to intemperance and all manner of vice, willing all to descend as low in their several trades as their necessities require. These are the characters to populate a ruin, answering to the owls and satyrs and dragons and other doleful creatures that congregated in the ruined cities of old, only more base and poisonous as they are more depraved. They are unclean spirits, bringing every one his seven to occupy the places that are empty. Thus, after a certain point is reached, the motion of every thing is downward. Religion, morals, society, all begin to sink in the common decay. No courage or hope being left, public spirit dies, and with that, public character, and with that, private character. Intelligence, industry, good manners, piety, every thing good yields to the common fate of decline, and nothing is left but a city of doleful creatures, who are lost to this world, and with about equal certainty, to the world to come.

Let us not then forget that prosperity, great as its dangers are, is yet the condition of virtue. Great and sudden calamities, such as conflagrations, fevers and plagues, falling on a city from God, bring no such results. Received as God's righteous judgments, they may soften a people to repentance and turn their thoughts to future worlds. Meantime they will never discourage effort and enterprise; for you will see the people rising up out of God's chastisements to rebuild what is perished and renew their works with greater vigor. Whereas, under a slow doom of decline, and especially where that decline comes of their own lack of duty and enterprise, there is no elastic spirit, no element of power and virtue left. They have lost the vital force—what then can the restorative agents, the stimulants of duty and religion do for them longer? They may possibly start a galvanic motion now and then, but they cannot maintain a vital action in the dead. Easier therefore, would it be to bring up a new but growing city into habits of virtue and religion, though composed like Rome itself of refugees and robbers, than to sustain the dying flame of piety in any such old, dilapidated town.

Nor in this do we draw upon our own judgment merely. I could point you to many examples for illustration. Like examples can even be cited from sacred history. It was in just such a state of national decline and despair, that a prophet was sent to rebuke the shameful wickedness and moral abandonment of his times; and the success he had was a good omen of what every preacher of God's truth will have to meet in like circumstances. The people are answered, as every desperate and hopeless community will—"It is vain to serve God, and what profit is it that we have walked mournfully before the Lord of Hosts?" Nor do they stop here. Having just enough of character left to feel the odiousness of the restraints of duty, but not enough to reap its reward, growing weary of paying tithes to ruin and hearing solemn lectures which they have no spirit of self correction to improve, they at last become utterly desperate. "And now," say they, "we call the proud happy, yea, they that work wickedness are set up, yea, they that tempt God, are even delivered. Let us be rid of the preachers and have it in our way. We shall, at least, have our vices and our pleasures, and these are better than to be worried and fretted by a religion that only robs us of enjoyment."

Thus it is in every poor community that has run itself down, by a lack of character and enterprise. Reduced to poverty by a want of industry and virtue, their poverty becomes, in its turn, a temptation, exasperates their depravity and makes them scoffers, at last, even against the principles of virtue. The want of character first makes them poor, and then the destruction of the poor is their poverty. Accordingly the wise caution of Agur—lest I be poor and steal—is oftener and more strikingly verified in the case of communities, than it is in the case of individuals; for it will be found in every such decayed, unthrifty community, or city, that the people become as abject in character as they are in fortune. Having too little virtue to thrive, they must yet live ; and therefore they descend to the basest employments and trades, that they may gain their bread. The loss of hope is followed by a loss of shame. Having no industry to earn a living and no character to lose, they are ready, of course, to steal. They appear as bandits on the highway, or, what is the same in principle, they become mountebanks, jugglers, strolling musicians, keepers of tippling shops, gambling tables, lottery offices, mock theatres, brothels,—cormorants of all sorts, living on the vices they are able to foster, and the prey they may gather from other men's earnings. Every decayed community swarms with creatures of this sort, and the more of them you see in any place, the more reason have you to think that the day of decline has come.

I look, therefore, upon the prosperity of our city, as connected with the best hopes of virtue and religion. If, as a man of business and of property, I should feel oppressed and discouraged by the prospect of its future decline, much should I, as a man whose office it is to stand for the law of God and the honor of his truth. If such a day shall ever come upon us, the worst business of all in Hartford will be that, whose labor it is to make men better.

IF, now, I am right in these views,—if it be true that a decline of prosperity is connected with results to morals and religion of a nature so disastrous, it follows irresistibly that it is our duty to prosper; only provided it be possible for us. For if God has given us the power, it cannot be less than a most sacred duty to save our city from a moral decay so abject and hopeless. It becomes, therefore, a serious question, whether it is possible to maintain our growth and prosperity.

Happily I have not one doubt that it is. And yet it may render the obligation that lies upon us more distinct, if we contemplate a few proofs that God has set in our way, to encourage our confidence and stimulate us to our duty. To cite all the passages of Scripture that represent and promise prosperity, as the reward of faith in God and virtuous industry, is impossible. There is no doctrine of Scripture so often obtruded on the reader. God claims the right, in fact, to show the worth of his favor, and the healthful power of his commandments, by the blessings he will let fall on the good. He tries all modes of appeal, invents all glowing figures, that he may set forth the established connection between obedience and virtue on one hand, and prosperity of every kind on the other. He speaks to the individual, declaring that "the righteous man shall be like a tree planted by the rivers of water, that bringeth forth his fruit in his season; his leaf also shall not wither, and whatsoever he doeth shall prosper." He speaks to communities, declaring that "when it goeth well with the righteous, the city rejoiceth;" and that "by the blessing of the upright the city is exalted." He accumulates examples of good men and times of public virtue, flourishing in luxuriance, as boughs planted by wells of water, whose branches run over the wall, and hang there laden with fruit before our eyes. Jacob under Laban,

Joseph in Egypt, David under Saul, Daniel at Babylon, Esther and Nehemiah at the court of Persia, and, not least, the godly and devout prince named in my text, and who may be taken as an example of all. He found the kingdom in a low and broken state, and surrounded by great and powerful enemies, but by means of good laws and a purified religion, he set every thing on a footing of prosperity, so that "he had exceeding much riches and honor. He made himself treasuries, we are told, for silver and gold, and for precious stones, and for spices, and for shields, and for all manner of pleasant jewels. Store houses also, for the increase of corn and wine and oil, and stalls for all manner of beasts. Moreover, he provided himself cities and posses. sions of flocks; for God had given him substance very much." Then, to conclude all, it is added,—"this same Hezekiah also stopped the upper water-course of Gibon and brought it straight down to the west side of the city of David. And Hezekiah prospered in all his works." In such and so many ways do the Scriptures represent to us the fixed connection between virtue and prosperity. It cannot, therefore, be any more difficult for this, or any other community, to prosper, than it is to be virtuous. And as one is certainly possible, so must also be the other.

Nor is it only by authority of Scripture that we receive such a conclusion. Nothing is better understood, or oftener proved, than that all virtuous industry is connected, by a fixed law of nature, with growth and success. Prosperity and virtue are interwoven, by God, in the scale of being itself. Virtue is the appointed spring of prosperity,—prosperity the badge and flower of virtue. Nor is it by any miracle, or special grace, that virtue receives her reward. For virtue is itself a creative power, in its own nature, and can no more exist without some attendant increase, than a substance without a shadow. It forbids idleness. It sets the powers in action. It produces self-government, and keeps all the passions and capacities, both of body and mind, in a healthy, conservative order. It proposes good aims and worthy ends, such as foster application, inspire energy, and amplify all the capacities employed. It represses vice and extravagance, moderates reckless impulses, becomes a spring of order, patience, frugality, temperance, and economy. Hence there is no so creative agent out of God's own nature as virtue. It is, in fact, a re-creative power under Him, building the world to its own model and likeness, and holding, as a rental for this purpose, all the laws and resources of his realm. It opens the mines, levels the forests, builds up cities and empires, covers the earth with harvests and the sea with ships, piles up its stores of plenty, and makes the world itself the treasure-house of its works. Wherever there is public virtue and character, therefore, there must be public prosperity; for it is the fixed ordinance of God, that all right industry shall bring increase of substance. Hence it will do for Mexicans, Neapolitans and Chinese, not to prosper, but it will not do for us. They are not dishonored by decay and thriftlessness, because they cannot be; but we, I trust, have yet enough of character and virtue left, to suffer some disgrace from a state of wasting and decline. However appropriate to them, it cannot yet be quite appropriate to us.

On the whole, though it may not be possible, in all cases, for the individual to prosper, there is almost never a community that cannot and will not, if it be only true to itself; for the chances that may overthrow an individual, such as a want of capacity, a loss of health, an unexpected fraud and the like, seldom comprehend a whole community. If a harbor is closed up by an earthquake,—if some rival city comes down with an armed force, as Florence did upon Pisa, to crush it; in these and other like cases, a city may be justified in its decline. But exceptions of this nature are few and need hardly be considered. The great truth is, that God favors industry, and has made the most bountiful arrangements to bless it. The scale of His Providence is liberal,—the laws of production are sure, so that any reasonable measure of effort and industry, is infallibly connected with growth and abundance. No matter how inauspicious the clime, or how sterile the region a people may occupy,—placed on a barren rock, in mid ocean, their industry will make a pasture of the sea itself, and wrest from the waters and the storms, a fund of wealth and regular increase. If ever men had a right to lose their courage and give themselves up to dismal wasting, it was the first planters of our own New England. The shore was bleak and wild, the climate severe, the soil a meagre, flinty heritage. They had every thing to create by their own patient industry, out of lean and scanty harvests, and without a market. And yet they multiplied their numbers and resources, spreading out from post to post,—conquering, by stern effort and economy, a wealth continually increasing, till now the most populous, richest, happiest portion of our great country, is that same hard, frowning region of rocks and snows, on which they began to battle for a heritage. Well and manfully is it proved what power there is in character and industry to conquer prosperity any where. And yet this people have done only what it was their duty to do. Had they failed, they would have dishonored the principles they were called to illustrate, and God would have charged it as their crime against them.

What, then, shall we say for Hartford, with such examples before us? If industry and duty can make any thing to prosper, it cannot be that a city possessed of so many advantages with so good a beginning, has a right to suffer any decline; or can, without some fault that is both dishonorable and criminal. I care not how many railroads compass us about, or how much of our former trade they withdraw. Be it that all our former resources and modes of increase are cut off. Still we have our hands and our wits left us. Our capital is ample; we hold a position at the head of a navigable river, in the bosom of a broad, fertile valley, surpassed by no other on the face of the globe for beauty and richness; we have a healthy and vigorous people, and, compared with any other community, a fair measure of genius and enterprise ; and, what is more than all, virtue dwells in our houses, and God is with us at our altars. To say, or to fear that such a people cannot prosper, is even criminal. We have only to do what becomes us, and we are safe. Many thought, when the West India commerce was cut off, that our city must be fatally ruined. Doleful prophecies were uttered in the streets, and doleful faces congregated to hear. But it has since been found, that there are other things in the world besides West India commerce; and so it will be found now, if we have courage to look for them, and a pliant skill to turn our hand with the times,—that there are other things besides country groceries and market waggons. I do not undertake to say what we shall do or whither we shall turn. I only say that God never made such a city as Hartford, and set it in a country like ours, where every thing is on a tide of progress, to go down into decline and prostration without some grievous and even shameful delinquency.

Besides, it will be a new thing in the history of mankind, if any city or people are ruined by works of improvement. Such works may change the courses of trade and the modes of production; they may work temporary losses and hardships, but they will always be found in the end, if there be a prompt and manly spirit to turn them to account, to promote even the advantage of those who most suffer by them. The growth of every city helps the growth of every other; the prosperity of the world assists the prosperity of every part of it. There is no real war between the interests of cities and communities. No real improvement is ever a source of permanent injury; for it is the fixed law of God that what advances the wealth and happiness of the whole, shall stand in final harmony with the good of every part. To believe, therefore, that railroads are going to destroy the prosperity of Hartford, if we have the spirit to do what becomes us, is to doubt a first and fundamental law of society. Rather should we judge that these instrumentalities, which seem to threaten a present injury, are destined, in the end, to establish our growth and invigorate our success.

Let us, then, accept it, as a fixed conclusion, that Hartford can and ought to prosper. Let us take it in charge as our duty, under God, to make it prosper; not doubting that if once we come to such a determination, the result is sure. Meantime, let me add some suggestions and stimulants, which may set us forward in the way of our duty, and thus in the way of success.

FIRST OF ALL, we must renounce every thought and scheme which looks for prosperity at the expense of others. The only sound law of increase is the law of production.—"Wealth gotten by vanity shall be diminished, but he that gathereth by labor shall increase." We cannot thrive by plunder, or by any kind of strategy, in which we seek to advance at the expense of others. The wealth that we desire we must also create, and what we are to add to ourselves must be measured by the values added, by our industry, to the common stock of the world's goods. We are not required to submit quietly to any kind of wrong, which under the pretext of improvement, robs us of our natural rights; but to every other kind of improvement, which assists the public good, however unfavorably it may affect us, we are bound to oppose no hindrance. To maintain that right enthusiasm, which is the first condition of all sound growth and success, we must be worthy to prosper in our own sight. Our plans too must have that enlarged and friendly character, that will make us worthy to prosper, in the sight of others. Therefore it must be our study, not how we may cripple or thwart any rival interest, but how we may build up our own—how to earn most, how to develop our own resources and improve our own advantages. I have a great respect for the mercantile profession, but there is one error into which they are specially liable to fall. Being ever on the rack to save themselves from the effects of fluctuating prices, or studying how to make their gain by the same, i. e. by what others lose; having it for their business to serve the public only by changing the locality of objects already produced and distributing them to consumers, not to fashion by their industry objects which represent the visible effects of labor, they are prone to assume (what really is not true in regard to their own profits) that whatever is gained must be gained by the loss of others. The impression of the mechanic is more likely to be the true one; for with him creation is the only source of income to be thought of. The values he creates appear in visible shapes and products, and his hopes are measured by the visible earnings of his industry. What is equally true of the merchant, or should be, but is slurred over and lost sight of under the indefinite and shapeless benefit of a transference; a distribution and a credit, is to him a first and only thought. The sooner we dismiss all thoughts but this the better for us. Had we done it years ago, I think I can see that we should be in a better and healthier state. The hope that we may somehow thrive by chances and wise schemes may do to amuse the present hour, but it becomes us to know that other communities have as many chances and wise schemes as we. And the more we play with such temptations, the more we debauch our courage and chill our enthusiasm for better and more earnest struggles. It is time for us now to propose a more serious and certain method, viz: lo gird on the harness of toil and go to the patient work of years, to create within ourselves the prosperity we desire. Not that we are to forsake merchandise and betake ourselves to manufactures. Merchandise is a power as truly creative as any other, only it does not show the values it creates as visibly. We are to set all our instruments and faculties at work together. We are to consider what possible improvements will assist our growth. We are to make up an inventory of our capital and the fund of creative powers we have in our people, and study in what way we may best employ and develope all---confident always of this, that we have only to be true to ourselves and nourish the seeds of growth we possess, to be sure of all the progress we desire.

In this view and as a mere matter of public economy, saying nothing of higher motives, we must endeavor to stimulate and perfect our schools. To unfold the creative talent and genius of our people, must be one of our first studies; for in this our best hopes of prosperity lie. We can better afford any waste than the waste of talent, and it is deplorable to reflect on the immense fund of talent we have slumbering in unconsciousness, or only half awakened, by reason of the defectiveness of our schools. The great first problem at the root of all prosperity, is to produce the most condensed virtue and intellectual capacity possible; for if we may give to one man the capacity of three, then he will produce three times as much, without consuming any more. So if you can open as much of manhood in ten as in thirty thousand people, (which is far from difficult) you will have only ten for expenditure and thirty for production. Therefore, if you wish to make a city of ten thousand swell to a population of thirty thousand, the readiest and surest way is to make the ten thousand worth thirty thousand, by the stimulus of a right education. Neither need you be concerned to find out beforehand how the ten thousand will produce a three fold value by their industry. They will determine that for themselves. Having so much of manhood in them, as a creative power, it will be sure to appear in ways of its own. Nothing is better understood than that a dull minded family of mechanics, receiving low wages, will barely subsist, while a family that is quickened to inventiveness and skill, will command as much higher wages, as the values they produce are greater, and these will thrive in property, rise in character, become influential citizens, and act as stimulants to every kind of prosperity. An active, spirited, and scientific body of mechanics is a want every where, and especially here, where the mechanical interest has hitherto been greatly depressed. We take up a prejudice that manufactures and trades of handicraft are unfavorable to a state of public virtue, a prejudice that is refuted by facts on every side of us; for there is no purely manufacturing town in New-England, that exhibits a waste of character and virtue, as deplorable as Hartford—actuated by this prejudice, we withhold our capital from enterprises that would quicken industry among us, and elevate its salutary hopes. And so, the prejudice we cherish creates a loss of virtue even worse than the loss it deprecates. A visible discouragement rests upon most of the trades among us, and the effect is seen in a want of life, progress, cultivation and character; consequently in want of that thrift and hopefulness which are the springs of industrious virtue. One great mechanic rising into wealth and public note among us, would rectify many false impressions and breathe new life and courage into all the mechanic professions. I could speak of one such, that we had in prospect, a few years ago. I watched his opening genius with no little hope and admiration. But whether by our fault, or not, I cannot say, he was scarcely ripe for action, before the better encouragement offered him elsewhere withdrew him from us. Others doubtless we have among us now, who are proving their genius in a similar manner, though unknown to me. Many others, we have, beyond all question, whose fine native capacity is rusting in dull obscurity and depression, never to be made conscious of itself, for want of a sufficiently quickening stimulus in our schools to bring it into action. For it is not nature alone that makes the man. Neither is it enough for us, when once a promising talent is unfolded to detain it, if possible, among us by adequate encouragements and aids to success. If we yielded all the encouragement to talent that we might, we should doubtless have more to encourage. But the living spark can be first kindled only by schools. It is the school that quickens curious thought, fills the mind with principles of science, and starts the inventive and creative powers into action. Therefore I say push your schools to the highest possible limit of perfection. Spare no pains, count no expense; for rely upon it, whatever you may do to make a city of men will go to make a city. Let every talent, every type of genius, in every child, be watched and nurtured by the city, as by a mother watching for the signs of promise in her sons.

At the same time, while we are endeavoring thus to create productive talent and power, it would be very unwise and absurd not to have an eye upon all the schools of destruction by which talent is blighted and industry corrupted. Here I touch a subject of which I have no words to speak as I could wish. It is appalling to the mind of every public spirited citizen, watching for the welfare and honor of the city, to see how many gates of ruin we have opening on our streets. If we support schools of knowledge and virtue, we are also supporting schools of vice and destruction. And these two kinds of schools are set one against the other; one to create, the other to destroy; one to bless, the other to curse; one to prepare industry, the other to blast every good habit; one to call out talent and capacity, the other to brutalize and damn every divine faculty that God has given; one to furnish and bring forth useful men, such as shall rise to honor and wealth in the virtuous callings of life, the other to rot men down into felons and paupers, and make them a burden and a tax on industry itself. I walk the streets and I see the cormorants who keep these dens of vice, coming up from below ground, or out from above ground, and even daring to look virtuous men in the face! as if they had a right to breathe the same air and walk the same streets with men of character and citizens who honor and serve the city! I know not what can be done. Of this however I am quite sure, that if our citizens who love the city and wish to see it prosper, had any right sense of what these men are doing, they would somehow find a way of relief. Suppose there were a military company quartered on our city by the government. How long should we submit to be thus preyed upon ? But these men add not a cent to our income. They create nothing that has value. They are all quartered on the city, living at the public expense, and what is worst of all, living on the consumption of talent, industry and all creative power. If the city were to take them all up as pensioners and support them and their families, at the public expense, it would be a real gain to our wealth; for then we should save, as clear profit, all which they destroy. We think little of the loss we suffer by these vicious instrumentalities, because it is so diffused and falls so extensively, in the first instance, on the obscure and the poor. The greater is it and the more vital on that account; for it falls upon the broader surface and paralyses the greater amount of power. Neither let us think that, because it is only the roots of the tree that are killed, the tree itself is clear of harm. Could we ever be fairly rid of these vicious instrumentalities, the saving would be equal, I am persuaded, in the mere scale of economy, to the accession of at least a half dozen wealthy citizens every year—an accession sufficient of itself to turn the scale of prosperity, in any town not larger than this.

Suppose now, for a moment, that by a right education, and a wise protection of the public virtue, we could start into high creative action, the whole lower stratum of our city, comprising the vicious, the idle, the unprogressive and thriftless of every sort, and set them all on the ascent; awaken their talents, encourage their undertakings, secure them in temperate and frugal habits, inspire them with a sense of character and a will to rise, what a mass of dead expenditure should we cut off!—another savings bank created, and another, and another, all overflowing with deposits; the families happy, and the city, by the mere development of its creative virtue, swelling in population and wealth, as never before in its happiest days. We should save enough out of the annual waste of our present city, to build another and a greater in a very few years.

While endeavoring, in these and other like methods, to unfold our internal talents and resources, it will sometimes be required of us to undertake enterprises of a more public character, that may assist our growth. And then it becomes us to understand, that what we do must be done promptly. I do not say hastily or blindly, but promptly. No man ever prospered who had not his eyes open, and did not stand ready to do the right thing, at the right time. It is not enough to talk of doing something, we must act, and act before it is too late to act successfully. "In all labor there is profit, but the talk of the lips tendeth only to penury." Let our city once begin to decline, —let it once go abroad that we are going down, and then every thing conspires against us. We shall want courage ourselves, and the public about us will help to rid us of what little we have left. To revive a decaying town is like raising the dead, for hope, which is the life of all enterprise, is gone. Therefore we must be beforehand. We must be alive to all our opportunities, and be ready to act for the public good as for our own—to strike at the right time, and strike the right blow.

Then again we must be united and strike together. "There be

four things which are little upon the earth, but are exceeding wise, and the locust family is one. They have no king, yet they go forth all of them by bands." Public spirit is a great organific power in communities, and no community that is thoroughly animated by public love, can ever be prostrated or defeated in its purposes. We must feel that we have one interest, and all ranks and classes must unite heartily in the pursuit of it. We must encourage the weak and lend what aid we can to the virtuous struggles of industry. Our men of business must support and strengthen each other. Those who have funds to invest should prefer investments here, even if it cost a nominal sacrifice. The best investment is that which most enlarges the heart, and no man who lets his bosom swell with public spirit to the city, and feels the conscious pleasure that flows from serving its welfare, will deem himself a loser because of any trifling sacrifice. There must be no sectional conflicts, no political or party jealousy, no sectarian distance or division. Forgive me if I suggest a fear that there is something in the state of society in Hartford which is peculiar and has a baleful effect on our prosperity. I speak of a certain religious clannishness, which draws us into circles of a sectarian complexion. Nothing is more undignified, or more opposed to the real object of society, which is to open the heart to man as man, and breed a state of courtesy and mutual regard between those who have different opinions, and wear the diverse colors of actual life. Nothing could be more fatal to anything like public spirit, or to any practical unity of force, in behalf of the common interest. We cannot flow together,—no warmth of feeling can be kindled for the public good. Society is divided, even down to the root. We are not people of Hartford, but we are Congregationalists, Episcopalians, Baptists, Methodists,—penned by our religion, impounded in it, as it were, for safe keeping. What I say is not literally and exactly true, but proximately, and the baleful effect is to be traced, in all our affairs as a city; creating a chill, souring the springs of feeling and producing a virtual enmity, out of that which should set us in love with all mankind. Such a habit of society cannot too soon be broken down. And if we cannot be otherwise rid of it, let us be exorcised. Sometimes we are moved either by the bigotry we have within us, or by provocation from without, to say what does not perfectly justify the kinder charities we feel, and it is most unhappy if by any such means we embitter the springs of social life. Let all such fences that we may have raised up be broken down. We must have union or we cannot have strength, and union implies something more than that we reside in the same city. There must be a fellow spirit, a social warmth, a living glow and a common aim.

But it is time for me to close. And let no one say that I have given you a discourse on the water project. I have only seized upon this occasion, when the question of your own prosperity is before you, as a favorable one to gain your attention to some useful suggestions. Ordinarily, the prosperity or success of a community is not like to be advanced by great artificial movements, though there are times and exigences when a somewhat violent blow needs to be struck. The prosperity of a city is commonly developed by a slow process within itself. It expands by force of its own virtues, and the creative power of its own industry. This is the main hope of every people, and what I have said has been chiefly designed for permanent effect in this direction,—to impart courage, to create public responsibility and public spirit,—to impress a conviction of the value of talent, and the ruinous and destructive power of vice, and thus to prompt us to united and vigorous action for all that concerns the common good. Neither let me seem to have meddled with that which is not within my sphere. I see blended in this great subject all the dearest interests of virtue and religion for ages to come. If we of to-day are recreant to our duty, and allow this city, which God has made our heritage, and that of our children, to go down into decline, the cause of virtue and the church of God will suffer as deeply as the fortunes of business; and that by a ruin as much more deplorable as they are more sacred and closer to immortality. To avert any such possible evil, every man is called to lend his voice and his influence. Nor is there any office too sacred to be employed in blessing the hopes of industry, and sanctifying the bonds of public love. Dismiss, then, every discouraged thought. Take it as a fixed truth that Hartford can prosper; therefore, that it ought; therefore, that it shall. Go then, every man to his own altar, and live a godly life; every man to his work, and do it manfully and well; and all together to the task of preserving the public virtue, and proving to mankind, in despite of all hindrance, the unalterable truth that growth and progress are the right, under God, of every people that will do their duty.

## PART III
# BARBARISM THE FIRST DANGER

A DISCOURSE FOR HOME MISSIONS

NOTE. The following Discourse was delivered in New York, Boston and other places, in May and June, 1847, and is now yielded to the American Home Missionary Society, in whose behalf it was prepared, for publication. H.B.

# DISCOURSE

*Then said Micah, Now know I that the Lord will do me good, seeing I have a Levite to my priest.*

— JUDGES 17:13.

A VERY unimportant chapter of biography is here preserved to us—save that if we take the subject as an exponent of his times, we shall find a serious and momentous truth illustrated in his conduct. He lives in the time of the Judges, that is, in the emigrant age of Israel. It is the time, when his nation are passing through the struggles incident to a new settlement, a time therefore of decline towards barbarism. Public security is gone. The people have run wild. Superstition has dislodged the clear sovereignty of reason. Forms are more sacred than duties, and a costly church furniture is taken as synonymous with a godly life. It is at just such times that we are to look for the union of great crimes and scrupulous acts of devotion. The villain and the saint coalesce, without difficulty, in one and the same character; and superstition, which delights in absurdities, hides the imposture from him who suffers it. Thus Micah enters on the stage of history as a thief, having stolen eleven hundred shekels of silver from his mother; but before the scene closes, he becomes, at least in his own view, quite a saint; and that too, if we may judge, without any great detriment to his former character.

Finding that his mother has invoked a solemn curse upon the thief, whoever he may be, that has stolen her money; and also, which is more frightful still, that she had actually dedicated the money, before it was stolen, to a religious use, even to make a molten image for himself, the superstitious fancy of the barbarian begins to worry his peace. To have stolen the money was nothing specially dreadful, but to have a parent's curse hanging over his head, and sacred money hid in his house—both considered to involve the certainty of some impending mischief that is fatal—is more than he has courage to support. Moved, of course, by no ingenuous and dignified spirit of repentance, but only by a driveling superstition, he goes to his mother and chokes out his confession, saying: "The silver is with me, I took it"! And what a beautiful evidence of piety, thinks the glad mother, that her Micah was afraid to keep the sacred money! So she pours out her dear blessing on him, saying: "Blessed be thou of the Lord, my son"! Then she takes the silver and from it has a molten image cast for her worthy and hopeful son, which he sets up in "the house of his gods," among the teraphim and other trumpery there collected. And as Micah is now growing religious, he must also have a priest. First, he consecrates his own son; but his son not being a Levite, it was difficult for so pious a man to be satisfied. Fortunately, a young Levite—a strolling mendicant probably—comes that way, and he promptly engages the youth to remain and act the *padre* for him, saying: "Dwell with me and be a father unto me." Having thus got up a religion, the thief is content, and his mental troubles are quieted. Becoming a Romanist before Rome is founded, he says: "Now know I that the Lord will do me good, seeing I have a Levite to my priest." That it would do him any good to be a better man, does not appear to have occurred to him. Religion, to him, consisted rather in a fine silver apparatus of gods and a priest in regular succession!

Set now the picture in its frame, the man in connection with his times, and you have in exhibition a great practical truth, which demands your earnest study. Nothing is more certain, as you may see in this example of Micah and his times, than that emigration, or a new settlement of the social state, involves a tendency to social decline. There must, in every such case, be a relapse towards barbarism, more or less protracted, more or less complete. Commonly, nothing but extraordinary efforts in behalf of education and religion, will suffice to prevent a fatal lapse of social order. Apart from this great truth, clearly seen as enveloped in the practical struggles of our American history, no one can understand its real import, the problem it involves, or the position at which we have now arrived. Least of all, can he understand the sublime relation of home missions, and other like enterprises, to the unknown future of our great nation. He must know that we are a people trying out the perils incident to a new settlement of the social state; he must behold religion passing out into the wilds of nature with us, to fortify law, industry and good manners, and bear up our otherwise declining fortunes, till we become an established and fully cultivated people. Just here, hang all the struggles of our history for the two centuries now past, and for at least another century to come.

We shall also discover, in pursuing our subject, in what manner we are to apprehend danger from the spread of Romanism. If you seem to struggle, in this matter of Romanism, with contrary convictions; to see reason in the alarms urged upon you so frequently, and yet feel it to be the greatest unreason to fear the prevalence here of a religion so distinctively opposite to our character and institutions; if you waver between a feeling of panic and a feeling of derision; if you are half frighted by the cry of Romanism, and half scorn it as a bugbear; you will be able to settle yourself into a sober and fixed opinion of the subject, when you perceive that we are in danger, first, of something far worse than Romanism, and through that of Romanism itself. OUR FIRST DANGER IS BARBARISM-Romanism next; for before we can think it a religion, to have a Levite to our priest, we must bring back the times of the Judges. Let us empty ourselves of our character, let us fall into superstition, through the ignorance, wildness and social confusion incident to a migratory habit and a rapid succession of new settlements, and Romanism will find us just where character leaves us. The real danger is the prior. Taking care of that we are safe. Sleeping over that, nothing ought to save us; for if we must have a wild race of nomads roaming over the vast western territories of our land—a race without education, law, manners or religion—we need not trouble ourselves farther on account of Romanism; for to such a people, Romanism, bad as it is, will come as a blessing.

I shall recur to this question of Romanism again. I only name it here as a preliminary, that may assist you to apprehend the true import of my subject. Let us now proceed to the question itself, How far emigration and a continual re-settlement, as in this country, involves a tendency to moral and social disorganization? In the discussion of this question, I shall draw principally on the facts of history; I only suggest here, as a preparative and key to the facts that may be cited, a few of the reasons why such a decline is likely to appear.

First of all, the society transplanted, in a case of emigration, cannot carry its roots with it; for society is a vital creature, having roots of antiquity, which inhere in the very soil-in the spots consecrated by valor, by genius and by religion. Transplanted to a new field, the emigrant race lose, of necessity, a considerable portion of that vital force which is the organific and conserving power of society. All the old roots of local love and historic feelingthe joints and bands that minister nourishment-are left behind; and nothing remains to organize a living growth, but the two unimportant incidents, proximity and a common interest.

Education must, for a long time, be imperfect in degree and

partial in extent. There is no literary atmosphere breathing through the forests or across the prairies. The colleges, if any they have, are only rudimental beginnings, and the youth a raw company of woodsmen. Hurried into life, at the bar, or in the pulpit, when as yet they are only half educated, their performances are crude in the matter and rough in the form. No matter how cultivated the professional men of the first age, those of the second, third and fourth will mix up extravagance and cant in all their demonstrations, and will be acceptable to the people partly for that reason. For the immense labors and rough hardships necessary to be encountered, in the way of providing the means of living, will ordinarily create in . them a rough and partially wild habit.

Then, as their tastes grow wild, their resentments will grow violent and their enjoyments coarse. The salutary restraints of society being, to a great extent, removed, they ˃ will think it no degradation to do before the woods and wild animals, what, in the presence of a cultivated social state, they would blush to perpetrate. They are likely even to look upon the indulgence of low vices and brutal pleasures, as the necessary garnish of their life of ad venture.

In religion, their views will, of course, be narrow and crude, and their animosities bitter. Sometimes the very life of religion will seem about to die, as it actually would, save that some occasional outburst of over-wrought feeling or fanatical zeal kindles a temporary fire. Probably it will be found that low superstitions begin to creep in, a regarding of dreams, a faith in the presentation of scripture texts, in apparitions and visions, perhaps also in necromancy.

Mean time, if we speak of civil order, it will probably be found that the old common law of the race is not transplanted as a vital power, but only as a recollection that refuses to live, because of the newness of the soil, and the varied circumstances which, in so many ways, render it inapplicable. It asks for loyalty where there is no demesne, offers a jury before there is a court, and sanctifies a magna charta where no plain of Runnymede is ever to be known. Hence, the need of much new legislation, consequently much of confusion and a considerable lapse of time, before the new body of law, with its tribunals and uses, can erect its trunk and grow up into life from a native root. Mean time it is well, if the social wildness and the violent resentments of the people do not break over all the barriers of legal restraint, and dissolve the very bonds of order.

If now, beside all the causes here enumerated, the emigrants are much involved in war to maintain their possessions, or if they are gathered from many nations having different languages, laws, manners and religions, the tendency to social decline is, of course, greatly aggravated.

. Indeed, where all the forms of habit, prejudice and opinion are found to impinge upon each other, and every recollection of the past, every peculiar trait of national feeling and personal character requires to be obliterated, before it is possible for the new elements to coalesce, what can save a people, we are tempted to ask, from being precipitated downward even below society itself?

Having glanced, in this rapid manner, at the causes of decline theoretically involved in emigration, (for emigration works no mischief by itself, but only as it provokes the malignant action of other causes,) let us now pass to some historic illustrations. And I begin with the emigration headed by Abraham, where the facts are already familiar, so that when you are engaged in tracing their import as illustrations of my subject, your minds will be distracted by no effort of attention to conceive the facts themselves.

There was never an emigration conducted under better auspices.

As in the original settlement of New England, the aim and purpose of the movement were strictly religious. The emigrants too, were shepherds in their habit, never attached to the soil, but accustomed to movement. They came out also as a family, for Lot appears to have been only a ward of Abraham; and in the family state-which is itself a patriarchate, the simplest and most unquestionable of all governments, as it is closest to nature—they had a complete frame of social order already provided. Though trained as a nomad and manifestly ignorant of certain moral distinctions familiar to us, Abraham yet evinces, in his character, a degree of beauty and princely dignity, such as seldom can be found under the politer forms of civilization. In his heroic pursuit and slaughter of the kings to rescue Lot, in the singular dignity of his meeting with Melchisedec on his return, in the generous and conciliatory terms by which he sought to avoid the quarrel already begun between Lot's herdsmen and his own, in his hospitality at the tent door in Mamre, in his burial of Sarah, in the whole manner of his life in short there is a grand, massive nobility of character, which, if we cannot call it civilization or refinement, is yet only so much higher and more charming, as it is closer to nature, more original and older than the days of accomplished heartlessness and drawing-room pretence. It is the pure, virgin character of a great and primitive manhood, which, in the simple, godly life of the east country, was not yet spent.

See now what a mass of barbarism is shortly developed out of this fair beginning. The character of Lot is not strongly fortified by religious principle, and the restraints of society being now removed, he soon falls into loose habits of virtue and, in the end, brings himself and his family to a very sorry figure. Thus out of Lot springs the wild race of the Moabites, a race as degraded in character, as the abominable and filthy rites of their god Baal Peor require them to be-enemies, of course, to Jehovah and the kindred stock of Israel, in all after times. The Ammonites are a branch of the same stock.

Meantime, Abraham himself is throwing off upon the world, in his son Ishmael, another stock of barbarians. Driven out with his mother, to seek his fortune as he may, among the wild tribes of idolaters that infest the country, the lad, we are told, grows up in the wilderness and becomes an archer. By which it appears that he betook himself to some secret cave or fastness, in the south, and there, by the use of his bow as a hunter and robber, maintained himself, and became the father of the Bedouin race. There he trained up the young Ishmaelites, otherwise called Arabs a name which, according to some, signifies westerners—a prolific, talented and powerful race of men, whose nature it has been to this hour to live by plunder, whose hand is against every man and every man's hand against them. Thus you have another wild people, a cruel, treacherous, lying stock of thieves and idolaters developed out of the emigration.

One generation later, viz.:—out of the family of Isaac, comes another. I speak of the persecuted Esau and the Idumeans or Edomites descended of him. These were a warlike and ferocious race, governed by dukes or great captains, and for long ages the sturdiest of all the enemies of Israel.

It is remarkable too that, when David is giving the roll, in one of his Psalms, of the great league of nations that were conspiring, at that time, against his country, he puts at the head of all precisely these three fierce and barbarous people, descended of Terah, the common ancestor both of them and of his countrymen. "For they have consulted together with one consent, they are confederate against thee, the tabernacles of Edom and the Ishmaelites, of Moab and the Hagarenes." Then follow the other nations who are led by these.

Meantime, if we consider the dastardly conduct of the ten brothers of Joseph, who for jealousy sell him into slavery, and then, by a solemn lie, convince their father that he is dead-remembering also and holding in comparison Abraham's noble and magnanimous treatment of Lot-we shall see that there has certainly been a very great falling off towards barbarism, in the chosen family itself.

But we must follow them further, even into this book of Judges, where they come to make their final settlement in the land. In Egypt they had become acquainted with agriculture, with cities and the settled modes of life; though degraded, to some extent, by their temporary subjection to slavery. But their freedom, connected with their strong legal discipline under Moses, the new sentiments and new social capacities, which had been formed under this protracted discipline of forty years, during which the old generation of slavery had become extinct, had prepared them to enter the country appointed and make a fair beginning. They took their places; for a time all was well. Still they were a people without roots, and they began, ere long, to fall into social anarchy. They served the Lord all the days of Joshua, and all the days of the elders that had overlived Joshua and had seen all the great works of the Lord that he did for Israel, and when that generation were gathered unto their fathers-so says the history "There arose another generation, which knew not the Lord, nor yet the works which he had done for Israel." Now came the dark time; for in every emigration, the moral and social trial commonly falls, not on the first generation, but more frequently on the second, third and fourth. So it was here, and it really seemed that the nation must utterly die, before it could get root. Three times it is said in the history, that "there was no king in Israel and that every man did what was right in his own eyes." By which we are to understand, not that royalty was discontinued, for it had not existed; but that there was no civil head, that government was utterly dissolved. It was, in truth, the paradisaic age of no government; a day when they had it, not for a theory, but for a fact. Wrongs were redressed by uprisings of popular impatience, by assassination or private revenge. In one case of outrage, which may be taken doubtless as a good specimen of the barbarity of the times, the tribes were roused to vengeance, in the manner of a riot, by sending round, as a proclamation, the pieces of a murdered woman's body! If at any time they had a government, it was commonly the government of a usurper, who butchered, as he came into power, after the method of the Turks, all the families that had any semblance of right to civil precedence, or any possible hope of succession. The roads were destroyed, and there was no passage through the country, save in by-ways, or across the fields and mountains. The arts perished; there was not even a smith left in the land, and they were obliged to go down to the Philistines to get an axe or a mattock sharpened. In one case, they fought a battle with ox goads, because they had no better implements. Their religion being all one with the laws, fell of course into the same confusion with them. As we see in the case of Micah, Jehovah and the gods, all stand upon a par! They have their molten images set up together in "the house of the gods," to be smoked by the same incense; and Micah's Levite probably has it for his duty to practice before them all! Such is the decline suffered by this emigrant nation, in the process of colonizing a new region and building up a new social fabric. But dismal as the picture is to which they have descended, we have it for our comfort, that they are not utterly lost. After they have sounded the lowest notes of misery and social debasement, a Samuel appears, collects the scattered elements, works them gradually towards order, and the new nation, taking root, begins to rise.

Passing over now the instructive lessons that might be drawn from the Egyptian, Grecian, Carthaginian and Roman colonies, we descend to the great American question itself. That the Mexican and the South American States have actually lost ground, since the emigration; that they have been descending steadily towards barbarism, in the loss of the old Castilian dignity, in the decay of society and manners, and the general prostration of order, is well understood. But it is commonly supposed, I believe, that our North American settlements, especially those of New England, have never suffered any similar retrogradation; that they have, on the contrary, steadily advanced or ascended to their present state. No impression could be more opposite to the real facts of history. Probably never before did any emigrant people resist, with so great promptitude and effect, the inherent causes of decline involved in a new state of society. Nor can it be said that the issue was ever doubtful. Indeed I am not sure that, if we consider the rough amount of character in the whole community, any real diminution was ever suffered. For if much was lost in the complete finish of the higher class, something was also gained in the sharpness, vigor and capacity of the lower. And if there was even a decay of virtue and good manners in all classes, there was yet a gain in all, as regards spirit, self-reliance, physical endurance and other like traits, which are essential as the staple of a perfect manhood. If there was more coarseness, so possibly there was more volume. If there was less of learning, there was also a more perfect deliverance from the restraints of learning. If they had less of society, they had as much more of action. If they finished nothing, they created more. But in taking such a view as this, which is the most favorable permitted us, it is implied, as will be observed by all, that there was, in certain very important respects, a marked decline.

This decline was most evident in the higher class, and in the cultivated manners and tastes, brought over by the emigrant families. The leading spirits of the first age were truly great and cultivated men—cedars of Lebanon, nay, the topmost branches of the cedars, that God had brought over to plant by the waters of the new world.

They were many of them scholars, who had received at the English universities, the highest advantages of culture furnished in that age. Their minds were matured and polished by severe study. They knew society. Some of them were persons who had travelled in foreign countries, who had figured in civil stations and were not unskilled even as courtiers. They were fellow disciples and compatriots with such men as Owen, Howe, Milton, John Hampden, Oliver Cromwell and the other great spirits, who were struggling in that age for the civil and religious emancipation of their country. But they came into the wilderness, as it were to be tempted of the devil, throwing themselves and their families, for a whole century to come, upon the severest struggles of toil and warfare, to provide and fortify their new home. For a long time, they had no market. In their modes of dress, their residences and their furniture, they were many of them restricted to supplies that were coarse and rude. Their means of education for the youth were defective, in that which is necessary to a finished and really accomplished character, though sufficient to give a good degree of rudimental force. And, more than all, society, that indefinable but powerful something, which gives a tone of refinement to literary tastes, and without which, feeling cannot rise to its highest dignity-this was a want, which no industry or care could supply. The trials and exposures were rough, the great world was far away, petty strifes and bickerings-always enveloped in the ill nature of the race, but restrained among a great people under the established forms of cultivated life-broke out and raged in their little communities. A painful subsidence of manners soon began to appear. In many families, a certian flavor of refinement passed, by tradition, and in fact was never wholly spent. Still it was evident, after the first race was gone, and the second and third had come into their places, that character had fallen to a lower type. The educated men were, in comparison, a rude or, at least, partially cultivated race. Their English style is loose. Elegance, well chastened thought, dignity of feeling do not appear. The spelling is even more irregular and capricious than it had been. And the public proceedings of courts and churches, if the records

are referred to, exhibit a certain rawness, that is quite characteristic. We feel, in short, that we have descended to an inferior race. It is somewhat as if a nest of eagles had been filled with a brood of owls.

The decline of manners and mental cultivation, consequent on a life in the woods, carried with it a correspondent decline of morals and religion. And the natural downward tendency was aggravated, by the wars in which they were compelled to engage. Thus, after the bloody war with Philip, the synod of Massachusetts, convened to deliberate on the state of virtue and religion, set forth the following mournful particulars: "a decay of godliness and secret apostasy among professors;" "pride and contention;" a "want of truth and promise breaking;" a "neglect of family prayer;" "profane swearing;" "intemperance;" "a common practice of travelling on the Sabbath day;" "inordinate passions and breaches of the seventh commandment." Allowing all that may be necessary for exaggeration in this picture, we are still obliged, when they speak of a common practice of travelling on the Sabbath day, to acknowledge that there must have been a very marked decline in their moral habit. Following too into the war the four companies, for example, of Connecticut Rangers, we find them quite at home in the woods, displaying, in their modes of warfare and their wild, rough spirit, the full grown Texan habit. On going to the church and court records of this period and onward, for the next fifty or seventy years, we discover mournful evidences of incontinence, even in the respectable families. As if, being cut off from the more refined pleasures of society, their baser passions had burnt away the restraints of delicacy, and the growing coarseness of manners had allowed them finally to seek, in these baser passions, the spring of their enjoyments. Shortly after this war, the wretched scenes of infatuation enacted at Salem, furnish us the proof that religion is dwindling towards superstition. Not that a belief in witchcraft was peculiar to New England, or to that age of the world, but only that a want of thorough mental discipline in the ministry and the courts, connected with a general taint of superstition contracted in the woods by the whole people, aggravated the public delusion and

finally suffered the whole body of society to go mad, in scenes which it is even horrible to contemplate.

Still the way is downward till we come to the "great revival," so called, and the times of the French wars. And here we find a period of thirty or forty years, where the dregs of decline and the seeds of new life are so intermixed, and the signs so crossed, one by another, that we hardly know what judgment to hold. Over and above all patriotic motives that may be conceived, there was a readiness to enlist in these wars, that indicates an adventurous and partially wild habit. The little State of Connecticut, containing at that time probably about 75,000 people, raised and equipped over 5,000 men, for three years in succession. As might be expected, when these two wars were over, the people were found to be reduced to a miserable state of poverty, and, what was yet worse, it was also discovered that their habits of industry and virtuous thrift had received a fatal shock. Then it was, that the people of New England seemed, for once, to want a spur to their creative activity, and a society was organized "For the Promotion of Industry"—a society which brought out three hundred women with their spinning-wheels on Boston common, to give an example to the other sex, of a virtue which they had so nearly forgotten. Mean time, the whole community, I may almost say, was unconsciously steeping itself in drink; and this also conspired with the wars, to break down the thrift of the people. In Massachusetts alone, when she had only 150,000 people, fifteen thousand hogsheads of rum were distilled every year, and a very large share of it was consumed by her own citizens; a fact in which you will see what the living men of that day did not-a certain doom of decline, towards social misery and brutality.

If

At the same time, when it even seems, in our view, that all the foundations are dissolved, and that every hope of a new American civilization has perished, there begin to rise symptoms of order, and possibly of a new era. the masses have been unsettled, they have also been made conscious of power. Or if they have been corrupted, in the same wars which have robbed them of their virtuous habits, certain great men, afterwards to be distinguished as

leaders in our history, have also had their apprenticeship - learned to be leaders, felt the elevation of power, received new impulses, prepared themselves to act with address and vigor in scenes of yet higher moment. Religion, too, has been reviving, and re-asserting its power, not of course in demonstrations the most unexceptionable or respectable, but in such as the times of the Judges will suffer. It is the wild chant of Deborah, or better still, it is the nail that was driven by Jael's hammer-not the ointment ministered by the graceful hand of Mary. This new quickening accomplished, in fact, for religion, what the French wars accomplished for liberty; it broke up the age of frost, and brought in a new era of power. We begin, therefore, shortly to discover that a new spring has been given to character. An upward motion is visible, which upward motion has continued even to the present time, save as the war of the Revolution produced a temporary decline.

Pardon me now, if I venture to fill out the view of my subject, by saying that New England society is still in the transition state. Compared with some portions of the old world, and in certain points of view, we are still in the rough-presenting to the eye a healthy living aspect, such as the old world cannot any where offer, but still a raw, unfinished aspect, which it remains for the next century to civilize and bring into full ornamental perfection. For as our history now begins to live on its own root, and to send up a vitalizing power into the social body; as wealth is unfolded; as schools and colleges are perfecting their standards of learning; as literature and art advance to maturity, we are rising steadily into noon, as a people socially complete.

But the great problem of American society is not solved, however much it may be illustrated, by the history of New England. Still we are rolling on from east to west, plunging into the wilderness, scouring across the great inland deserts and mountains, to plant our habitations on the western ocean. Here again the natural tendencies of emigration towards barbarism, or social decline, are displayed, in signs that cannot be mistaken. The struggle through which we have passed, is continually repeating itself, under new modifications. We see the same experiment involving similar jeopardies; and we draw out of our own experience warnings to make us anxious, and encouragements to make us hopeful for our country-a double argument of fear and hope, to make us doubly faithful in our christian efforts for its welfare.

In some respects, this westward emigration is secured by advantages which our own colonial emigration had not; in others, it is beset by disadvantages quite as decided. Among the advantages are these-First, a better and more available market for the sale of its products, and hence, a much greater facility in rising to a state of outward comfort. Secondly, a good and well established government, able to protect the beginnings made, exerting also an important moral constraint over all tendencies to lawlessness and public disorder. Thirdly, a connection with the eastern and older portions of the country, by which they are made to feel the moral effect of association with a more advanced state of manners, of social culture and religious virtue. Fourthly, a history; for it is not as when our fathers forsook a history to plant themselves in this new world; but the emigrant, wherever he strays, remembers that he is an American still. He looks out from his hut of logs on the western border, and feels the warmth of a distinct nationality glowing round him, like the clear warm light of day itself. On the other hand, these manifest advantages are counterbalanced by disadvantages. First, the western emigration is not religious, but is instigated by mere personal interest and adventure. Secondly, it does not carry with it a homogeneous or a well educated people. Together with a portion of enterprising, well qualified young men, who are rushing westward after their fortune, it gathers in the rude minded and ignorant masses of western Pennsylvania; the luckless and impoverished families flying from slavery in Virginia, Kentucky and Tennessee; together with such hordes of foreigners, as the over-populated countries of Europe are obliged to sparemen of all habits, characters and religions-and these it pours along in a promiscuous flood, to people the new world, and settle into social order as best they may. Then, thirdly, a considerable portion of the new west, has a social and historical connexion with slavery, which is continually doubling the inherent perils of emigration itself.

And here, since this institution of slavery, entering into the fortunes of our history, complicates, in so many ways, the disorders we suffer, I must pause a few moments to sketch its characteristics. Slavery, it is not to be denied, is an essentially barbarous institution. It gives us too that sign, which is the perpetual distinction of barbarism, that it has no law of progress. The highest level it reaches, is the level at which it begins. Indeed, we need not scruple to allow that it has yielded us one considerable advantage, in virtue of the fact, that it produces its best condition first. For while the northern people were generally delving in labor, for many generations, to create a condition of comfort, slavery set the masters at once on a footing of ease, gave them leisure for elegant intercourse, for unprofessional studies, and seasoned their character thus with that kind of cultivation which distinguishes men of society. A class of statesmen were thus raised up, who were prepared to figure as leaders in scenes of public life, where so much depends on manners and social address. But now the scale is changing. Free labor is rising, at length, into a state of wealth and comfort, to take the lead of American society. Meanwhile, the foster sons of slavery-the high families, the statesmen-gradually receding in character, as they must under this vicious institution, are receding also in power and influence, and have been ever since the revolution. Slavery is a condition against nature; the curse of nature therefore is on it, and it bows to its doom, by a law as irresistible as gravity. It produces a condition of ease which is not the reward of labor, and a state of degradation which is not the curse of idleness. Therefore the ease it enjoys cannot but end in a curse, and the degradation it suffers cannot rise into a blessing. It nourishes imperious and violent passions. It makes the masters solitary sheiks on their estates, forbidding thus the possibility of public schools, and preventing also that condensed form of society, which is necessary to the vigorous maintenance of churches. Education and religion thus displaced, the dinner table only remains, and on this hangs, in great part, the keeping of the social state. But however highly we may estimate the humanizing power of hospitality, it cannot be regarded as any sufficient spring of character. It is neither a school, nor a gospel. And when it comes of self-indulgence, or only seeks relief for the tedium of an idle life, scarcely does it bring with it the blessings of a virtue. The accomplishments it yields are of a mock quality, rather than of a real, having about the same relation to a substantial and finished culture, that honor has to character. This kind of currency will pass no longer; for it is not expense without comfort, or splendor set in disorder, as diamonds in pewter; it is not airs in place of elegance, or assurance substituted for ease; neither is it to be master of a fluent speech, or to garnish the same with stale quotations from the classics; much less is it to live in the Don Juan vein, accepting barbarism by poetic inspiration-the same which a late noble poet, drawing out of Turks and pirates, became the chosen laureate of slavery-not any or all of these can make up such a style of man, or of life, as we in this age demand. We have come up now to a point, where we look for true intellectual refinement, and a ripe state of personal culture. But how clearly is it seen to be a violation of its own laws, for slavery to produce a genuine scholar, or a man, who, in any department of excellence, unless it be in politics, is not a full century behind his time. And if we ask for what is dearer and better still, for a pure christian morality, the youth of slavery are trained in no such habits, as are most congenial to virtue. The point of honor is the only principle many of them know. Violence and dissipation bring down every succeeding generation to a state continually lower; so that now, after a hundred and fifty years are passed, the slave-holding territory may be described as a vast missionary ground, and one so uncomfortable to the faithful ministry of Christ, by reason of its jealous tempers, and the known repugnance it has to many of the first maxims of the gospel, that scarcely a missionary can be found to enter it. Connected with this moral decay, the resources of nature also are exhausted, and her fertile territories changed to a desert, by the uncreating power of a spendthrift institution. And then, having

made a waste where God had made a garden, slavery gathers up the relics of bankruptcy, and the baser relics still of virtue and all-manly enterprise, and goes forth to renew, on a virgin soil, its dismal and forlorn history. Thus, at length, has been produced what may be called the bowie-knife style of civilization, and the new West of the South is overrun by it—a spirit of blood which defies all laws of God and man; honorable but not honest; prompt to resent an injury, slack to discharge a debt; educated to ease, and readier, of course, when the means of living fail, to find them at the gambling-table or the race-ground, than in any work of industry-probably squandering the means of living there, to relieve the tedium of ease itself.

Such is the influence of slavery, as it enters into our American social state, and imparts its moral type of barbarism, through emigration, to the new west. Hence, the Mexican war, which has its beginning and birth in what I have called the bowie-knife style of civilization—a war in the nineteenth century, which, if it was not purposely begun, many are visibly determined shall be, a war for the extension of slavery. It was no one political party, as some pretend, who made this war, but it was the whole southwest and west rather of all parties, instigated by a wild and riotous spirit of adventure, which no terms of reason or of christian prudence and humanity could check. And if this war results, as probably it may, in the acquisition of a vast western territory, then is our great pasture ground of barbarism so much to be enlarged, the room to run wild extended, the chances of final anarchy and confusion multiplied.

We are now prepared to complete our view, by passing directly to the subject of western emigration itself. And what are the moral and social results here preparing? That I can draw a picture of western society, which will be universally approved, is more than I have any right to expect. I can only give such a sketch as the facts seem to require, and without exaggeration; observing, however, that if any western man should be dissatisfied, it will, by no means, convince me that I am wrong; for to conceive a people rightly it is not sufficient to know them; they must be viewed from a stand point without. And just as the character of New England cannot be rightly drawn, save as it is viewed from abroad, so no western or westernized man, coming directly out from the scenes of western life, is qualified, on that account, to estimate their social standing and prospects. On the contrary, he may even be partially disqualified, by the experience under which he has fallen. At the same time, let it be understood, that in what I may say, however the public may receive it, I do not consider myself as reflecting any necessary dishonor on the west, or on western society. It is no dishonor in them, any more than it was to New England, to suffer what they must, from the very laws of society itself. On the contrary, if the west puts forth a manly struggle to breast the laws of decline involved in a new social state, it may even display the more heroic qualities, because of the adverse elements it has the spirit to master. Much the same allowances, too, are to be made here, that were supposed to hold in reference to the decline of New England. It is not general or universal. It includes only a portion of western society, and this portion only in regard to certain particulars. Probably there is no decline, but an improvement rather, if we take in all, and regard what I have called the total amount of character. Many of the emigrants from Pennsylvania, Virginia, and yet further south, were at a very low point of character when they removed, and these, brought within the reach even partially of schools and churches, are rapidly improving. If the emigrants from New England lose ground, in manners, piety and habits of intelligence, they also gain in spirit, freedom, self-reliance, and other qualities that are certainly desirable. Besides, we are making strenuous efforts to save the west from the decline that would otherwise appear; so that, while there is a certain tendency to barbarism in their new condition of society, that tendency, we may believe, is held in check and, in many cases, displaced, even from the beginning, by signs of improvement.

Western character has many powerful and promising qualities, but it wants the salt of religious virtue, the sobriety of discipline, and the modesty of true intelligence. It is frank, bold, earnest and positive, but somewhat rude and extravagant, and specially destitute of the genial sentiments which enrich the more settled and cultivated forms of society. A very large portion of the western community, it is well known, are already so far gone in ignorance, as to make a pride of it, and even to decry education as an over-genteel accomplishment. They hold, of course, their manhood in their will, not in their understanding; which is the same as to say that law is weak, and passion violent. Hence, the many public murders, committed in the newer states of the west and south, which are never legally investigated. Or, perhaps you will even see an ambitious young city, mustering itself in a military mob, to murder an inoffensive christian minister and citizen; and when it is done, when the fit of passion is over, the law, instead of rising up to re-assert its rights, as we see it do in older and less barbarous communities, still sleeping in its violated majesty. Or, if you will discover how near it is possible to come, and within how short a time, to a complete dissolution of civil order, you may see the executive power of a a sovereign state standing by, for six months, to look on, as a spectator, while two organized military parties of its own citizens are prosecuting an open war, one to defend, the other to capture an American city! Where shall such disorders stop? and what is the limit towards which they run? If, in the days of the Judges, Pennsylvania rebelled against the excise of whiskey, and now Illinois substitutes the camp and the siege, in place of justice itself and the ordinary methods of legal redress, what shall by and by appear, in some new state as far west of Illinois, as that is of Pennsylvania? What are we to expect as this reign of passion, spreading onward across the vast regions yet unoccupied, grows yet more violent as it is deeper in ignorance, and wilder still, as it is more remote from the haunts of christian civilization? Is it not well understood that a partially wild race of men, such as cannot any longer be properly included in the terms of civilization, is already formed? I speak of what is sometimes called the pioneer race. They roll on, like a prairie fire, before the advance of regular emigration; they have no fixed habits, and do not care to appropriate the soil, consequently have no education or religion. They live mainly by hunting and pasture; and, when a regular settlement begins within an hour's ride, they feel the proximity too close, quit their hut of logs, which is in fact only their tent, and start on, by another long remove, into the wild regions beyond them. These semi-barbarians too, are continually multiplying in numbers, and becoming more distinct in their habits. Ere long, there is reason to fear, they will be scouring in populous bands, over the vast territories of Oregon and California, to be known as the pasturing tribes-the wild hunters and robber clans of the western hemisphere-American Moabites, Arabs and Edomites!

Or if it seem extravagant to speak of any such result, let it not be forgotten that one emigrant family of the Saxon race has already sunk into barbarism, since our history begun. I speak of the Dutch Boers in South Africa. They are Calvinistic Protestants; they began their settlement at Cape Town, in the year 1651. And now they are virtually barbarians; for they are scarcely less wild in their habits than the Hottentots themselves. They subsist by pasture, roving from place to place. Lynch law and private revenge are the principal methods of redressing injuries. Their habits are filthy. Their women do the work. Education is forgotten, and the cruelties they practice in their sanguinary wars, are such as resemble them to beasts of prey. They are now a race of nominally christian barbarians-barbarians under the synod of Dort, a standing proof that Protestants, and they too of the Saxon blood, may drop out of civilization, and take their place on the same level of ignorance and social brutality with the barbarous tribes of the earth. Let no American that loves his country refuse to heed the example.

Many are accustomed to regard the exposure of our western country to Romanism with extreme horror, regarding a possible lapse into this corrupt form of religion as the climax of all possible disasters. In that opinion there is quite as little to approve, as there is in the overconfident opinion of those who declare that Romanism cannot spread in this country. Nothing is necessary to make room for Romanism, but to empty us of all opposing qualities; and it will not take a long period of ignorance and religious anarchy to do that. Nor do I mean to imply, in thus speaking, that Romanism can coexist only with barbarism, much less to sharpen a point of satire against the Romish church. Under this we know are gathered many great and accomplished men, and many nations farther advanced, in some respects, than we. only mean, that while it is possible for a people brought up in Romanism to become socially advanced under it, a free minded people, brought up in mental and moral habits wholly opposite, never can be led into it, save through the gate of superstition; which gate of superstition never can be opened, save by a loss of knowledge, social order and religion, such as approximates to barbarism. There may be cases where a cultivated man, wearied out and lost in the mazes of fantastic speculation, throws up suddenly the prerogatives of reason, and takes it for certain that God will do him good, if he has a Levite to his priest. There may be truly godly men-men, so to speak, of an overgrown religious sentiment, who see no consistent issue short of Romanism to assumptions already made, and whose nerves are too weak to go back and manfully sift these assumptions-there may be such, who fall a prey to their own delicate illusions, and drop into the Romish church to settle their peace. But these are only caprices, accidents, idiosyncracies, which support no general conclusion, save that between opposite superlatives, the sublimities and follies of mankind, there is often a natural brotherhood. Thus, over-cultivation may sometimes join hands at the church door with barbarism, both entering as fellow proselytes together. Thus over-speculation will sometimes throw up private judgment in disgust, and place itself on a par, with those who have no private judgment to lose. But the great danger of Romanism, the only danger of any moment, is from the multiplication of the latter class those who have no private judgment to lose; and it is a real danger. Man is a religious being, and if he cannot come to God through his intelligence, he will come to what sort of God his superstitions offer him.

When, therefore, I consider how certainly an ignorant soul is prepared to superstition, remembering also the vast amount of ignorance that prevails among the western people, I want no other proof that superstition has already a wide and terrible sway over the western mind. Or if I suffer a doubt, the great Mormon city and temple rise as proof visible before me-proof, however, that does not accrue as against the west alone, save that it shows how all fantastic errors and absurdities will assuredly congregate there. Who could have thought it possible that a wretched and silly delusion, like that of the Mormons, could gather in its thousands of disciples in this enlightened age, build a populous city, and erect a temple, rivalling in grandeur, even that of the false prophet at Mecca? And when we see, in facts like these, how readily material may be gathered to represent the times of the Judges, it is vain to imagine that Romanism can find no affinities prepared among us, or that none can be found, who will think it a religion, to have a Levite to their priest. Romanism can do any thing in this country which we will help it to do, and we ought not to complain if it does no more. Or if we persist in training a barbarous people for its use, let us indulge no regrets that Romanism gives them such a religion as they are capable of receiving.

I have led you thus over a wide field, and yet the subject is not exhausted. But I can pursue the argument no farther. If now you ask what is to be the conclusion of the great problem we have on hand; shall we go clear, at last, of all these perils; shall we rise into order, law, intelligence and religion; or will parts of the nation go down, at last, below the capacity to rise? I care not to answer that question. Indeed it is a question to be answered, not in speeches or conjectures, but by our works! The answer hangs, not on what we may think or reason, but on what we shall do! We can make it what we desire; we can make it as bad as we have power even to fear! Enough that we understand the magnificence of the problem, and the tremendous perils incident thereto, viz: that we have it on hand to struggle up, for a half century or a century

to come, against the downward currents of decline, and bear up the nation with us, into a settled condition of christian culture and virtue; which, if we do, the critical point of our destiny is turned. We are then to be the most august and happiest nation that has ever appeared on earth, the leading power of the world's history. Was there ever a struggle offered to the good and great of mankind, so fit to kindle enthusiasm, or nerve the soul to patient sacrifices!

WHAT, THEN, SHALL WE DO?

First of all, we must not despair. There is no cause for despair. Dark as the picture is that I have given. I do not, for one, suffer a misgiving thought. In many portions of the field, the crisis is already past. In others, it soon will be. And every new state, or section added to the parts already secure, brings an accession of aid and a more preponderant weight of influence. Of the new regions, we may say that Vermont, Western New York, and a part of Ohio, are already gained, and are now side by side with us, helping us to support the downward pressure of the emigrant masses. We have only to make sure, in like manner, of all the States this side of the Mississippi, and then the critical point is, in my estimation, past. Much will remain to be done; but the result will be sure. For when once the vast region this side of the Mississippi is seen to be ascending with us into order and christian refinement, the regions beyond will scarcely be able to drag themselves down into anarchy. The die of our destiny is cast. Seeing then the momentous perils that hang about us, let them only quicken us to a more fixed and heroic devotion. It must be a faint heart that cannot bear up, in a struggle so evidently temporary. Nothing is more certain than that, if we deserve to triumph, we shall triumph; and if that be not enough to sustain our courage, we are worthy of no such cause as this.

And what next? We must get rid, if possible, I answer, of slavery. It aggravates every bad tendency we suffer. We cannot, as American christians, be at peace with it longer. Not forgetting the moderation that belongs to every just cause, we must lift our voices against it, and must not desist from all proper means to secure its removal, till the work is done.

We must also return, as soon as possible, to a condition of peace, and maintain it, as the only hope of moral and social progress in our country. War is the proper work only of barbarians—the bane, therefore, of all social order and virtue. Even New England itself, as I have shown you, came near sinking into a fatal debauchery of character in the wars she encountered. For a war exasperates all the evils incident to emigration, postpones all settled habits, and turns all sobriety to madness.

If something could be done to civilize the manner of American politics, to abate the rudeness of political animosities, to establish candor and courtesy and dignity of feeling between opposing parties and their leaders, it would greatly expedite the progress of refinement in our people. And I know of no more ready or proper expedient, than for every christian man to look at the most interior merits of every cause or question, and stand ready to support the right, bear what name it may.

Be it also understood, that the sooner we have railroads and telegraphs spinning into the wilderness, and setting the remotest hamlets in connexion and close proximity with the east, the more certain it is that light, good manners and christian refinement, will become universally diffused. For when the emigrant settlements of Minesota or of Oregon feel that they are just in the suburb of Boston, it is nearly the same thing, in fact, as if they actually were.

Education, too, is another and yet more sacred interest which we are to favor and promote by every reasonable means. Colleges are a great and pressing want; but we want only a few. Indeed, we have enough already for the next twenty years, if only they were fully organized and sufficiently endowed. Subordinate schools, and especially rudimental schools, are a much more pressing want; but these, in order to have any value, must be created and

supported principally by the people for whose benefit they exist. The most, therefore, which can be done is to stimulate the demand for such schools, in every convenient

manner.

This brings me to speak, last of all, of that which is really the chief, the all-important work, viz: to provide a talented and educated body of christian teachers, and keep them pressing into the wilderness, as far as emigration itself can go. These mixing with the families, and entering into their new struggles, will stimulate the demand fo~ instruction, assist in the founding of schools and academies, and become the guardians of every good interest We must throw ourselves out, therefore, upon HOME MIS SIONS as the first and sublimest christian duty which the age lays upon us.

Religion is the only prop on which we can lean with any confidence; and Home Missions are the vehicle of re ligion. In no form of human society is there any law o self-support and self-conservation. There is no shape o society, least of all any shape of new society, that wil not rot itself down and dissolve, unless there descend upon it from above, a conserving power which it has not in itself. Nothing but religion, a ligature binding society to God, can save it. No light, save that which is celestial, no virtue but that which is born of God, no power of motivity, but that which is drawn from other worlds, can suffice to preserve, compact and edify a new social state. It was religion that sustained and finally turned the crisis of New England. It was religion, dispensed by the old Missionary Society of Connecticut, and other sister institutions of a later date, which finally turned the crisis of Vermont, Western New York, and Eastern Ohio. Among these later institutions, and as the most vigorous and powerful too of all, we are to class the Home Missionary Society, for which I now speak-a Society which is now hovering over Michigan, Indiana, Illinois, Wisconsin, Iowa, and other new regions beyond, as once it did over the regions just named. It has now a spiritual army six hundred strong, in these fields, and waits to make its hundreds, thousands. For it has undertaken the most magnificent work ever yet appropriated to any human

institution, with a zeal proportioned to its grandeur. In this institution, for I speak this evening only to its friends, we are enlisted, as I trust, with whatever of christian determination God permits us to exercise. Here we feel that we have the future in our charge, and we mean to see the trust faithfully fulfilled. To save this mighty nation; to make it the leading power of the earth; to present to mankind the spectacle of a nation stretching from ocean to ocean, across this broad continent; a nation of free men, self-governed, governed by simple law, without soldiers or a police; a nation of a hundred millions of people, covering the sea with their fleets, the land with cities, roads and harvests; first in learning and art, and all the fruits of genius, and, what is highest and best of all, a religious nation, blooming in all the christian virtues; the protector of the poor; the scourge of oppression; the dispenser of light, and the symbol to mankind, of the ennobling genial power of righteous laws, and a simple christian faith-this is the charge God lays upon us, this we accept and this, by God's blessing, we mean to perform, with a spirit worthy of its magnitude. I say not that we must forsake other and more distant fields of duty. God will never call us to that. I only say that there can be no other duty at all comparable to the duty of saving our country; none that God so manifestly imposes. What less than a romantic folly could it seem, to any sober mind, if such indeed were the alternative, to be pouring out our mercies into the obscure outposts of heathenism, and leaving this great nation, this brightest hope of the ages, to go down as a frustrated and broken experiment!

It is time also to understand, that if we are to fill this great field with christian churches and a christian people, we must have a spirit of life in our breasts, and a tone of christian devotion such as we have not hitherto exhibited. Here is the only real cause of discouragement I know. It is not money, it is not men, it is no mere human outlay that can bear up such a work as this. We want the unworldly spirit; that which knits us, and through us knits our great country to God. And then also, we want that intense and Christ-like humanity, which will attract the feeling of our whole country towards us. For it is not in op

positions, it is not in raising a crusade against Romanism, or filling the air with outcries of any sort, that we are to save our country. We must rise upon it as the morning, in the tranquillity of love. We must rain righteousness upon it, as a genial shower.

It is beautiful also to see that God designs, by the very work we undertake, to fill out and finish our own christian type of character and society. In the case of our fathers, it seems probable that nothing but the strong pillars of high Calvinism held them up, or could have held them up, till the critical point of their history was passed. There were no missionaries coming over unto them. Nothing could hold them up but an internal force, such as they had in these doctrines-doctrines that were incorporated in their souls, as the spinal column in their bodies. Thus, when their manners were grown wild, their sentiments coarse, and their ill-trained understandings generally incapable of nice speculation, still the tough questions of their theology kept them always in action; still they could grasp hold of the great iron pillars of election, reprobation and decrees, and their clumsy-handed thoughts were able to feel them distinctly. Whoever could distinguish a thunderbolt could surely think of these, and it mattered not so much, whether they thought exactly right, as that they kept thinking, and in their thinking brought down God upon their souls. So they took hold of the iron pillars that held up the theologic heavens, and climbed and heaved in huge surges of might, and kept their gross faculties in exercise, till the critical hour of their trial was passed. The themes they handled kept them too before God. They dwelt in the summits of divine government. They looked upon the throne, they heard the thunders roll below, and felt the empyrean shake above, at the going forth of God's decrees. Such a religion as they had could not be distant, or feeble. It had power to invest the coarse mind with a divine presence, and make Jehovah felt as an element of experience. Never was there a better foundation for a grand, massive character in religion; and now God means to finish out this character, by uniting in it the softer shades of feeling, and the broader compass of a more

catholic and genial spirit. We go forth now to a people, who unite all manner of opinions, and we go in company with christians of other names and other creeds, who are undertakers also in the same great work. We cannot, therefore, spend our strength now upon exclusive and distinctive dogmas, but we must proceed in a catholic and comprehensive spirit. Otherwise we shall be at war with each other, and shall only spend our force, in demolishing all the force we have. Thus, the Methodists, for example, have a ministry admirably adapted, as regards their mode of action, to the new west-a kind of light artillery that God has organized, to pursue and overtake the fugitives that flee into the wilderness from his presence. They are prompt and effective in action, ready for all service, and omnipresent, as it were, in the field. The new settler reaches the ground to be occupied, and, by the next week, he is likely to find the circuit crossing by his door, and to hear the voice of one crying in the wilderness, "The kingdom of God is come nigh unto you!" Our Methodist brethren have put on their armor too against the enemies of learning among themselves. They are building colleges, and one among the number, which they mean to make the most complete and best endowed university in the west. If sometimes their demonstrations are rude, and their spirit of rivalry violent, still it is good to have such rivals, for their labor is still ours, and when they have reached the state of intelligence they are after, they are sure to become effectually, if not formally, one with us. Therefore let there be, if possible, no controversy with them; but let us rather encourage ourselves in a work so vast, by the fact that we have so vast an army of helpers in the field with us. So of all the other christian families, who are going into the field to do a work for their Master. There should be not only concord of spirit, but also an actual understanding; so that we may cover together as much ground as possible. And then we should all go forth together, to calm the angry divisions of controversy and sweeten the bitter prejudices of sectarian strife. Earnest for the truth, we must also remember, that truth itself is catholic and comprehensive. We must shun that vapid liberalism, which instead of attract

ing us into unity, will only dissolve us into indifference, and yet we must be willing to stretch our forbearance and charity even to Romanists themselves, when we clearly find the spirit of Jesus in their life. In this manner, God will instruct us by our work, and make our work itself our reward. Engaging with our utmost ardor to save the wilder portions of our country, we shall carry on thus our own noble beginnings to completion, and finish out a character, as earnest in its sacrifices and catholic in its charities, as it is firm in its original elements. May we not also hope to draw down from the skies, upon us and upon all the regions for which we labor, such a baptism of love as will melt both us and them, and all the families of Christ in our land, into one christian fraternity.

Thus will we go on and give it to our sons and daughters to come after us. We will measure our strength by the grandeur of our object. The wilderness shall bud and blossom as the rose before us; and we will not cease, till a christian nation throws up its temples of worship on every hill and plain; till knowledge, virtue and religion, blending their dignity and their healthful power, have filled our great country with a manly and a happy race of people, and the bands of a complete christian commonwealth are seen to span the continent.

AND NOW, Jehovah God, thou who by long ages of watch and discipline, didst make of thy servant Abraham a people, be thou the God also of this great nation. Remember still its holy beginnings, and for the fathers' sakes, still cherish and sanctify it. Fill it with thy Light and thy Potent Influence, till the glory of thy Son breaks out on the western sea, as now upon the eastern, and these uttermost parts, given to Christ for a possession, become the bounds of a new Christian Empire, whose name the believing and the good of all people shall hail name of hope and blessing!

## PART IV

# THE FATHERS OF NEW ENGLAND

An Oration Delivered before the New England Society of New York, December 21, 1849, and published at their request.

# ORATION

GENTLEMEN OF THE NEW ENGLAND SOCIETY:
It is a filial sentiment, most honorably signified by you, in the organization of your Society, and the regular observance of this anniversary, that the founders and first fathers of states are entitled to the highest honors. You agree in this with the fine philosophic scale of awards, offered by Lord Bacon, when he says, "The true marshalling of the degrees of sovereign honors are these: In the first place, are *Conditores*; founders of states. In the second place, are *Legislatores*; lawgivers, which are sometimes called second-founders, or *Perpetui Principes*, because they govern by their ordinances after they are gone. In the third place, are *Liberatores;* such as compound the long miseries of civil wars, or deliver their countries from servitude of strangers or tyrants. In the fourth place, are *Propagatores*, or *Propugnatores imperii*; such as in honorable wars enlarge their territories, or make noble defence against invaders. And in the last place, *Patres patria*, which reign justly, and make the times good wherein they live."

Holding this true scale of honor, which you may the more heartily do, because you have fathers who are entitled to reverence for their worth as well as their historic position, you have undertaken to remember, and with due observances to celebrate, each year, this twenty-second day of December, as the day *Conditorum Reipublicæ*. Be it evermore a day, such as may fitly head the calendar of our historic honors; a day that remembers with thoughtful respect and reverence the patience of oppressed virtue, the sacrifices of duty, and the solemn fatherhood of religion; — a register also of progress, showing every year by what new triumphs and results of good, spreading in wider circles round the globe, that Being whose appropriate work it is to crown the fidelity of faithful men, is Himself justifying your homage, and challenging the homage of mankind.

MEANTIME, be this one caution faithfully observed, that all prescriptive and stipulated honors have it as their natural infirmity to issue in extravagant and forced commendations, and so to mar not seldom the reverence they would fortify. We pay the truest honors to men that are worthy, not by saying all imaginable good concerning them least of all can we do fit honor, in this manner, to the fathers of New England. It as little suits the dignity of truth, as the iron rigor of the men. If it be true, as we often hear, that one may be most effectually "damned by faint praise;" it may also be done as fatally, by what is even more unjust and, to genuine merit, more insupportable, by over-vehement and undistinguishing eulogy. We make allowance for the subtractions of envy; but when love invents fictitious grounds of applause, we imagine some fatal defect of those which are real and true. There is no genuine praise but the praise of justice:

> "For fame impatient of extremes, decays
> Not less by envy, than excess of praise."

In this view, it will not be an offence to you, I trust, or be deemed adverse to the real spirit of the occasion, if I suggest the conviction that our New England fathers have sometimes suffered in this manner — not by any conscious design to overmagnify their merit, but by the amiable zeal of inconsiderate and partially qualified eulogy. In particular, it has seemed to me to be a frequent detraction from their merit that results are ascribed to their wisdom, or sagacious forethought as projectors, which never even came into their thoughts at all; and which, taken only as proofs of a Providential purpose working in them, and of God's faithful adherence to their history, would have yielded a more reverent tribute to Him, and raised them also to a far higher pitch of sublimity in excellence. The very greatness of these men, as it seems to me, is their unconsciousness. It is that so little conceiving the future they had in them, they had a future so magnificent — that God was in them in a latent power of divinity and world-disposing counsel which they did not suspect, in a wisdom wiser than they knew, in principles more quickening and transforming than they could even imagine themselves, and was thus preparing in them, to lift the whole race into a higher plane of existence, and one as much closer to Himself.

And just here is the difficulty that most consciously oppresses me in the engagement of the present occasion. It is to praise these great men justly— to say what is fit to them and not unfit to God. It is to make unconsciousness in good the crown of sublimity in good; to set it forth as their special glory, in this view, that they executed by duty and the stern fidelity of their lives, what they never propounded in theory, or set up as a mark of attainment so to meet the spirit of the occasion, and to raise in you the fit measure of enthusiasm, by the sober wine alone of justice and truth.

Do I then deny what has been so often observed in the great characters of history, that they commonly act their part under a visible sense or presentiment of the greatness of their mission? Is it a fiction that they are thus exalted in it, made impassible, borne along as by some fate or destiny, or, to give it a more Christian name, some inspiration or call of God? Nothing is more true; it is in fact the standing distinction, the sublimity itself of greatness.

> "Souls destined to o'erleap the vulgar lot,
> And mould the world unto the scheme of God,
> Have a fore-consciousness of their high doom."

Ignorant of this, we cannot understand what greatness is. To us it no longer exists. But we need, in the acceptance of a truth so ennobling to human history, to affix those terms and restrictions under which it is practically manifested, else we make even history itself fantastic or incredible.

Whoever appears to assert any great truth of science or religion, wanted by his age, ought to feel an immovable conviction that the truth asserted will prevail, else he is no fit champion. But as regards the particular effects it will produce in human society; these he cannot definitely trace. He can only know that, falling into the great currents of causes, complex and multitudinous as they are, some good and beneficent results will follow, that are worthy of its divine scope and order. In like manner, the hero of an occasion, exalted by the occasion to be God's instrument, we may believe is sometimes gifted with a confidence that is nearly prophetic, and by force of which he is able to inspire others with a courage equal to the greatness of the encounter. Thus it was that Luther, in virtue of a confidence that other men had not, became the hero of the Reformation. But when we speak of inventions, institutions, policies, migrations, revolutions, which are not single truths or occasions, but inaugurations of causes that can reveal their issues only in the lapse of centuries, the projectors and leaders in these can be sure, at most, only of the grand ideal that inspires them; but by what medial changes and turns of history God will bring it to pass, or in what definite forms of social good it will finally clothe itself, they can but dimly conceive.

And this is what I mean, when I speak of the unconscious, or undesigning agency of the fathers of New England, considered as the authors of those great political and social issues which we just now look upon as the highest and crowning distinctions of our history. Their ideal was not in these, but in issues still farther on and more magnificent, to which these are only Providential media or means. Occupied by the splendor of these medial stages of advancement, and unable to imagine any thing yet more glorious to be revealed hereafter, we conclude that we have reached the final result and historic completion of our destiny; and then we cast about us to ask what our sublime fathers attempted, and settle a final judgment of their merits. Sometimes we smile at their simplicity, finding that the highest hope they conceived in their migration, was nothing but the hope of some good issue for religion! We secretly wonder, or, it may be, openly express our regret, that they could not have had some conception of the magnificent results of liberty and social order that were here to be revealed. And in this view, we often set ourselves to it, as a kind of filial duty, to make out for them what we so much desire.

Who of us, meantime, is able, for once, to imagine that the shortness may be ours, the prophecy and the greatness theirs? We want them to be heroes, but we cannot allow them to be heroes of faith. This indeed is a great day for heroes, and our literature is at work, as in a trade, upon the manufacture. But it will some time be discovered that, in actual life, there are two kinds of heroes — heroes for the visible, and heroes for the invisible; they that see their mark hung out as a flag to be taken on some turret or battlement, and they that see it nowhere, save in the grand ideal of the inward life; extempore heroes fighting out a victory definitely seen in something near at hand, and the life-long, century-long heroes that are instigated by no ephemeral crown or more ephemeral passion, but have sounded the deep base-work of God's principle, and have dared calmly to rest their all upon it, come the issue where it may, or when it may, or in what form God will give it. The former class are only symbols, I conceive, in the visible life of that more heroic and truly divine greatness in the other, which is never offered to the eyes in forms of palpable achievement. These latter are God's heroes-heroes all of faith; the other belong to us, flaming as dilettanti figures of art in romances; protruding as bipedal gods in the windy swell of pantheistic literature; or it may be, striding in real life and action over fields of battle and pages of bloody renown. If our New England fathers do not figure as conspicuously in this latter class of heroes as some might desire, may they not sometimes be seen-when the main ideal of religion is fulfilled-to have been the more truly great because of the remoteness and the sacred grandeur of their aims? And if the political successes in which, as Americans, we so properly indulge our pride, are but scintillations thrown off in the onward sweep of their historic aims and purposes, little honor can it do them to discover that these scintillations are the primal orbs and central fires of their expectation.

Let us offer them no such injustice. They are not to be praised as a tribe of successful visionaries, coming over to this new world, in prophetic lunacy, to get up a great republic and renovate human society the world over. They propound no theories of social order. They undertake not, in their human make will or wisdom, to be a better Providence to the nations; no promise of the end they will put to all the human ills, or of melting off the ice of the poles to cap them with a "boreal crown" of felicity.

Had they come to build a new future, in this manner, by their will, according to some preconceived theory of their head, the first awful year of their settlement would have broken their confidence, and left them crying, as home-sick children, for some way of return to their country. The

> —"craven scruple
> Of thinking too precisely of the event,—
> A thought which, quartered, hath but one part wisdom,
> And ever three parts coward"—

would have shaken their fortitude with an ague as fatal as that which, in the first dreadful winter, assailed the life of their bodies — giving us, in their history, one other and quite unnecessary proof, that man is the weakest and most irresolute of beings when he hangs his purpose on his expectations. But coming in simple duty, duty was their power — a divine fate in them, whose thrusting on to greatness and triumphant good, took away all questions from the feeble arbitrament of their will, and made them even impassible to their burdens. And they went on building their unknown future, the more resolutely because it was unknown. For, though unknown, it was present in its power — present, not as in their projects and wise theories, but as a latent heat, concealed in their principles, and works, and prayers, and secret love, to be given out and become palpable in the world's cooling, ages after.


Nor is this suggestion of a latent wisdom or law present in their migration, any conceit of the fancy; for as in the growth of a man or a tree, so also in the primal germ of nations and social bodies, there is a secret Form or Law present in them, of which their after-growth is scarcely more than a fit actualization or development. This secret germ, or presiding form of the nascent order, has the force also of a creative, constitutive instinct in the body, building up that form by a wisdom hid in itself; though conceived, in thought, by no one member. By this instinctive action languages are struck out as permanent forms of thought, in the obscurest and most savage tribes, squared by the nicest principles of symmetry and grammatic order, having hid in their single words whole chapters of wisdom that, some thousands of years after, will be opened by a right explication, to the astonished gaze of the philosophic student. By the same instinctive germinal force, unconsciously present in a people, the future institutions and forms of liberty will be constructed; just as the comb of the hive is built by the instinctive geometry of the hive, though not by the geometric science of any one or more single bees in it. And somewhat in this manner it was that our institutions were present in the fathers and founders of our history. They had in their religious faith a high constructive instinct, raising them above their age and above themselves; creating in them fountains of wisdom deeper than they consciously knew, and preparing in them powers of benefaction that were to be discovered only by degrees and slowly to the coming ages. If you will show them forth as social projectors or architects of a new democracy, they stubbornly refuse to say or do any thing in that fashion. They are found protesting rather against your panegyric itself. Or if they have come to your acquaintance overlarded in this manner, so that you really regard them as the successful and deliberate revolutionizers of the modern age, you will need to wash off these coarse pigments and daubs of eulogy, as with nitre and much soap, and set them before you shining in the consecrating oil of faith, before you can truly conceive them as the fathers of American history. Their greatness is the unconscious greatness of their simple fidelity to God — the divine instinct of good and of wisdom by which God, as a reward upon duty, made them authors and founders of a social state under forms appointed by Himself.

It has been already assumed in this general outline of my subject, that the practical aim or ideal of our fathers, in their migration to the new world, was religion. This was the star of the East that guided them hither. They came as to the second cradle-place of a renovated Messiahship. They declare it formally themselves, when they give, as the principal reason of their undertaking, "the great hope and inward seal they had of laying some good foundation for the propagating and advancing the kingdom of Christ, in these remote parts of the world." — *Young's Chronicles*, p. 47.

It appears, however, that they had a retrospective reference, in their thoughts, as well as the prospective expectation here stated. Thus, it is affirmed by Mr. Hildersham, who had full opportunity to know their precise designs, that the colonists, as a body, before coming over, "agreed in nothing further, than in this general principle — that the reformation of the Church was to be endeavored according to the word of God." — *Cotton Mather*, p. 18. But precisely what, or how much they intended by this, will be seen nowhere else, with so great clearness, as in the ever memorable parting address which Robinson made to the Pilgrims, at their embarkation. Here we behold the real flame of their great idea. He said:

"I charge you before God and his blessed angels, that you follow me no further than I have followed Christ. And if God shall reveal any thing to you, by any other instrument of his, be as ready to receive it as you ever were to receive any thing by my ministry; for I am confident that God hath more truth yet to break forth out of His holy word. I cannot sufficiently bewail the condition of the Reformed churches, who have come to a period in religion, and will go no further than the instruments of their reformation. The Lutherans cannot be driven to go beyond Luther; for whatever part of God's will he hath further imparted by Calvin, they will rather die than embrace it. And so also the Calvinists stick where Calvin left them — a misery much to be lamented. For though they both were shining lights. in their times, yet God hath not revealed his whole will to them. Remember now your church covenant, whereby you engage with God and one another, to receive whatever light shall be made known to you from His written word. For it is not possible that the Christian world is so lately come out of such thick antiChristian darkness, and that full perfection of knowledge should break forth at once." — *Young's Chronicles*, p. 396-7.

A most remarkable passage of history, in which this truly great man is seen asserting a position, at least two whole centuries in advance of his age. His residence abroad, among so many forms of opinion and of order, has quickened in his mind the germ of a true comprehensive movement. He also perceives the impossibility that the full maturity of truth and order should have burst forth in a day, as distinctly as a philosophic historian of the nineteenth century. The Reformation, he is sure, is no complete thing — probably it is more incomplete than any one has yet been able to imagine. And then he has the faith to accept his own conclusion. Sending out the little half-flock of his church, across the wide ocean, he bids them go to watch for light; and there, in the free wilderness of nature, unrestrained by his own teachings, to complete, if possible, the unknown measure of Holy Reformation.

This was the errand he gave them, and in this we have the fixed ideal of their undertaking. And they meant by "reformation," all that God should teach them and their children of the coming ages, by the light that should break forth from His holy word — all that was needed to prepare the purity and universal spread of Christian truth, and open to mankind the reign of Christ in its full felicity and glory. They fixed no limits. It might include more than they at present thought, or could even dare to think. Still they had courage to say — "Let the reformation come in God's measures, and as He himself will shape it." And for this, they entered, with a stout heart; upon the perils and privations of their most perilous undertaking. Doubtless they had the natural feelings of men, but they were going to bear the ark of the Almighty, and could not painfully fear. Robinson had said — and he knew what was in them — "It is not with us as with other men, whom small things discourage, and small discontents cause to wish themselves home again." — *Young's Chronicles*, p. 61. Confidence most sublime! justified by a history of patience equally sublime. We shall see before I close, whether the errand of religious reformation, thus accepted, was an illusion, or whether it contained, in fact, the spring of all our political successes, and of other and still greater that are yet to come.

LET us pause a moment here and change the scene. We will leave the "pinched fanatics" of Leyden, as they are sometimes called, weeping 'their farewell on Robinson's neck, and turn ourselves to England. Ascending out of the dull and commonplace level of religion, we will breathe, a moment, in the higher plane of wisdom and renowned statesmanship. The philosopher and sage of St. Albans, hereafter to be celebrated as the father of modern science, sits at his table, in the deep silence of study, preparing a solemn gift of wisdom for his countrymen. His brow hangs heavy over his desk, and the glow of his majestic face, and the clear lustre of his meditative eye, reveal the mighty soul discoursing with the inward oracle. The noble property-holders and chartered land-companies of the realm are discoursing, every where, of the settlement of colonies in the new world, and discussing the causes of failure in the settlements heretofore attempted — he has taken up the theme, and is writing his essay "Of Plantations." And the advice he offers to their guidance is summarily this — Make a beginning, not with "the scum of the people," but with a fair collection of single men, who are good in all the several trades of industry. Make as much as possible of the spontaneous products of the country, such as nuts and esculent roots; but expect to support the plantation, in great part, by supplies from the mother country, for the first twenty years, and let the supplies be dealt out carefully "as in a besieged town." "As to government, let it be in the hands of one, assisted with some counsel, and let them have commission to exercise martial laws with some limitations." "When the plantation grows to strength, then it is time to plant with women as with men."

Need I stay to imagine, before an American audience, what kind of history must follow a plantation ordered in this manner — a plantation without the family state, without the gentle strengthening influence of woman, governed by a single head, under martial law!

Behold the little May Flower rounding, now, the southern cape of England — filled with husbands and wives and children, families of righteous men, under "covenant with God and each other" "to lay some good foundation for religion:" — engaged both to make and to keep their own laws, expecting to supply their own wants and bear their own burdens, assisted by none but the God in whom they trust. Here are the hands of industry! the germs of liberty! the dear pledges of order! and the sacred beginnings of a home!

That was the wisdom of St. Albans — this of Leyden. Bacon is there — Robinson is here. There was the deep sagacity of human statesmanship — here is the divine oracle of duty and religion. O religion religion! true daughter of God! wiser in action than genius itself in theory! How visible, in such a contrast, is the truth, that whatever is wisest in thought and most heroic in impulse, flows down upon men from the summits of religion — and is, in fact, a divine birth in souls! We can only say of her as the poet of woman herself — rejected here by the masculine wisdom of theory, and welcomed by religion as a needed support in her sturdiest trials of duty —

"All higher knowledge, in her presence, falls
Degraded. Wisdom, in discourse with her,
Loses, discountenanced, and like folly shows."

We are not, then, to conceive, and must not attempt to show, that our fathers undertook the migration with any political objects in view; least of all as distinctly proposing to lay the foundations of a great republic. Their end was religion, simply and only religion. Out upon the lone ocean, feeling their way cautiously, as it were, through the unknown waves, exploring, in their busy fancies and their prayers, the equally unknown future before them, they as little conceived that they had in their ship the germ of a vast republic that, in two centuries, would command the respect and attract the longing desires of the nations, as they saw with their eyes the lonely wastes about them whitening with the sails and foaming under the swift ships of that republic, already become the first commercial power of the world. The most sanguine expectation of theirs I have any where discovered, which, however, was not political, but religious, was ventured by Gov. Bradford, viz. — "That as one small candle may light a thousand, so the light kindled here may, in some sort, shine even to the whole nation!" This one small candle lighting the thousands of all England, is not quite as bold a figure of enthusiasm now as it was when it was uttered, and will probably be somewhat less extravagant, a hundred years hence, than now. No! they cross the sea in God's name only, sent by Him, as they believed, to be the voice of one crying in the wilderness — Prepare ye the way of the Lord, make his paths straight. But whither those straightened paths will lead, and in what shape the new kingdom of the Lord will come, they as little conceive as John the Baptist himself.

LET US NOT BE SURPRISED, then, neither let it be any derogation from their merit, if we find them actually opposed, in thought or speculative view, to the very opinions and institutions, now regarded as being most distinctively American. In this I partly rejoice; for some of the distinctions we boast, it is their most real praise, not to have sought or accepted. Thus we boast that we have made solemn proof to the world of the great principle, that civil government has its foundation in a social compact — that it originates only in the consent of the governed — that self-government is the inalienable right of every people — that true liberty is the exercise and secure possession of this prerogative — that majorities of wills have an inherent right to determine the laws — and that government by divine right is only a solemn imposture. I will not deny that, in some very partial and qualified sense, these supposed doctrines of ours may be true. But taken in the more absolute sense, in which they are boasted by many, they compose a heap of as empty and worthless chaff as ever fed the conceit of any people in the world.

What are formal compacts, what is self-government, what are majorities of wills, taken as foundations of civil order? What stronger bond in these, to hold a community, than in those recent compacts made to share the gold of our western Ophir — all dissolved, as by a breath of air, the moment the adventurers touch the shore? Or, if we speak of right, what right is there of any kind, which is not divine right? Or, dropping all such refinements, what truth can there be in abstract principles of order, discovered by us, which make every other government that has existed in the world, for six thousand years, an imposture, or a baseless usurpation?

But if it be conceived that there are three distinct orders of government, adapted to three distinct stages of social advancement — the government of force, the government of prescription, and the government of choice — and then that the particular terms of order just named are most appropriate and happiest for us, taken as modes or machinery of government, and not as theoretic principles and moral foundations; if we say these will best accommodate our liberties, and secure us in the high position to which God has raised us, it is well. But then we need to add that law is law, binding upon souls, not as human will, or the will of just one more than half the full grown men over a certain age, but a power of God entering into souls and reigning in them as a divine instinct of civil order, creating thus a state — perpetual, beneficent, the safeguard of the homes and of industry, the condition of a public feeling and a consciously organic life. This it is that makes all government sacred and powerful, that it somehow stands in the will of God; nay, it is the special dignity and glory and freedom of our government, that it rests, so little, on the mere will or force of man, so entirely on those principles of justice and common beneficence which we know are sacred to God. And it is the glory also of our founders and first fathers that they prepared us to such a state. Had they managed to weave nothing into our character more adequate than we sometimes discover in our political dogmas, we should even have wanted the institutions about which we speculate so feebly, and should have been as hopeless of any settled terms of order, as we now are confident of our baseless and undigested principles.

I cannot withstand the temptation to recite, just here, another passage from Robinson. I do it, partly because it so exactly meets the genius of our institutions, and reveals so beautifully the moral springs of our history, and partly because it prepares a way so aptly for other suggestions yet to be offered. He gives the Pilgrims on their departure, a written letter of advice to be carried with them, in which are contained the following remarkable words — words which I could even wish were graven in tablets of stone, as the words of a father before Washington, and set up over the doors of our Congress, our State Legislatures, our town halls and political assembly rooms, there to stand, meeting the eyes of our people as long as the nation exists certain always of this, that when the spirit of the words is wholly gone, the nation will exist no longer.

"Lastly, whereas you are to become a body politic, using civil government amongst yourselves, and are not furnished with any persons of special eminency above the rest [no knights or noble orders] to be chosen into office of government, let your wisdom and godliness appear, not only by choosing such persons as do entirely love and will diligently promote the common good, but also in yielding unto them all due honor and obedience in their lawful administrations; not beholding the ordinariness of their persons, but God's ordinance for your good; nor being like the foolish multitude, who more honor the gay coat [understand the stars and ribbons of nobility] than either the virtuous mind of the man, or the glorious ordinance of the Lord. But you know better things, and that the image of the Lord's power and authority, which the magistrate beareth, is honorabie in how mean persons soever. And this duty you may the more willingly and conscionably perform, because you are, at least for the present, to have only them for your ordinary governors, which yourselves shall make choice of for that work." — *Young's Chronicles*, p. 95.

BUT, while our founders stand right, when viewed in relation to what is most really fundamental in our institutions, we must not expect them to concur in all that we now regard as most properly and distinctly American.

They had no sehemes of democracy to execute. They were not, in fact, or in their own view, republicans in their ideas of government. When Robinson's doctrine of church order was assailed as being a scheme of Christian democracy, he repelled the imputation as a slander, insisting, instead, that it was a plan of order "plainly aristocratical." — *Punchard*, p. 348. They were all, to a man, royalists and true Englishmen — pleased with the hope of "endeavoring the advancement of his Majesty's dominion." — *Cotton Mather*, p. 6. Some of them delighted in being able to write "Mr." before their names, and the others would have cast out any man as a leveller and disorderly person, who dared to controvert the validity of that high distinction. Does any one the less certainly know that their whole scheme of principle and order was virtually and essentially republican, even from the first?

They as little thought of raising a separation of church and state as of planting a new democracy. They accepted in full and by formal reference the English doctrine on this subject, and Robinson even professed his willingness to accept the "oath of supremacy," which acknowledges the king as the rightful head of the church. When a new settlement or town was planted, they said, not that the settlers were become a body politic, but that they were "inchurched." And when Davenport preached on the terms of suffrage, the problem stated was, "how to order a frame of civil government in a plantation whose *design* is religion." — *Bacon*, p. 289.

And yet we can look back now and see as distinctly as possible, that their very doctrine of church-membership must necessitate a final separation of church and state. For, if none but the true members of Christ can be included in the church, and none but such as are included can have the right of suffrage, then it must shortly appear that many good neighbors and virtuous sons and brothers are reduced to the condition of aliens in the commonwealth. Accordingly, we find that the settlers of the Hartford Colony, who had begun to see the pernicious consequences of the restricted suffrage in Massachusetts, in the beautiful constitution they adopted — the first written constitution of a purely representative republican government known to human history — opened the right of suffrage to all whom the several towns might elect as freemen. And thus, in less than twenty years after the settlement of Plymouth, the separation of church and state is visibly begun — a step is taken which can possibly issue in this alone, though the result is not completely and formally reached, till a hundred and fifty years have passed away.

I wish it were possible to claim for our fathers the honor of a free toleration of religious opinions. This it would seem that they might have learned from their own wrongs and sufferings. But they were not the men to think of finding their doctrines in any woes of their flesh. They had, in fact, a conscience against toleration, lest the state, "whose end is religion," should seem to connive at false doctrines and schismatic practices. Therefore, when Cromwell was proposing toleration in England, the Synod of Massachusetts even protested against the measure as licentious. And one of their ministers, the eccentric pastor of Ipswich, was stirred up to publish in England, a most violent diatribe against it. He delighted in the old maxim that "true religion is *ignis probationis*," — a test of fire. Indeed this narrow-spirited man had lived in the midst of toleration, upon the continent, and had not discovered its Christian beauty. "I lived," he says, "in a city where a Papist preached in one church, a Lutheran in another, a Calvinist in a third; a Lutheran one part of the day, and a Calvinist the other, in the same pulpit. The religion of that place was but motley and meagre, and their affections leopard-like." — *Cobbler of Agawam*, p. 5. Alas! for the brave pastor of Ipswich, how clear is it now, that the toleration he so much dreaded really belonged to all but the rather testy prejudices that he took for a part of his religion. The old *ignis probationis*, too, whose smoke had so lately been wafted over England from Smithfield and Tyburn — which however he did not mean, I trust, to commend in its most literal and orthodox sense — is gone out for ever the world over. And as to the "leopard-like" religion, just that which compelled a separation of Church and State, has doubtless compelled a sufferance also of this, even in his own parochial Ipswich itself. Or if free opinion be a leopard, spotting over the Church, or dissolving it into so many motley groups of division, it will ere long be seen that this unruly leopard is fulfilling the prophecy, forgetting his instincts of prey and schism, and lying down with the kids of love, in a catholic and perennial unity..

It need scarcely be added, that our fathers had as little thought of a separation from the mother country and as little desire of founding an independent commonwealth, as of the other distinctions just named. England was their home, they loved the monarchy. They would even have doubted their piety itself, had they found a single unloyal thought in their bosoms. And yet they were compelled to be jealous, even from the first, of any too close implication with the political affairs of the mother country, lest it should finally involve the security of their liberties. They formally declined, in this view, to connect themselves with Cromwell's Parliament by any application to it, and also to appear by deputies in the Westminster Assembly of Divines. — *Bancroft*, vol. i. pp. 450-1. It may be taken also as a singular and most omnious fact, that the Hartford Colony in arranging the new constitution just alluded to, made no mention either of king or parliament. This constitution required an oath of allegiance directly to itself, and even asserted a supreme power — "In which General Court shall consist the *supreme power* of the Commonwealth." — *Trumbull*, i. p. 532. And this supreme power they, in fact, exercised for ever after; subject to no negative, under governors of their own choice, creating their own tribunals and holding them without appeal, and even openly resisting the royal levies as an infringement of their rights. Here was, in fact, a little, independent, unconscious republic, unfolding itself by the banks of the Connecticut, on its own basis, under its own laws; so that when the war of independence came, instead of being dissolved by the state of revolution and required to reorganize itself, it stood ready in full form for action, and was able, in the first twenty-four hours after the outbreak, to set twenty thousand men upon the march, fully appointed with officers and arms. The people had never set up for independence. They were loyal — in their way. But they had been sheltered under the very singular privileges of their charter, as well as by their more retired position; and had actually grown apart, unconsciously and by force of their own moral affinities, into a free republic. The condition of Rhode Island was similar: and the same general process was going on also in the other colonies, only under many restraints from royal governors and the qualified privileges of their charters.

NOW THERE IS a class of writers and critics in our country, who imagine it is quite clear that our fathers cannot have been the proper founders of our American liberties, because it is in proof that they were so intolerant and so clearly unrepublican often in their avowed sentiments. They suppose the world to be a kind of professor's chair, and expect events to transpire logically in it. They see not that casual opinions, or conventional and traditional prejudices are one thing, and that principles and morally dynamic forces are often quite another; that the former are the connectives only of history, the latter its springs of life; and that if the former serve well enough, as providential guards and moderating weights, overlying the deep geologic fires and subterranean heavings of the new moral instincts below, these latter will assuredly burst up, at last, in strong mountains of rock, to crest the world. Unable to conceive such a truth, they cast about them, accordingly, to find the paternity of our American institutions in purely accidental causes. We are clear of aristocratic orders, they say, because there was no blood of which to make an aristocracy; independent of king and parliament, because we grew into independence under the natural effects of distance and the exercise of a legislative power; republican, because our constitutions were cast in the moulds of British law; a wonder of growth in riches, enterprise, and population, because of the hard necessities laid upon us, and our simple modes of life.

And the concurrent action of these causes must not be denied, we only must not take them as the true account of our successes. As good accidents were enjoyed elsewhere as here. There is the little decayed town of St. Augustine, settled by a Spanish colony even earlier, by some years, than Boston, which nevertheless we were just now called to rescue, by a military force, from the incursions of the savages! There are Mexico and the South American states, colonized by Spain, even a hundred years prior to the settlement of Plymouth, — when Spain too was at the height of her glory, and even far in advance of England, as regards the state of wealth and civil order, — fellow republics indeed in name, but ignorant still of what liberty is, thirty years after they have gotten the right to it; poor, unprogressive, demoralized by superstition, and the oldest and strongest of them all actually contending, at this moment, with the aborigines, to save large towns and old and populous settlements from extermination! A glance in this direction is enough to show how much must be referred to the personal qualities and principles of the founders of a nation, how little to the mere accidents of circumstance and condition.

BESIDES, there is yet another view of this question, that has a far higher significance. We do not understand, as it seems to me, the real greatness of our institutions, when we look simply at the forms under which we hold our liberties. It consists not in these, but in the magnificent Possibilities that underlie these forms, as their fundamental supports and conditions. In these we have the true paternity and spring of our institutions, and these, beyond a question, are the gift of our founders.

We see this, first of all, in the fixed relation between free. dom and intelligence, and the remarkable care they had of popular education. It was not their plan to raise up a body of republicans. But they believed in mind as in God. Their religion was the choice of mind. The gospel they preached must have minds to hear it: and hence the solemn care they had, even from the first day of their settlement, of the education of every child. And, as God would have it, the children whom they trained up for pillars in the church, turned out also to be more than tools of power. They grew up into magistrates, leaders of the people, debaters of right and of law, statesmen, generals, and signers of declarations for liberty. Such a mass of capacity had never been seen before, in so small a body of men. And this is the first condition of liberty — the Condensation of Power. For liberty is not the license of an hour; it is not the butchery of a royal house, or the passion that rages behind a barricade, or the caps that are swung or the *vivas* shouted at the installing of a liberator. But it is the compact, impenetrable matter of much manhood, the compressed energy of good sense and public reason, having power to see before and after, and measure action by counsel — this it is that walls about the strength and liberty of a people. To be free is not to fly abroad, as the owls of the night, when they take the freedom of the air, but it is to settle and build and be strong — a commonwealth as much better compacted in the terms of reason, as it casts off more of the restraints of force.

MUTUAL CONFIDENCE also is another and fundamental condition of free institutions. When a revolution breaks out in Mexico or in Paris, and the old magistracies are swept away, then immediately you shall see that a most painful question arises. Power must be deposited somewhere, with whom can it safely be trusted? Is it already in the hands of a committee? then can this committee be trusted? Is a military commander set up to maintain order for a time with greater efficiency? what shall restrain the commander? Whoever is in power, the signs are jealously watched and morbidly construed. Well is it if some faction does not spring up to usurp the sovereign power, by a new act of revolution, justified by the pretext of saving the public liberties. Here you have the whole history of Mexico for the last thirty years, and, with fewer and less frequent alternations, the history of France, for a longer period. There is a fatal want of mutual confidence which nothing can supply, for the simple reason that there is nothing in which to confide. Power is known only as power, not as the endowment of obligation.

We are distracted by no such infirmity. We have never a thought of danger in the immense powers we confide to our rulers, simply because we can trust one another. We know so well the good sense and the firm conscience of our people as to be sure that, if any magistrate lifts the flag of an usurper and throws off the terms of his trust, all power will instantly drop out of his hands, and nothing will be necessary but to send a constable after him, even though he be the head of the army itself!

Now this matter of mutual confidence, fundamental as you see it to be to all strength in our institutions, or peace under them, has a very humble, unpretending look. Scarcely ever has it crept into the notice of history. It has never been celebrated, I am sure, in any epic poem. No! but it is the silent exploit of a great history. Let Mexico ask for it, and offer the mortgage of her mines to buy it; let France question her savans, or lay it on the mitred priesthood at her altars to provide the new republic with this most indispensable gift, and alas! they cannot all together guess where it is, or whence it shall come. It is the silent growth of centuries, and there is no seed but the seed of Puritan discipline, out of which it was ever known to grow.

IT IS another and most necessary condition of free institutions, that the people should be trained to a special exercise of personal self-government. For it is the distinction of a republic that it governs less and less violently, substituting a moral in place of a public control. It is an approach towards no government, grounded, as a possibility, in the fact of a more complete government established in the personal habits of the subjects themselves. No republic could stand for a year, if it were compelled to govern as much, and with as much force as the English people are governed. Force must be nearly dispensed with. For,

"What are numbers knit
By force or custom? Man who man would be,
Must rule the empire of himself; in it
Must be supreme, establishing his throne
Of vanquished will, quelling the anarchy
Of hopes and fears, being himself alone."

Under this high possibility or condition, punishments are mitigated, the laws are fewer and more simple, the police are at their own private employments and come only when they are sent for, domestic fortresses and standing armies nowhere appear to annoy the sense of liberty. A foreigner passing through the republic and hearing the sound of government in no beat of the drum, seeing the government in no parade of horse or foot or badges of police, concludes that the people are put upon their good behavior to-day; but when he is told that they were so yesterday, and will be to-morrow, he imagines that a doom of anarchy is certainly close at hand. The fears of Washington and the most sober patriots of his time, that our government had not strength enough to stand, were justified by all human example, and were not to be blamed. And yet the course of our legislation has, to this hour, been a course of discontinuance. We seem to be making an experiment, with how many laws it is possible to dispense. We are anxious many times for the result, and yet we do not suffer. We have gone a length in this direction which to any European will appear incredible. When I ponder, not without fears I confess, this sublime distinction of our country, holding in contrast what has been heretofore, and forecasting what God may be intending to bring forth here in the future ages, I am swallowed up in admiration of that power by which our faithful fathers were able to set our history on a footing so peculiar. They gave up their all to religion, knew no wisdom but simply to live for religion, and were it not for the intermixture of so many foreign elements which at present disturb our condition, we might almost imagine that in some good future, when the moral regimen of self-government is complete in our people, the external government of force and constraint may be safely dispensed with, the civil state subside in the fulness of the spiritual, and God alone be left presiding over the grand republic of wills by the sufficiency of his own divine Spirit and principles.

CLOSELY ALLIED with this great possibility of self-government, as a ground of republican order, is another, if indeed it be another, which must needs be prepared also. I speak of the displacement of loyalty, and the substitution of law. Loyalty is a sentiment, law a conviction or principle. One is the tribute yielded to a person, the other is the enthronement of an abstraction simply, or a formal statute. In the sentiment of loyalty, taken as a tribute of homage to high-born persons, to the starred noble, or the reigning prince of a royal house, there is a certain beauty which naturally fascinates the mind. The sentiment partakes of chivalry. In such a distribution of the social state, there is a fine show of distinctions that sets off a romance, or a play, and even gives to society itself the courtly air of a drama. Government is here seen in the concrete, set off by dress and title and scales of precedence, and the loyal heart rejoices in the homage it yields to the gods of the eye. Such a government is better adapted to a people generally rude and uneducated, or low in moral culture, because it is a government of show and sentiment, and not of reason. But, with all the captivating airs it has to the mere looker on, it is, in fact, a government of authorized caprice, and obedience a state, too often, of disappointed fealty. If it is pleasant to look upon the fine livery of a noble, it is far less so to be imprisoned as a public malefactor for a slight breach of the game law. The splendor of nobility is too often corruption; the protection, contempt and insult. Moreover, it will be found that a merely personal and sentimental homage is of a nature too inconstant or capricious ever to be confidently trusted. It may possibly hold a dog to his fidelity, but it never held a race of men. There, accordingly, has never been a government, standing on the basis of loyalty, that was not obliged to fortify loyalty by a display of steel and of military squadrons, more conspicuous than its noble orders.

Now the problem is, in founding a republic, to prepare a social state without artificial distinctions, and govern it by abstractions and formal constitutions in place of persons. The "gay coat" of Robinson, the royal pageants and the starred nobility are withdrawn from the eye, and the laws and constitutions — in one view nothing but invisible abstractions or terms of public reason — must be set in that inward homage which can never be shaken. The problem, though it be the most difficult ever attempted in the history of mankind, is yet, for once, accomplished. Consider the terrible surging of party and passion, displayed in one of our Presidential elections. See a whole nation, vast enough for an empire, roused to the intensest pitch of strife and tearing, as it were in the coming out of a demon. The old Guelph and Ghibelline factions were scarcely more violent or implacable. But the day of election passes without so much as the report of an outbreak, and the day after the whole nation is as quiet as if there were but one mind in it — all by the power of Invisible Law! Nay, we had a President at the head of our great republic who had no party in the Congress, and few friends among the people. During four whole years he occupied the seat of power, dispensing a patronage greater than that of the Queen of England, with not a soldier visible to assert the majesty of order, and yet without even the symptom of a disturbance. Never, in all the history of mankind, was displayed a spectacle of moral sublimity comparable to these four years of American history — sublimity the more sublime, because we were wholly unconscious of it ourselves, and had not even a thought that it could be otherwise!

And the fundamental cause, if you seek it, is that law with us is the public right and reason. It is mine, it is yours, and being for all as public reason, it is God's. To rebel against it, therefore, is to rebel both against ourselves and God. And if you ask whence came this conviction, how was it so firmly established? By the life, I awswer, and the religion of our fathers. Whether true or false is not now the question, but their religion was a religion only of judgments and abstractions. For these they renounced comfort, country, property, and home. These they preached. On these they even fed their children. Honors and pageants of distinction were out of sight. They could not be saved in the easy drill of forms. No mitred order, no priesthood came between the worshipper and his God to act the patron for him, and be the conduit of heaven's grace to his soul. He must enter with boldness into the holiest himself. There was besides in Calvinism, as a religion, just that which would give abstractions the intensest power and the most awful reality to the mind. It took its beginning at the sovereignty of God. It saw all men lying in a common plane of equality below. The only princes it knew were God's elect. And this kind of knighthood it was no easy formality to gain. It was to believe and accurately hold and experimentally know the iron base-work of an abstractive theology. The mind was thrust into questions that compelled action — eternal decrees, absolute election, arbitrary grace, imputed sin, imputed righteousness. On these head anvils of abstraction the blows of thought must needs be ever ringing, and when the points were said to be cordially received, it was meant also that they were dialectically bedded in the framework of the man.

Hence the remarkable power of abstractions in the American mind. The Germans can live in them as their day-dreams, but we can live upon them and by them as our daily bread. Our enthusiasm is most enthusiastic, our practical energy most energetic and practical just here — in what we do, or hope to do, under the application of great principles, whether of science, government, or religion. And thus it has come to pass that the gulf between loyalty and law is effectually crossed over. The transition is made, and we are set by it on a new and, as time will show, a much higher plane of history. In one view, there is something ungracious in our American spirit. We are nearly as ignorant of the loyal feeling as a tribe of wild animals

— unrespectful often to worth and true precedence. And yet we have a feeling as truly national as any people in the world. If the traveller in England begins to count the pictured Oaks and Lions, the royal or princely names stuck upon all shows and shops of trade and chop-houses, and even petty wares, down to soaps and razors — riding always on "Royal" roads, sleeping at "Royal" inns, and washing in the water of some "Royal" aqueduct — if he is nauseated, for the time, by what appears to be the inexhaustible servility of that great people, he is sure to smile at his own impatience when he returns, and recall the sentence he had passed. He takes up the newspapers at his hotel, and finds how many headed by cognomens ingeniously compounded with "People," "Democracy," "Republic," "Constitution," "Independence," and "Nation." He runs his eye down the advertising columns and along the signboards of the street, and it falls on how many titles to patriotic favor, ranging in all grades, from the "People's Line" of steamboats and the ship "Constitution," down to the "Jefferson Lunch" and the "New Democratic Liniment." In one view, these demonstrations have a most ludicrous air; in another, they are signs of the deepest significance — showing that we, as truly as the most loyal of nations, have our public feeling; a feeling not the less universal and decided, because its objects are mostly impersonal.

And, by force of this public feeling, it is just now beginning to appear that the government of this vast and, as most persons would say, loosely compacted republic, is really the strongest government in the world. What can be stronger than a government that has no enemies, and the subjects of which do not desire and would not suffer a change? They have looked out from their fastnesses and the loop-holes of fortified order in Europe, prophesying our speedy lapse into anarchy; they have said, how can a people be governed without a personal embodiment of authority in princes and noble orders? but now, when their thrones are rocking on the underswell of popular movement, and their princes flying in fishermen's disguises from the splendid millinery that was to captivate the loyal eyes of their loyal people, they begin to cast a look across the ocean, to the new republic, whose impalpable throne of law is every where acknowledged by all as a friendly power — and is not this, they ask, the real strength and stability of order?

Yes, and so I trust in God it shall prove itself to the coming ages. When twenty years hence, and twenty years after that, the successive waves of liberty roll high across the fields of Europe, and the old prescriptive orders and powers are drifted onward and away till not even the wreck can be found, this better throne of law I trust shall stand, as the guardian to us and the promise to mankind of the freedom and the righteous peace they long for.

Do I then affirm that our fathers foresaw these magnificent results, now revealed in our political history? I have even made it a part of their greatness that they did not. They stood for God and religion alone. They asked for nothing, planned for nothing, hoped for nothing, save what should come of their religion. They believed in the Bible and in God's decrees, and they came over to profess the one and fulfil the other. They had not so much as thought of giving the universe or the world a 'Revised Constitution.' They did not believe in predestination by man — therefore had nothing in common with our modern prophets of 'science,' who promise to re-organize society from a point without and by a scheme imposed, not by any remedial forces of faith and duty, acting from within and through its secret laws. They did not begin at the point zero in themselves, or in their own human wisdom, but at duty; and they represent, at once, the infallible success and the majestic firmness of duty. Compared with the class of ephemeral world-renovators just named, they stand as the firm, granitic, heaven-piercing Needles, by the *mer de glace* of human unbeliefs and the unwisdoms of pretended science; and while that is cracking below in the frosts by which it is crystallized, and grinding down its bed of destiny, to be melted in the heat of practical life and be seen no more, they rise serenely, as ever, lifting their heads above the storm-clouds of the world, and stand — still looking up! They will do below only what they seek above. They will give us only the reward of their lives, and what may be distilled from their prayers. And in these, they give us all.

Ah! the sour, impracticable race, who, by reason of their sinister conscience, could not kneel at the sacraments, and must needs stand up before God Himself, when kings and bishops kneeled; barbarians of schism, who revolted to be rid of the Christian civility of priestly garments; who could not be in the spirit on the Lord's day under the excellent prayers of the Parliament, and preferred to insult the king by dying, rather than to yield him an inch of Church reformation! — so they are described, and I am not about to deny that they made as many sharp points in their religion as Christian charity and true reason required. When God prepares a hammer, it will not be made of silk. If our fathers were uncomfortable men, what great character ever lived that was not an uncomfortable man to his times? If they cast off the decrees of Parliament, and took in the decrees of God in their place, was it not to be expected, both from what they had cast off and from what they had taken, that there would be a little more of stiffness and punctilious rigor in the issue than was requisite ? Or, if they had found a true Pope in the Bible, what should follow, but a most literal obeisance, even to the slipper of the book? As the world too of past ages had received their salvation, with tremulous awe, in a little sprinkling of holy water, or a wafer on the tongue, and they had now learned to look for salvation in what they believed, what should they do but stand for their mere letters of abstraction, as exact and scrupulous, as if the words of faith had even as great dignity, as ablutions of the finger or a paste in the mouth? It could not be otherwise. That was no age for easy compliances and flowing lines of opinion. Whatever was done, must have the cutting edge of scruple and over-punctual severity. Only let our fathers be judged with that true historic sympathy, which is the due of all men, and I ask no more. Then it will even be confessed that, by the strictness which exceeded reason, they only proved that close fidelity and sacred homage to reason, which is itself but a name for true spiritual honor and greatness. For

>—"Rightly to be great
>Is not to stir without great argument,
>But greatly to find quarrel in a straw,
>When honor's at the stake."

I have spoken thus at length of the successes of our political and social history, for it is chiefly in these that we have our prominence before the world, and seem also to ourselves to have achieved results of the greatest brilliancy and magnitude. But my subject requires me to believe, and I think the signs also indicate that results are yet to come, far transcending these in their sublimity and their beneficent consequences to mankind. Indeed, what now we call results of history, seem to me to be only stages in the preparation of a Great and Divine Future, that includes the spiritual good and glory and the comprehensive unity of the race — exactly that which most truly fulfils the grand religious ideal of Robinson and the New England fathers.

Their word was "Reformation" — "the completion of the Reformation;" not Luther's nor Calvin's, they expressly say, they cannot themselves image it. Hitherto it is unconceived by men. God must reveal it in the light that breaks forth from Him. And this He will do, in His own good time. It is already clear to us that, in order to any farther progress in this direction, it was necessary for a new movement to begin, that should loosen the joints of despotism and emancipate the mind of the world. And in order to this a new republic must be planted, and have time to grow. It must be seen rising up in the strong majesty of freedom and youth, outstripping the old prescriptive world in enterprise and the race of power, covering the ocean with its commerce, spreading out in populous swarms of industry — planting, building, educating, framing constitutions, rushing to and fro in the smoke and thunder of travel along its mighty rivers, across its inland seas, over its mountaintops from one shore to the other, strong in order as in liberty, a savage continent become the field of a colossal republican empire, whose name is a name of respect and a mark of desire to the longing eyes of mankind. And then, as the fire of new ideas and hopes darts electrically along the nerves of feeling in the millions of the race, it will be seen that a new Christian movement also begins with it. Call it reformation, or formation, or by whatever name, it is irresistible because it is intangible. In one view, it is only destruction. The State is loosened from the Church. The Church crumbles down into fragments. Superstition is eaten away by the strong acid of liberty, and spiritual despotism flies affrighted from the broken loyalty of its metropolis. Protestantism also, divided and subdivided by its dialectic quarrels, falls into the finest, driest powder of disintegration. Be not afraid. The new order crystallizes only as the old is dissolved; and no sooner is the old unity of orders and authorities effectually dissolved, than the reconstructive affinities of a new and better unity begin to appear in the solution. Repugnances melt away. Thought grows catholic. Men look for good in each other, as well as evil. The crossings of opinion, by travel and books, and the intermixtures of races and religions, issue in freer, broader views of the Christian truth: and so the "Church of the Future," as it has been called, gravitates inwardly towards those terms of brotherhood in which it may coalesce and rest. I say not or believe, that Christendom will be Puritanized, or Protestantized; but what is better than either, it will be Christianized. It will settle thus into a unity, probably not of form, but of practical assent and love — a Commonwealth of the Spirit, as much stronger in its unity than the old satrapy of priestly despotism, as our republic is stronger than any other government of the world.

And this, I conceive, is the true issue of that "great hope and inward zeal" which impelled our fathers in the migration. Our political successes are but means to this magnificent end — instruments, all, and powers of religion, as we have seen them to be its natural effects and fruits. All kinds of progress, political and spiritual, coalesce and work together in our history; and will do so in all the race, till finally it is raised to its true summit of greatness, felicity, and glory, in God and religion. And when that summit is reached, it will be found that, as Church and State must be parted in the crumbling and disintegrating processes of freedom; so, in freedom attained, they will coalesce again, not as Church and State, but in such kind of unity as well nigh removes the distinction—the peace and love and world-wide brotherhood, established under moral ideas, and the eternal truths of God's eternal kingdom.

GLORY ENOUGH, then, is it for our sublime Fathers, to have filled an office so conspicuous in the preparation of results so magnificent. I am not unaware of the defects in their character. Nay, I would rather see and confess, than to hide them; for, since we cannot be gods ourselves, it is better to be descended of a race of men than of gods. But, when I consider the unambitious sacrifice they made of their comforts and their country, how little they were moved by vagrant theories and projects of social revolution, how patient of hardships, how faithful to their convictions, how little they expected of men, how confidently they trusted their unknown future to God, and, then, what honor God has put upon them, and what greater honor he is preparing for their name, before the good and the free of the blessed ages of the future; I confess that I seem even to have offended in attempting to speak their eulogy. Silence and a bare head are a more fit tribute than words. Or, if we will erect to them a more solid and yet worthier monument, there is none so appropriate as to learn from them, and for ourselves to receive, the principle they have so nobly proved, that — THE WAY OF GREATNESS IS THE WAY OF DUTY.

# PART V

# GOD'S THOUGHTS FIT BREAD FOR CHILDREN

A Sermon Preached before the Connecticut Sunday-School Teachers' Convention, at the Pearl-Street Congregational church, Hartford, Conn., Tuesday Evening, March 2, 1869.

# INTRODUCTORY NOTE.

At the opening of the State Sunday-School Convention for Connecticut, at Hartford, March 2, 1869, the Rev. Dr. Bushnell preached, by special invitation of the Committee of Arrangements, a sermon to the assembled teachers. This discourse so fully met the high expectations entertained of it, and with such clearness and force presented the whole subject of Christian Teaching, and the Claims of Children on Church and Ministry, that the desire was general among its hearers to obtain copies of it for further study, and for permanent preservation.

The following resolution was passed unanimously by the Convention:

> "Resolved, That the Chairman of the State Central Committee be instructed to make, if practicable, some arrangement with the Rev. Dr. Bushnell for the publication of his valuable address at the opening of the Convention."

It is in response to the call thus made, that the distinguished author has submitted the discourse to the officers of the Connecticut Association; and it is with peculiar satisfaction that those having the matter in charge, now present it in this form to the public, in the confident belief that the interests of the dear Saviour's work among children will be promoted by its wide circulation and perusal.

GEORGE LANGDON,<br>
Chairman of State Central Committee.

*PLYMOUTH, Conn., May 29, 1869.*

# SERMON

How precious also are thy thoughts unto me, O God! How great is the sum of them!

— PSALM 139:17.

It is a common fault of our preachings, teachings, and faiths, that we take every thing too externally; as if beholding God from without, and only doing or thinking something about him. In the beautiful and glowing utterance of the divine singer, as here cited, it is not so. He had been thinking, as we see in the preceding verses, of the curiously wrought substance and organism of his own person; how his members were written out beforehand in the registry of God's book, when as yet imperfect; growing as it were in God's depths, even as the precious gems are distilled in the lowest parts of the earth. Whereupon, he breaks out, as one living among God's very thoughts themselves, "How precious also are thy thoughts unto me, O God! how great is the sum of them!" He does not go prosing about God as the architect and artificer of his frame, shaping him on the outside plastically by his hand; but he beholds himself and the dear gift of his body and spirit crystallizing, so to speak, in the bosom of God's fatherhood, meditated there and fashioned and curiously wrought. It is as if he grew in the womb of God's thoughts, and God's thoughts lived within him as he grew.

Let us follow and develop, a little way farther, this interiorizing utterance and apostrophe of the psalmist; and then we shall be ready, I trust, to gather in what we have learned upon our present occasion, setting it in close relation with all we have on hand, and making it a kind of institute in itself.

Two points, in particular, invite our attention here: first, that God is a being who thinks—doing all deeds, creating all creations, appearing in all beauty, towering in all heights of excellence, by his thoughts, which are therefore infinitely precious; secondly, that there is a possibility and way of arriving at the knowledge of God's thoughts, such as the psalmist found, else how could they be so adoringly prized by him?

I. God is a being who thinks, and whose thoughts, being the creating powers of all good, are infinitely precious. Of course, being infinite and filling all space, he cannot be supposed to move or travel in space; but the everlasting going on of thought within him is none the less possible. All the goings-on of things without do but represent, in fact, the eternal potentiality of his mind within. His immutability is not, as the Eastern sophists imagined, the necessary cessation of thought, but is rather his immutable freedom and vitality in it. His greatness does not stifle his mind, leaving him to be blind Fate, or still-born Nature, or a great king-dreamer, Brama, recumbent on the stars. In his word of revelation, he says indeed, — "For my thoughts are not as your thoughts;" — but he means by this only that his thoughts are better, or perhaps full formed and perfect; for there is no progress in his thinking, but only in the events he moves. He does not think distractedly, as we do under our sin; and then he does not infer, ascertain, compute, conjecture, or in that way learn any thing. His memory recalls nothing, for nothing is absent. His internal movement is not a rill, in which drop steals after drop, one single thought after another, but it is the sea containing all drops at once, a boundless fulness moving tidally with no drop lying dead and still. Holding this view, all events are at bottom his thought; and precisely here, in the stripping off of their external husk of commonness, we arrive at their secret potentiality and behold their preciousness. They have all God's dispositions moving back of them, God's plans contriving in them, God's beauty shaping them, God's patience waiting by them, God's justice filling their quiver with arrows, God's creations, providences, spiritual visitations coursing inwardly through them; and so beholding in them, as it were, the secret distillations of God's bosom, they become all thoughts of God, — our precious things, our gems of knowledge, even as the diamonds curiously shaped and fashioned in the secret laboratories of the world, become a precious kind of dust, which we now call dust no longer. Every commonest event and thing has a base-work of divine thought and idea under it, in which it is precious.

II. There is a possibility and way of arriving at God's thoughts, or the knowledge of them, in which we make a large stride of advance in our subject.

In certain matters this point is readily and always perceived, even though we think of no such possibility in other things. We assume it, for example, as the test of all right thinking, in matters of absolute truth and duty, that we think the thoughts of God. For there can be no two kinds of righteousness, truth, moral beauty, moral perfection : whatever standard reigns in the mind of God must be standard law and verity to us. God's ideal law of right and truth is our ideal law of the same. Not that every particular act seen to be conformed to right by God is infallibly seen to be by us, or that every particular affirmation seen to be true by him is infallibly seen to be by us. Under these ideals, God sees every particular rightness and trueness; whereas we distinguish the same only dimly and doubtfully. And yet, if we live rightly in or under these ideals, and adhere to them faithfully, we shall be constantly gravitating towards the mind of God in all such particular matters, and shall come at last to think more and more closely the thoughts of God himself. Clouds of dust and grains of false mixture may partly obscure our seeing still, when they do not his, but we shall approximate him; and, as far as we may go, what is truth to us will be truth to him; and every good and pure emotion we may have will have the precise quality of his. What, in fact, can be more absurd, than to suppose that we can think any thing fit to be thought, which is contrary to or different from the thinking of God? And that, of course, implies that we may so far arrive at the thoughts of God.

And exactly this, I now go on to say, is what he means for us. For, to this end, first of all, he creates us in his own image, giving us just such a mind as, apart from wrong and sin, tends naturally, by its own internal law, to think what he thinks, — precisely that and nothing less. And then he constitutes the creation itself, so as to put our mind at school by his own. Thus, we think out certain mathematical laws of circles; and we turn to the heavens, where God has hung out his machinery, and we find that his notions of circles and their laws correspond exactly with ours, and ours with his. Hence the ecstatic, half-bewildered, gloriously rational outcry of Kepler, when he puts his problem finished on the stars, and finds it exactly fit: "O God, I think thy thoughts after thee!" And just so the chemist, when he goes down into the secret chambers of matter, unyoking the atoms and recomposing them again by their laws, finds them ready for new partnership, only in the strictest laws of arithmetic — so many of this kind, with so many of that, in eternally fixed proportions; showing that God builds the earths and the stones in numbers,` and puts the atoms to school in them, even as we teach our children the same. And what are they doing thus early in their studies of arithmetic but arriving, so far, at the thoughts of God?

We read the mind of God also on a broader scale of perception, when we take the natural expression of things. For they bear a look of meaning or intelligence in their faces, and recite and sing, as it were, of God about us. His cloud, his thunder, his dew, the flush of his morning, the shadows of his evening, every form of beauty, and plenty and gladness and power and terror discourses to our hearts' feeling somehow of feelings, dispositions, meanings, thoughts, somewhere, that are consciously not our own. And the lowest, dullest minds are caught by these impressions, — clowns, poetasters, poets, prophets, all are taken by them in their way. And yet there is a wonder more wonderful than this; viz., that every word of every human language is based, as every scholar knows, on some object or event naturally significant, provided for it in the grand universal dictionary called the creation; in which we see that thought is in it everywhere. And whose thought is it that packs this dictionary, this immense word-factory of expression? God's, of course. "Day unto day uttereth speech; night unto night showeth forth knowledge of him. There is no speech nor language where their voice is not heard."

So far we go in arriving at God's thought, as we trace the interior laws and behold the exterior expression of mere nature; far enough to see plainly that he is here permitting us and carefully training us to such deep interior acquaintance with himself. But we open now his supernatural word, his book of revelation, and our impression is not so much that we are arriving at God, or the thoughts of God, as that they are arriving at us. In the very first chapter of the book, where the creation-story begins, he allows us, as it were, to overhear him in the deliberative council of his thoughts, saying, "Let us make man in our image," &c., taking us back, so to speak, into the chambers of his eternity, where we may see him planning, from a day before the world, to have a family round him bearing his likeness, and sharing, if they will, his blessedness. Next follows the dread fatality of sin, and the general undoing, by which our good possibilities are blasted. God's own verdict thereupon is, "that the imagination of their thoughts is only evil, that they know not the thoughts of the Lord." Misthoughted now all through, filled with misruling passion, —hate, lust, proud self-worship, blind world-worship, — God engages here to recover us by a great supernatural salvation, and finally to recompose our life in his divine order, casting down imaginations and bringing our every thought into chime and coincidence with his own.

Let us now ascend this bible stair and look onward, along down the lines of the story, and see how God's great thoughts are waiting and working for us in it, — waiting and working to be felt and welcomed, and become the law and blessing of our own. This old-world history is not any thing precious, viewed externally, but is only a very coarse mixture of idolatries, judgments, wars, barbarities: a religion shut up in formalities and transacted in a slaughter-yard of sacrifice, where gluttonous priests are watching for their part of the meat; the civil history is wild and oppressive; the social is treacherous and cruel : and yet, if we go down under the externalities deep enough to find what God is meditating there, we shall say at every turn, "How precious are thy thoughts!" Underneath the outward story, we distinguish signs that are preluding everywhere a gospel day. Enoch walks with God, till by God's loving thought he is lifted and taken away. Abraham has found that God provides himself a lamb, and gotten full discovery thus of God's loving thought to him. Jacob has seen angels of God ascending and descending on him; and by that sacred telegraphy had his communication with God. Moses has had his bush and put off there his shoes before Him whose title of mystery is, *I am that I am*. Little Samuel has had his call; and Isaiah has cried "Woe is me, for I have seen the King;" and David has got so wonted in God's dispositions, purposes, sympathies, self-sacrificing patiences, and meditations of mercy, that he prays by God's thoughts, — "Have mercy upon me, O God, according to thy loving kindness; according to the multitude of thy tender mercies blot out my transgressions." Meantime God is calling out all along down the ages, himself, to the sottish people of transgression, "Come, let us reason together." Come, that is, and put yourselves alongside of me, your mind by my mind, your thoughts by my thoughts, that we may think alike and be one for ever. And so, if we take all these old books of story, biography, and prophecy, and join ourselves to these old hymns of worship, we seem to be insphered among God's very thoughts, — let in deep into the discerning of them. And we are lifted by the swell of a certain deific undertone in them, which is the Eternal Mind heaving up through, in great inspirations and tides of thought that have no human measures. Somehow the "precious thoughts" have arrived and found discovery in us.

Now, at last the fulness of time is come; and the New-Testament chapter is opened. And here the remarkable thing is, that every turn of the story is so palpably meant to give us God, and let us into the deepest possible discovery of his interior working and thought. Trinity lies on the face of the story, and it is a most gloriously practical and grand use of trinity, not often observed, either by those who believe in it or those who deny it, that it crowds all mind directly in upon the most searchingly inward ways of viewing God. We cannot think Him superficially now any more; but we must go far enough in, deep enough down, to be mining, as it were, in his nature. And then after this ante-chamber of tripersonal mystery is passed, the remarkable thing is, that every thing divine is made so palpable, so exceedingly obvious. God is manifest in the flesh. In his human person, Jesus is the incarnate word of the Father. By great works and all divinest charities he shows the precious thoughts and becomes the express image of God's inmost mind. He has no difficulty in saying, "I and my Father;" and as little in saying, "He that hath seen me hath seen the Father." Herein is love, herein are all God's dispositions, all God's patiences, condescensions, tendernesses, forgivenesses, all the righteousness; and the sacrifice of the cross declares them as in one comprehensive act of expression. God is visibly out, so that an apostle is moved to say, "For God hath shined in our hearts, to give the light of the knowledge of the glory of God in the face of Jesus Christ." The revelation is facial, so to speak, as if the cross of sacrifice were some inside-out forthcoming. And when he is declared as "the Lamb slain from the foundation of the world," what are we to understand but that in God's previous eternity of thought and character there was a bleeding side of sacrifice, a cross, which John saluted when he recognized the Lambhood of Jesus: "Behold the Lamb of God, that taketh away the sin of the world"? And when he dies — this Lamb of God — how far in opens the gate upon God's inmost counsel and feeling? We behold the one great, world-forgiving thought, we are fully atoned, our gospel of life is born!

Nothing more is wanted now but the gift of the Spirit, to come up from within, as Christ has come down from above, and be his interpreter in us, re-revealing Christ inwardly, as we believe in him, and helping us to believe in him, by such inward revelation. And then how far off are we from the discovered thought of God, when the Spirit witnesseth with our Spirit; when our natural man is gifted by him with a spiritual discerning of the things of God; when not knowing what to pray for, the Spirit helpeth us, groaning silently in our groans, to mould our intercession for us according to the very thought and will of God! And so, at last, as God is arriving at us, he makes our grace complete by putting spirit in our faith, that we may arrive at Him. Now the discovery is full, and we are sealed by it everlastingly. God is no more beyond sea that we must go after him, or above, that we may bring him down; but we have him in our mouth and in our heart, and are of him for ever. And this is our redemption.

ARE YOU NOW BEGINNING, my friends, to ask what is all this for? Has it any thing to do, and by any possibility what, with this particular occasion? My answer is, 'that it has, and will be seen to have just every thing to do with the occasion. The very design I have in it is to corner in your minds at a very important matter in which a whole great chapter of counsel will be opened. I bring you out here on this summit-level of the gospel, at a point where the day-star rises, and the day-bath of God's light floods all believing minds, that you may have a grand revision here, both of the matter which has called you together, and of yourselves as related to it. My design is to put our preaching and teaching ideas in measure with the real gospel, at its best and most central point of view.

It appears to me, though perhaps I am wrong, that we hold this Sunday-school work in a very light way, such as demands a kind of re-institution to put it on a right footing. The unfortunate word *school* appears to let up, a good deal, the pressure of Christian ideas. Who teaches, in what manner, with how much or little responsibility, is not so much considered, save by a specially conscientious few. And the work is a good deal secularized to the children; as if the making up of a good time for them were a considerable part of the plan. The jolly, no-religion songs, the amusing stories and droll illustrations that illustrate nothing, the uncaring manner of the memorizing, school-training recitations, — all these produce, when taken together, an atmosphere of general unchristliness. As it was and still is the manner of parents to bring up their children for a future conversion, so the vice creeps in here of teaching only for some benefit future, and letting every thing stop short, by consent, of touching the main thing. Palestine is taught, the mountains round about Jerusalem, Jerusalem about the temple and the cross, and all that is about God, but not God himself. It is not expected that the children will know God himself, but something about him.

And there is, in fact, a secret assumption that no such thing is possible. The true knowledge of God, as in friendship, is possible to adults, but not to children; whereas, the real fact is, that children are a great deal more capable of it. The boy child, Samuel, could hear the call when old Eli could not. Children may not think the gospel experiences as well, but they can have them a great deal more easily. Tell the child how present God is, how loving he is, how close by he is in all good thoughts, and he will take the sense a great deal better than the adult soul, that is gone a doubting so far, and speculated his mind half away in the false intellectualities miscalled reason. Ah! my friends, "Of these, of such is the kingdom of heaven:" so Christ says, and we make almost nothing of it. These children can make room for more gospel than we, and take in all most precious thoughts of

God more easily. The very highest and most spiritual things are a great deal closer to them than to us. Let us not wonder and not be offended if they break out in hosannas on just looking in the face of Jesus, when the great multitude of priests and apostles are dumb, along the road, as the ass on which he rides.

Consider next how much it means for us, that we may teach from Jesus, having him revealed thought-wise in us, in all the divine flavors of his life. As he came to draw himself, so we can draw; for we can bear him about visibly in our body and become each one a Jesus in our places. And we shall teach him thus, not by over-much digging at lessons, not by contrived arguments, and made-up speeches. A great many, meaning to be faithful teachers, study too much, reason their way too hard, practise their interpretations too indefatigably, and run so far always to arrive at Jesus, that they never arrive. They come short, they faint for exhaustion; they get so many detentions upon them in the surroundings of Jesus, that they do not really find him much of the time, and come in where he is. No man teaches a gospel, whether in his pulpit or at his table or in his school, who does not know Jesus, and he cannot know Jesus out of any book by simply knowing the book, whether it be Bible or any thing else; but he must know the being, the very person: indeed, he must become a Jesus, in some very important sense, himself. And here again, it will not be enough to go through some gusty phase of experience, some inward commotion, some turbulent heat, some vision of a flighty brain. You will fitly represent Jesus only when you are much with him, getting into his thoughts, and being carefully practised in them. You must be new-charactered in him, and that requires a great deal; a large meditation of the combined qualities that make up his beauty and set the equilibrium of his dignity, — his gentleness, unfearingness, impartiality, unsparing truth, deference to the humble, the burden of his sorrow, the love he seals by his death. If you had the whole four gospels at your tongue's end, if you understood all the occasions, times, conjunctions, harmonies, and had every thing elaborated in most scientific terms of argument, that would not qualify you. Simply to see Jesus in you, hear him in your voice, trace him in your patiences and charities, behold his gentleness in your walk, breathe his love in the flavors of your pure concern for godless men: this would signify more, preach more gospel, I might almost say, without a word beside. Your people, your house, your class, your school, living in such atmosphere, will have all Christly power upon them.

Another great matter will thus be secured; viz., unity of impression. It is a great source of failure, in the preachers and teachers that fail, that there is no constant element in their action, and of course no unity in the impressions they raise. They do many things in as many moods; they get up new subjects, fine arguments, wonderful discoveries, all varieties of expedients, and go darting round hither and thither, full of industry and just as full of nothingness. If they raise a little effect of some kind to-day, it will only make room for some other kind of effect to-morrow; all because they are working under key, down among things or questions that are not in Christ, or up to Christ at all. Whereas you will observe that one who is really in the hidden life of God — one who abides there in God's peace, and works from it — has a way of continuity, and keeps on rolling his work steadily forward, by a certain unity of meaning. He does not strain himself as hard as teachers often do, acting from a lower key: he will not do as brilliant things perhaps, or invent half as many expedients; but he will be filling this or that child's bosom with Christ, simply because of what is in him. Something precious from God will appear to flavor all he does; and that precious something will be catching, as it were, in other minds by a law. "How does he do it?" this and that other teacher and preacher will ask; and they never will find how, till they discover how all best power rests principally in what we are, and not in what we do. No doing, at least, is of any great consequence which is not steadied and quickened by what we are.

Sometimes the teacher who is not in and of God's thought, and knows not how to sing "How precious," will get visibly stalled in matters below the gospel, — questions of Bible antiquities, questions of geography, questions of commentary, questions of opinions, travels, chronologies; all of which may have a genuine interest and importance, but the misery is that it is so easy for him to stop in these matters, and build tabernacles there which Moses and Elias and Christ will not care to occupy. Some will be wanting so much to be popular with their class, and will do so many things for it, that they become subservient, and the class shortly has them in their power. Others will be so intent on results, as to quite weary out their pupils by over-much personal talk and intercession. Oh, if they could only be one degree fuller of the precious things, and let their simple fulness talk by its own silent flavors of sweetness and joy! That has no dinning in it; that will not hammer out the patience even of a child.

In all these matters now, and a thousand others which could be named, false aims, false means, false manners will be rectified, almost of course, if only the teacher is a saint or believer who has been set, or is now trying to be, in God's full equipment. If he truly lives with Christ and with God on the footing of a joyous friendship and full private acquaintance, he will have a certain divine propriety in him, and God's silent dew will be distilling on every thing he does.

But there are two very important matters, of a more general nature, that now ask your attention here, as in full view of a subject that presents the very highest, most spiritual, and most inwardly perceptive notions of Christian experience. One is this: Is there any modified way of organization or exercise that may do more than simply teach the classes matters about God, — bring them in to know even God himself? If we do not fear to drop the word "conversion," as a word more proper to the conditions of adult minds, is there any way of inchristing childish minds so immediate as to put them at one with him by their direct impressions? Of course, they will be converts in reality, but not as beheld in their external demonstrations.

I believe that there is a way of doing just this. The Moravians train their children largely by the singing of hymns that centre in Christ and true Christ-worship. So, dismissing partly the idea of a school, and organizing a discipleship in hosannas, we may put our children through songs of the Lamb — chants, litanies, sonnets, holy madrigals, and doxologies, — such and so many, and full of Christ's dear love, that they will sing Christ into their very hearts, and be inwardly imbued and quickened by him. At the same time, there will be rehearsed, with these, scripture lessons, that have the sense of God's authority and power and forgiveness and divine pastorship and child-cherishing friendship in them; every thing, in short, that most appreciates God and the precious thoughts of God; every thing that belongs to a penitent, adoring, tender, faithfully kept, patiently enduring, bravely steadfast, gloriously trustful character. And these rehearsed responsively, or by all together, and blended with high song, will make up a taking-in exercise, whereby Christ will be entered more and more deeply into the secret life of the children. For observe, that whoever hears or is taught something is only put on consideration, or helped into consideration, by the matter received; whereas the worshipping, praying, praising soul is put as far as possible into the very life of the sentiments rehearsed. We may teach about God and Christ altogether too much, putting our teachings right in the way of a due receiving. But if we come in with our children, full of worship ourselves, and open out our souls into that which waits to be opened into theirs, how receptive will they be, and how certainly will they sing the songs and pray the confessions and prayers into the deepest lodgements of their nature! We shall not have a small trained choir of singing boys to entertain or move the grown-up people in attendance; but we shall have a beautiful assembly of singing boys and girls offering their own hosannas to the Lamb, and he fast by them, waiting to be graciously installed in the chorus they sing to his name. Have we nothing to learn, nothing to gain, by a reconsideration of this whole matter? Is it our wisdom to lay every thing on teaching, and set every thing we do upon the score of private judgment, saying, "There, we have taught you how it is; and now you must be wise for yourselves." Have we not a more excellent way? And if we take our afternoons regularly for this kind of exercise, and have it as a common church privilege for all, will it not be quite as common, and quite as much valued, as if we were all become children together? At any rate, we should know what it means, that "of such is the kingdom of heaven;" for the kingdom would be there.

A single thought more, in which I will be brief, though it asks a large discussion. Is it not our privilege and duty, as preachers of Christ, to do more preaching to children? I think of nothing in my own ministry with so much regret, and so little respect, as I do of my omissions here. We get occupied with great and high subjects that require a handling too heavy and deep for children, and become so fooled in our estimate of what we do, that we call it coming down when we undertake the preaching to children; whereas it is coming up rather, out of the subterranean hells, darknesses, intricacies, dungeon-life profundities of old, grown-up sin, to speak to the bright daylight creatures of trust and sweet affinities and easy conviction. And to speak to these fitly, so as not to thrust in Jesus on them as by force, but have him win his own dear way, by his childhood, waiting for his cross, tenderly, purely, and without art — oh how fine, how very precious, the soul equipment it will require of us! I think I see it now clearly: we do not preach well to adults, because we do not preach, or learn how to preach, to children. Jesus did not forget to be a child; but if he had been a child with us, we should probably have missed the sight of him. God's world contains grown-up people and children together: our world contains grown-up people only. And preaching only to these, who are scarcely more than half the total number, it is much as if we were to set our ministry to a preaching only to bachelors. We dry up in this manner, and our thought wizens in a certain pomp of pretence that is hollow and not gospel. The very certain fact is, that our schools of theology will never make qualified preachers till they discover the existence of children. Let every young man who is going to preach put himself to it, first of all, in that afternoon service we just now spoke of, there to begin a ministry wise enough and rich enough in gospel meaning, to take the heart of children.

Some of us, I know, will say that they have, alas! too much thinking to do for this other exercise. It puts them to the strain and shapes their habit, and how can they unstring their bow? Yes, brethren, we have all much thinking to do; but if we are up among God's thoughts, it will not strain ust to think them, and scarcely more to have ascended the level where they are. Up through all created being and scripture knowledge, we shall be climbing, out of all darkness and obscurity, mounting fast and far toward the light; we shall go steadily over the rough hills of obstruction; we shall ascend the highest peaks to watch for the day; and when we see the east begin to be streaked with gray, the gray changing into purple, and the purple into gold, shall it not be much, that, if we have our children with us, they will see God's light as clearly and be as glad in it as we?

# PART VI

# CRISIS OF THE CHURCH

Published in 1835.

# SERMON

THERE are times, when the combat and career of human things seem to have spent themselves, and the world has sunk to rest; or, if not into absolute rest, there remains only a dull and vegetative motion, in which as in sleep, it recruits for some new but yet unknown crisis. At such a time, religion too, with little comparative detriment to its strength and safety, may compose itself to sleep beside its altars. But when a long age of repose has lulled and freshened the world, when the spirit and power of a new era are out, and the stirring motions and the sounding forces and all the struggling portents proclaim that a mighty crisis is at hand, then also must religion gird herself in the might of her God, and go forth among the fervid elements, to command and sway them to herself. If she fail of this, it will be seen when the great throe is past or the crisis accomplished, that if not shut out by violence, she has at least fallen out by inaction, from any place in the result.

And such, followers of Christ! is manifestly the era in which we live. For more than three hundred years, the reformation has been moving as a mighty leaven among the nations of men, and stirring them up to a more fervid and potent, activity. It has awakened; it has unbound; it has annihilated; it has created; it has developed new principles, projected new plans, raised up new institutions, offered new hopes to man; till now we may clearly discern, amid the swiftness of things and their approaches to concourse, that its grand moral crisis is near. This wonderful celerity which stimulates every thing, indicates a force that is hastening either to exhaustion or to victory; and bids us also haste, in our Christian labors, as we see the day approaching.

This admonition, we know, has already taken hold of the Church. She is putting on her armor and girding her strength, as for a great triumph. But whither will she lead?--this is an important question--into what field will she press, to accomplish the issue and seal the destiny of this mighty impulse, that now moves the world? Undoubtedly she is to prefigure to herself a result as broad as the benevolence of Christ and the scope of his salvation — even the day, when it shall be published from the heart of China, or sounded from the steppes of Central Asia, that the world is converted to God. This is the true goal of the Christian faith — we can rest in no hope less magnificent. But is this the crisis, upon the eve of which we now stand, or is it some other subordinate to this? To us at least there is another; and whoever duly considers what God has devolved upon this nation, will not deem it presumptuous to affirm, that in us the world also completes an era and seals a volume of its history.

To this subject, every lover of his country and of Christ is now called to give a special and considerate attention. In the considerations here to be offered, it is not disguised that an important change is contemplated, in the tone of our religious operations. It is believed that our enterprises abroad, though not too great, are vastly disproportionate to our efforts at home; and especially when we consider the peculiar and -pressing claims of our own country at this particular crisis. Not that our foreign operations. should be suspended, or the interest we feel in them given up; but that we are called, by signs too clear to be mistaken, to take up the cause of our own country, as the first and most imperative duty we own to humanity and to God.

IN ORDER to a due impression of this subject, there are three principal topics, which require special consideration: — that our nation holds a very peculiar position in the world; that now preeminently is its formative age; and that just 'at this crisis it is beset with peculiar dangers.

The position of our country is peculiar to a degree that is seldom realized. Our youth is peculiar, our enterprise, our advancement, and still more the happiness we have enjoyed as a people for the last fifty, or we might say the last fifteen years. In all these respects, and especially the last, we are vastly more distinguished abroad, than we are in our own estimation. We are occupied and often saddened, with the clouds that overhang our prospect, and, as it ever is with men, we are too uneasy under the little ills we suffer, to form any grateful estimate of the good we enjoy. Sometimes we even yield to discontent, and are ready almost to deny that we have any peculiar privileges. But could a fair and just balance be struck, it would doubtless appear, that we have suffered vastly fewer evils and enjoyed more real blessings, during the period I have mentioned, than any other people of any other era in the world. At this moment, we are advancing in population and national wealth at such a rate as almost astonishes belief — it is absolutely unparalleled in the history of nations.

But our position is chiefly peculiar, as a position of moral power. We stand to represent certain great ideas and principles, the success and validity of which, among other nations, depends in a chief degree upon us.

It is scarcely possible to estimate the power, which this infant nation has already exerted, upon the civil institutions of both hemispheres. At first our nation stood alone to represent the principle of Self-Government. In the very birth of its independence, it overthrew, partly as the accident and partly as the proper effect of that event, one of the most ancient and established monarchies of Europe; and from that hour to the present, it has wrought silently but mightily, to unsettle the grasp of arbitrary authority, in all the kingdoms of the world. It has dazzled by no splendor of wealth, it has not advanced by any peculiar arts of diplomacy, or striven with the force of arms; but its very name has carried with it a power, which no splendor of wealth, or art of diplomacy, or force of arms ever had. It cannot be pronounced, without calling up the vision of a young but mighty nation; governed by equal laws; spreading itself in a few years over a territory as large as half of Europe; whitening every sea with its commerce; advancing in wealth beyond example; projecting the most magnificent enterprizes; and showing, in its simple but beautiful form of self-government, the capabilities of man, under the power of freedom and a pure religion. How many nations have already been revolutionized, by the name of these United States? How many of those that remain upon their old foundations have relaxed the severity of their principles, and now begin to tremble for the issue of that power, which is gradually, but irresistibly working in the breasts of the people? Great Britain has exerted a tremendous moral power over the destinies of the world; but yet it is not such a power as goes forth from us. She is thought of as an ancient kingdom, proud of her laws and her sublime constitution; mistress of the seas; patron of learning and the arts; nurse of heroes and of great and holy men; — always it is the nation, Great Britain, rising in her greatness and glory. But when the United States are thought of, it is Man, man only, rising up from the dust to be, what God has ever meant he should be, self-poised and arbiter of his own destiny! This is the power, the peculiar power, which has wrought so mightily in the civil institutions of Christendom, for the last fifty years; and by which, if it continue for another fifty years, they must all be softened down to a salutary form, or revolutionized by the outbursting of popular force. No one, who understands how public opinion moves, or by what powerful contagion it propagates itself, will deem it possible for them to withstand the force now assaulting their establishments.

But this is rather the superficial and obvious view of our position than the real one. We are not more distinguished in representing the principle of self-government, than we are in representing the Protestant Faith; or, at least, whatever distinction may be ours in the former light, is due only to the fact, that Protestantism and Christianity have come to their head in us; and here, in our American institutions have passed out, for the first time, to make experiment of their virtue.

It will be granted that complete Protestantism is pure Christianity. It will also be granted, that neither had ever been able to develope its power unmixed and unperverted in the civil state of a nation. When Christianity was given, it was given to an old world. When Protestantism was given, it was given to an old world. In the former case, it found the ancient marks, maxims and establishments of tyranny and idolatry; and in the latter those beside of chivalry and Romanism, so deeply wrought into the fabric of nations, that no power could well eradicate them; and whatever power the religion of Christ might exert, indirectly, upon the social or civil state, yet the result was ever a joint product; of which no one could tell what part was due to Christ, and what to a thousand opposing and malignant forces. No! a new world was necessary, where the pure religion might begin at the beginning and call up around itself its own proper institutions. And He who apportions all events to their times with a sovereign wisdom, had reserved such a world unknown, — and doubtless for this very purpose — a vast continent of forests still in the wildness of nature. Behold now, across the howling waters they come to these western shores! Wherefore do they come? They bring the Protestant faith — God has sent them to try it in this new world!

Now Protestantism in its complete form is believed to be congregationalism, and this to be the simple original Christianity. Nor let this be deemed invidious. Episcopacy, for example, was

Protestantism in England, carried as far as existing establishments would permit. To carry it farther would have been revolution and perhaps defeat. But whatever may be thought of this, it is believed that no sect of American Christians, at the present day, are wont to receive any as lords over God's heritage — the ecclesiastical support and regimen are *in effect* popular in them all. Now this is the congregational spirit, though the form may be diverse; and this, it is conceived, is the spirit of pure Christianity. It is also the spirit of complete Protestantism.

And does any one doubt, that our republicanism is born of this spirit? Philosophically it must have been; historically it was. Self-government in religion passed over, by a natural and necessary consequence, to beget self-government in law; and that same equality, which was held in the church of God, extended itself to the civil state. Had it been a Romish emigration, religion itself would not only have furnished it with tyrants but with a due submission also. Turn your eye southward and see what it would have been! But, a band of Congregational Protestants, emigrating to this new world, neither did establish nor could have established, any other than a popular government. The language of their preamble ever was — "we do associate and conjoin ourselves:" and it was common to add, (for they scarcely knew as yet whether to deem themselves churches or incipient nations,) "for the purpose of maintaining the *liberty* and purity of the gospel." Their constitutions were all simple and popular, containing the same great elements, which mark our institutions at the present day. Even that confederacy, under which our independence was achieved, and upon which our Federal Constitution is based, was itself based upon the confederacy of the United Colonies of New England. The whole frame-work of these free states, in short, and of this free nation, is drawn out from the bosom of the Church; or rather it is the frame-work of the Church itself. It was Protestantism, in religion, producing republicanism in government. And the form of the latter was as perfectly developed in the first ten years of our history as it now is. It may well enough amuse the ears of an idolatrous people, or feed the growth of some new Jacobine sect, to boast the name of Jefferson or any infidel compeer, as father and founder of republicanism. History will not say it — philosophy scorns the presumption.

Schlegel, the Catholic philosopher of Vienna is not to be disputed here. In the celebrated lectures, which he delivered in that city in the year 1828, it was his set purpose to show, as the true philosophy of history, that Protestantism is the natural kinsman of republicanism; and, that when carried to its legitimate limits and checked by no pre-existing establishments, it cannot fail to call up the latter as its concomitant. But the philosopher is more definite still. Speaking of those contagious disorders which of late have troubled the quiet of European monarchies, he says — "The true nursery of all these destructive principles, the Revolutionary school for France, and the rest of Europe, has been North America." Yes, North America! — we hail the distinction — we are the grand experiment of Protestantism! Yes we — it is our most peculiar destiny — we are set to show, by a new and unheard of career of national greatness and felicity, the moral capabilities and all the beneficent fruits of Christianity and the Protestant faith; or if we fall, the deceitfulness of its promises. It is a new position; it is a signal position. God even reserved a world for its development. And what is another magnificent trace of divine thoughtfulness, God sent us hither to make this signal experiment, not alone, nor by contrast only with the old world, but also by contrast with Romanism in the new. There shall be no mistake. He therefore sends over, side by side with us, our Enemy; that we may prove ourselves together on the American shore. Behold the result!

Do we not also present a peculiar aspect, to one who is searching for the Power, that is to send the gospel through the world? Are we not compelled to feel, that it rests mainly with us and the British nation, which has hitherto led us in this heavenly enterprise, to accomplish it? And though it may seem a vain disparagement, or a poor extravagance, for us to speak of the British nation as limited in its resources, yet the American of another generation will have a different feeling. If God preserve us entire, to lead on the natural expansion of our forces, how long ere a hundred millions of freemen walk our soil; how long ere such resources of wealth, are developed here, as in no nation beside, whether of ancient or modern times? It is obvious, in the mean time, that societies cannot proceed in this work beyond certain limits. There is a natural limit to the funds, which charity will commit to an association; and if there were not, such establishments are rather fitted to give the prime impulse to so mighty a work, than to conduct it skilfully to a complete issue. Ere long then a people will be demanded, upon whom it can be thrown, as a work of private obligation. And what people so likely to take up individual or personal duties as the American people? What people so ready for undertakings? What people so facile. to adapt themselves to new circumstances, so skilful to plan, so powerful to execute? Is it not well nigh a proverb, that nothing can disconcert, or discourage an American? Then consider also, that our commerce flies into every clime, as if prepared to carry thither the ministers of our God and commend them to the heathen, under the favorable name of a nation, that will soon be known every where, as a name of promise to man. Can any one consider these facts, without feeling that the American people are meant to be the missionaries of the world?

Such, upon a very imperfect survey of it, is our peculiar position. We represent the principle of self-government; we represent Christianity and the Protestant faith; we are also the despositaries, in no subordinate degree certainly, of that light which is to illuminate the world. We are respected, we are felt. How has tyranny sickened in the old world within the last fifty years! How has man been excited to loftier hopes and better thoughts of himself, in every region where our name is spoken! In the mean time how decisive is the testimony we have given for religion. Romanism has been excited to copy our institutions; — how miserable and disastrous the failure! Infidelity even has risen up to rival us; — how signally is it proved that freedom is the birth alone of Christ! What nation ever did as much in fifty years, to soften the condition of man, and prove the faith of the cross? If but a hundred more such years are given us to unfold our growth, what spectacle so august! what power so commanding over the destinies of man!

Our next topic was the fact, that this is preeminently the formative age of the American nation. The principles of our civil institutions, as I have already shewn, were given by Protestantism; or (which is the same thing) by religion -restored to its original simplicity; which of course implies, that some portion of the nation was already formed to these principles. And had they not been territorially extended beyond the spirit of which they sprung, they would have had a people fully formed to them at the first. But it is well known that forces philosophically repugnant, entered into our national institutions at their birth, and even into the struggle which gained our independence. To a part of the nation, the republican principles were legitimate; to another part they were suppositious. To a part they were inbred and in a sense natural, to another they were adopted and theoretical merely. To a part they were principles of the conscience, and were coupled there with a deep reverence for the majesty of law and a religious fear of God; to another part they were rather the boastings of infidelity and a licentious philosophy. Between these two opposing forces there has, of necessity, been a continued struggle. Up to this moment, the grand question has been whether the former should fit the latter, or the latter should unfit the former, for the common doctrines and principles of both. The question has never once been dropped for an hour. In some form or other, (for it has taken a thousand shapes,) it has continued to agitate the people. Sometimes it has been a question of measures, sometimes of men; sometimes a question between local or sectional parties, sometimes, (and more especially of late,) between parties diffused and intermingled; — but always it has been easy, however disguised or complex the form, to discern the ancient mother-spirit of religion struggling against atheism, deism, irreligion, no-religion, and the common medley of licentiousness. In some parts of the country, though nothing has been lost in the real principle of religion, but much has been gained; yet the baser materials of society, formerly overawed by worth, have been drawn to a head in themselves and held in countenance by political affinities abroad. In other parts, a real and marked advance has been made in the power of religion, and extensive communities have been raised up to strengthen the hearts and the hands of those who stand for the faith on older ground. In the meantime, all the sects of the Protestant faith in all parts of the nation, have become more distinct from the contact of irreligion, more assimilated in spirit and more friendly to each other. They have all, we hope, the spirit of subordination and of sound liberty; and they begin to feel that they have one cause. And what indicates that we have now come to the turning point, the very crisis of our formative age is, that the Great Question has now ceased for the most part to be local or territorial and become diffuse. The elements of life and death are now every where in the nation, and somewhat nearly in the same proportions; and we come up, as it were a whole nation together, to try the final struggle and decide what we shall be. In a few years this question will be decided — the greatest question ever at issue on earth, short of man's redemption; for if religion be cut short of her perfect work and driven back from the field, it is not to be disguised that this mighty nation so blessed of God, so powerful over the world — the Bright Example of true freedom — the Hope of man — must sink into the dust. Infidelity cannot sustain it. Romanism cannot sustain it. Nothing but that pure and complete Protestantism, in which it was born, can sustain it. And behold how swiftly the forces move! The old states are yielding, the new states are forming, and others still are spreading out before the emigrant as fast as he can travel. Our own teeming people flood the channels of migration, foreigners are hovering in clouds upon our coast, the inhabitants of all states and nations mingle in towns and neighborhoods, the forests are falling, new institutions rising — all is agitation and swiftness, and all the great elements of the east, the west, the south, and the north are shaken up together as it were, soon to settle down and be fixed forever.

O that God would stir up the Christians of this land to understand the day they live in and comprehend the scenes in which they live! No mind can measure the interests, that wait upon this hour. We stand at the pitch of such a crisis as the world never knew. Tyrants are amazed before us. Chains cry out to us. Prostrate man looks up from his dust. Protestantism owns in us its completion. Religion rests her triumph in us. God sends us forth to offer a new era of hope to the world, and now the scale of our destiny poises! — Soon it will turn decisively, and with it an amazing destiny of good or evil to the future ages of men!

JUST AT THIS most solemn crisis it is, thirdly, that we are beset with peculiar dangers. I name as the principal, slavery, infidelity, Romanism, and the current of our political tendencies.

Slavery was always a great evil to our nation, but it is greater now a hundred fold than it was at the first, and is every day increasing. Numbers multiply, territory expands, all its effects grow aggravated and direful. Now

the great danger of slavery to our nation, (for of that alone I am now to speak,) is not from the physical force of the slaves, but from the moral evils that are gendered by it. If law could but govern the masters, they might easily govern their slaves. But here is the point where it will ever prove itself alien to the spirit of our institutions. That respect, that conscientious obedience to the majesty of law, which is so necessary to the stability of republican institutions, is the last thing which slavery teaches. It begets rather stormy and imperious passions and a general impatience of restraint;-to obey is rather the part of a slave than of a man. Has it not shown us already, on what slender pretexts subordination may be violated. Has it not more than once, within a few years resisted the supreme law, and trampled our eagle in the dust? Is it not ever teeming with the rankest jealousies? Is it not too sensitive for salutary control, and ready on all occasions to sunder or revolt, at the slightest imaginary grievance? Such should not be the temper of a free people; and had no steadier principle been associated, our constitutional fabric would long ere this have passed away, with the thousand visions of liberty and abortive schemes of theoretic legislation. It is a very anomalous freedom, as any one may see, whose breath and subsistence are slavery. And though it may strive to compensate to itself by a louder clamor of equality, for enslaving half the species; yet still the equality which it boasts, is rather that of petty tyrannies than of men. Such a republicanism is rather forced than natural. It has its seat in the will rather than in the conscience; and all its moral affinities from the first, have accordingly been adverse, and have operated to depress that noble virtue, which gave birth to our institutions. It had a more natural sympathy and would have coalesced more readily with the abortive theories of French liberty, than with that spirit which caught its fire, from the pure altars of God in New England. How full. of excitement too is this unhappy subject! We have scarcely ceased to feel how the pillars of the nation shook, when it was only proposed to limit the extent of this dire evil. And it is but a few months since a great city here at the north was involved in tumult and outrage, for three successive days, by the mere discussion of the subject. The whole material of slavery--all the moral elements, which it supplies to our institutions, are inflammable and violent. At almost any hour, it may explode the foundations of the republic.

Infidelity has existed to a gloomy extent, in some parts of our land ever since we became a nation. And it has been easy to trace it, gradually infecting the health of our government from the first. It has not been ambitious however of extension, and has been mostly confined to men of some thought and consideration, who have shown it, rather in the way of their political tendencies, than by open attacks upon religion. But within a few years, a new sect of infidelity has risen up, which holds a less dignified and respectable course. It is distinguished for no new reasonings, but only for a new spirit and mode of operation. It embraces principally the low and the ignorant of both sexes, whom it assembles every sabbath to be entertained with a blasphemous and obscene ridicule, of every thing good and respectable. There is now a considerable number of these congregations in the United States. They are organized to act in concert with each other. Their numbers are said to be increasing with fearful rapidity. They poison the youth of our cities. They scatter their tracts, in the great thoroughfares of public travel, and especially in the western states; which they innundate with their corrupt effusions. If it were only argument with which they assail religion there would be little to fear; but their main hope is to enlist the bad passions, which cannot be reasoned against. They not only deny the being of God and immortality, but they proclaim a division of property and the spoils of decency. They name a trinity of evils — Religion, Private property and Marriage; and so they unite irreligion, rapacity and lust. They draw in the poor by declaiming against the rich, and what they have not the industry to imitate they are taught to hate. The licentious fall in to participate in their orgies, for an object more profligate still. How far God will allow these impious men to carry their cause we cannot tell. But there is a large class of the poor whom they can easily enlist in any attempt against the rich. They dignify their cause too, by claiming the society and countenance of infidelity in the older and less corrupt school.— They have moreover no small sympathy in universalism and other kindred forms of infidelity. They are active beyond example; and the sudden growth they have had, augurs a degree of success to their cause, at which every christian and every lover of his country must shudder.

Romanism also has set in, with a new enterprise upon our liberties. The alarm on this subject, we have hitherto felt to be premature and unnecessary. Popery, we have supposed, was such an extravagance as could not be inflicted upon the American people; we have even been so confident of Protestantism as to smile at any attempt upon it from that quarter. But we hear of such advances in a distant part of the country and so well attested, that we can close our eyes no longer. Besides it is evident, beyond a reasonable doubt, that here is a settled and fixed design upon our free institutions. I have already cited, from a recent work on this subject, (which every christian and every American should read,) the language of Schlegel in his lectures at Vienna. In the year 1828, when he was in effect a member of the Austrian Cabinet, he declared and doubtless proved, that North America is the Nursery of all those destructive principles, which are disturbing the monarchies of Europe; and likewise that Romanism is the natural ally of absolutism. In the very next year, the St. Leopold Foundation, so called, was organized, for the purpose of "promoting Catholic missions in the United States." The all-managing Metternich was made a chief manager and the King himself enrolled as patron. And this is the society, which is flooding our country with Jesuits, erecting nunneries and establishing schools in all the western valley. In the two years previous to 1835 this institution expended $100,000 for the spread of Popery here. It is constantly advancing in its liberality and enlarging the sphere of its operations. More than six hundred persons of the church — jesuits and nuns — are said to have landed on our shores, within the last year. — Observe too how carefully the Pope justifies the eulogium of Schlegel. In his encyclical letter of 1832 he says — "from this polluted fountain of indifference, [toleration] flows that absurd doctrine, or rather raving, in defence of *liberty of conscience*." "Hence that pest most of all others to be dreaded in a state, unbridled *liberty of opinion*." "Hither tends that worst and never to be sufficiently execrated *liberty of the press*." Such are the doctrines, with which Austria would enlighten the American people! Can any doubt, that here is a deliberate design upon our institutions? It is impossible. — And what advances have they made? We cannot tell, but very great as we are every day assured. They flatter the people to believe that their religion is greatly changed. It has no longer any spirit of persecution; it does not even forgive sins, but only prays for their forgiveness; nay, if you will trust the priests, it is the most eminently democratic religion in the world! It draws in parents by means of their children, and children it allures by gratuitous education; for the church is also patroness of knowledge as well as of democracy! In the mean time, Catholic emigrants are pouring into the country, in a manner altogether unexampled. Every one of them and their descendants are meant to be our enemies, and most of them probably will be. The converts, which they gain, are said also to be numerous. And yet our country sleeps! — the secular press has not even begun to be alarmed. It smacks the slightest breath of aristocracy or uneasiness to equality, it cries out at once upon the intolerance or fanaticism of religion, when it moves any attempt to amend the public virtue; and yet with the utmost coolness, it commits our institutions to the Power that has ever opposed and still opposes the simplest ideas of liberty — the Power that has filled the world for ages with fires and groans of torture — nay it even trusts the Jesuits! whom it has ever been a standing maxim with all men to suspect and guard against. Alas! we have been humbled to see our own American press, bent to the earth and fawning with flatteries and caresses, that it might propitiate the votes of these alien enemies! And what are we to hope in future? Have not the priests a power over their people that is nearly absolute? — can they not lead them after whatever candidate they please? And what does this prove to us, but that a natural alliance will ever exist between them and the worst of our politicians; these caressing with good opinions and covert aids to the advancement of their cause, those supporting at the polls and the altar of confession. And so, between the corruptions of political strife, and the arts of a corrupt religion, mutually supporting each other, the work of our degradation is to be fearfully expedited. We have supposed that Popery could not be acclimated here; but we now begin to see that it could not have greater facilities for advancing itself than it has, when considered in connexion with our elective system. Holding the place they do, the priests of Rome will never cease to be courted, they will never want for sympathy and confidence. Alas! how long shall North America disturb the peace of Europe by her destructive principles!

Out of these elements, or in conjunction with them — slavery, infidelity and Romanism — spring our political tendencies. The political tendencies of slavery have always been adverse to our free institutions; and a bad leaven from that source has been continually extending its ferment through the nation, from the very beginning of our establishment. It has drawn to its political sympathies, and thus to boldness and prominence, the worst ingredients in the other states; and claiming to itself the monopoly of liberty, it has even surpassed its own arrogance in the reckless and corrupt elements it has cherished abroad. — Nor is it to be disguised, that the whole system of our political canvassing has operated badly, and worse every year from the first. It has given to intemperance the steady countenance of its sympathy; it has fed its flames and fanned their rage. It has drawn to a head and more frequently erected to office the basest elements. It has gendered a fearful spirit of radicalism and demolition. It has even far advanced in making us a venal people. In short, it has hurried us farther and farther from that lofty purity and those incorruptible principles, which imparted their dignity to our institutions in earlier times. How reckless of truth to a great extent is the press! — How licentious its abuse of moral worth and of whatever is good or respectable! And to what miserable arts do the candidates often stoop, grasping after the hand of that rabid infidelity, which blasphemes all that is holy; spurns every principle of right, and abjures even the form of chastity! — fawning too in the steps of despotism itself — the Prime Head of despotism and of every cruel machination against the freedom, the illumination and the moral glory of man! All the political tendencies of the nation are bad; and if some check be not interposed, we are soon to be whelmed in a vortex of ruin as deep and dreadful as our worst enemies could desire!

Such followers of Christ! is the position we hold, the crisis at which we stand, the dangers that beset us. At this sublime climax of peril, we stand not alone — we meet here the world. To this point the reformation has been ever reaching on, in its grand career, and here its issue poises— here wait the anxious ages and nations of men to know the things that shall be! How amazing the interests which God has here committed to our guardianship! And what shall we conclude? What can we, but that God now calls us to undertake a mighty effort in behalf of our own land? Let our foreign operations be sustained, in full efficiency; but it is not the time to project new conquests abroad. God now summons us, with a voice too clear to be mistaken, to stand by our own altars and arrest the ruin of OUR OWN COUNTRY!

Nor deem this a benevolence too narrow for the Gospel. What can be more shameful to a Christian, than to prove that he is not a patriot? Is it so — is it to be confessed, that when we follow Christ we cease to love our country? Is it to be written of us hereafter, that we so loved the Islands of the sea, or the heathen of some Eastern nation, as to sacrifice to them our own country, the brightest realm of light and religion upon the earth? And if we do sacrifice this nation, what Christian heart, what people of the earth will not feel an irreparable loss? Why if China with all her millions, could be converted to God in a day at the expense of these United States, it would be a blessing too dearly purchased. What should we say of that father, who on pretence of general benevolence, should take no more care of his own children, than he could bestow on all other children beside? There are cases where a general benevolence requires a special solicitude. Such is the case of a father. Such is the case of a citizen. What then shall be said of an American citizen — in this peculiar land, at this peculiar crisis, and surrounded by these peculiar dangers — if he fail to enlist his main strength in the cause of his country? There has been a wonderful supineness on this subject. We have lulled ourselves in false security. We have undervalued our own institutions. We have almost fancied, that if our country should be lost, our charities would raise up some other, and perhaps brighter Hope among the nations. Where shall it rise? A hundred years of effort in India, with all the wealth and all the power of the Church, could not raise up a nation, like these United States: so full of enterprize, so elevated, so vast in resources, so powerful over the destinies of the world. It is not an easy thing to make nations like this. Such a destiny can be reached only by long ages of conflicts, reverses, and struggles, aided by many prayers and mightily cherished by the Spirit of God. Shall we then give up? shall any pretext move us to compromise this holy inheritance, in which are incorporate the labors, the tears, the blood, the prayers of so many ages; sanctified as they were and made fertile by the God of our fathers? We had better abolish our Foreign Missionary Boards and summon back the Missionaries, and burn up their establishments; nay, if we had a hundred fold more in the field than we now have, we had better do it, than risk at all the fate of this nation. But this is unnecessary. Our means are ample, they are inexhaustible. How then can we hope for the blessing of God at home if we renounce our undertakings abroad?

But what shall we do? how shall we proceed to accomplish the work?

In the first place, we must drop our contentions. What mean we that we seize each other by the throat, for some trifle of supposed difference, or variant shade of opinion, when the enemies of God and man are dashing against our Heaven-born liberties and the very altars of our faith? When this sun of Protestantism has set and the legitimates of Austria and Rome have pealed their hymn of exultation over our fall, will it please our unhappy children to remember, that we stuck for the very words of agreement, and fell, amid the pillars of the nation, still fighting with each other? Unholy fire! Infatuated and miserable zeal! No, the American Church should rise rather simultaneous and lift up its heart as one unto God, till it call down a true fire from the skies, that shall blaze over it and embosom it and bear it onward in flame, like the prophet's chariot of God! Animosities should cease, they should be drowned in tears of repentance; the sects even should be almost forgotten, and all, who love the Protestant faith, should be of one mind and one spirit and stand forth together to sustain the altars!

Nor should we yield to discouragement. We have many who talk despairingly. But our cause is by no means desperate. It is only critical, to just such a degree, as may tempt the heroic spirit of the Church. Christians at the North do not consider that a grand process of assimilation has been going forward in the nation, and that while we have only seemed to lose, NewYork, Kentucky, Tennessee, and more lately, Ohio and Illinois have made a real advance. They do not consider, that we have only lost in a political aspect and not in the force of pure religion. They do not consider that the hostile forces, which have grown upon us so rapidly have grown only in boldness: that even now they would be crushed by the force of public opinion here, were they not held in countenance by political affinities elsewhere: and that if we can but turn this point and bring the whole nation to a moral condition as sound as that which we now deplore in New-England, religion is safe, and her triumph complete. They do not consider, that the excellent piety, which kindles so many hearts in the slave holding States, is soon to task itself with some plan for the extirpation of slavery, which will exercise and increase its vigor a hundred fold; and that the public opinion of the world is pushing it forward and prompting its courage, as if on purpose to give it a triumph on its own territory. And more than all, they do not consider that GOD is with us — therefore they despond. No more of this! — The Lord maketh a way in the sea and a path in the mighty waters. He bringeth forth the chariot and the horse, the army and the power. Is it the way of a Christian to distrust the God of his fathers! On the difficult subject of slavery we should act with firmness, but with moderation also, and with much prayer. At present we do not see the subject clearly, or at least we do not see it harmoniously. But if we only fall into the right spirit, if we only seek to do justly and love mercy as did the Savior of mankind, God will teach us the way.

Difficult as it seems to devise any plan of promise to the master or the slave, positive, nay, imperious as the tone of slavery now is, he who promises it a continuance of fifty years, has poorly estimated the forces that are now moving against it. It is not for the half of a free nation, to stand against the world in such a matter. It will find some issue to the evil, and one we doubt not that God will approve.

Let this corrupt and boisterous infidelity also be duly met; — its rage against a God with the ever-happy love of such a being, which is the best of arguments; its impurity with purity; its hatred of distinctions with that most excellent of all distinctions, — christian love and condescension. It is a sacred duty that no Christian admit to his favor except on the ground of moral worth. No man will dare rail at such distinctions. But if we will be proud of our family or our estate, in violation of the very first principles of Christian simplicity and love, if we will compel the worthy, when they rise, to break through our pride and contempt, as well as the natural impediments of poverty and a low education, we need not complain of that rabid infidelity which would pluck down all distinctions of property and caste. We make it for ourselves — it is the natural product of our own vanity.

That corrupt alliance too, which will naturally subsist between the worst of our politicians and the priests of Romanism, must be checked and counteracted. To this end the Church, comprising all who love our Lord Jesus Christ of whatever name, ought at once to resolve itself into a great Balancing Power, retiring from every alliance with party, and holding its forces ready to support only the best men. The Church will take her position then as it were on a lofty eminence. Below will ever be ambition assorting her factions and combining her forces. Now it will be seen that Rome is no longer to be courted, but virtue. Such candidates must now be offered as will propitiate that tremendous power, which is to come down at the election, and turn the scale which ever way it please. What right has the follower of Christ to become the follower of a party? And how clearly do we see in this case, what is an universal truth, that the position of duty is that of power! Nor let the Church lose a moment in occupying this ground. Here she may stand for ages, and steady the nation in its worst emergencies and give it a wholesome and salutary government.

But last of all, and holiest of all our solicitudes, what shall we do to save the pure religion. of our Lord and Master? Is it not evident, that our greatest enterprises and efforts in religion should be made at home? We have sat under the shade of our institutions, and enjoyed their fruits, the happiest nation upon earth; we have seen ourselves the footsteps of evil, and again and again have we been called to rise and save our land. Hitherto we have lent but a feeble and reluctant charity. Nay, while religion abroad has rejoiced in us and the friends of man have blessed us, we have scarcely felt that our country was worth the saving! The enemy has risen up in the mean time like a flood, and now at the last hour, we wake to see how God has blessed us and how little we have esteemed his blessing! O let every Christian repent of this ingratitude and purify his heart of it, that he may pray for his country! Even now when we behold the storm rising and hear its forces sound their rage, when the world is looking upon us and Christ is bending from the skies and calling us forth to the field, let us bow in repentance and tears before God and take upon us designs worthy of the great cause of religion and of man!

To the Home Missionary enterprise and kindred objects auxiliary to this, the Church is now called to give a more efficient support — here should be the centre of our charities. All the young men of promise who are not able to educate themselves, should be educated — some for preachers of the gospel and some for teachers. Missionaries and teachers should be poured into the new states at the West, like an army of crusaders. The gospel should be preached in every rising village, and secular schools, if necessary free of expense, should be established every where. I know that the expense will be great, but the cause also is great; and farther, God has given us the ability. What! cannot we do as much to save our country as our enemies can to destroy it? Is hatred more self-denying than patriotism or Christian love? Why it is a case in which I can conceive it to be a duty even, and solemnly demanded of God, that we sell the very soil we live on and make ourselves and our children hirelings on the inheritance of our Fathers. Every man has private obligations here which he may not trifle with except upon peril of his soul. Christianity, the Protestant faith, the World wait upon the footsteps and sue at the heart of every Christian; and He who is the patron and avenger of them all, will soon bring him to judgment. The young men of our churches have most seriously to consider what God has devolved upon them. Their course of life is not yet established, the fire of youth is in their blood, and O, is there not something of a christian patriot's fire also there! Of those who have families many undoubtedly should emigrate. Wealth, honor, ease, home should be sacrificed. Every heart should be expanded to the measure of our holy enterprise, every nerve of labor strung, and faith should fast embrace the altars of her God, praying Him with ceaseless voice to preserve our religion and our liberties.

Rise then O Men of Christ! And thou O God of the land, arise! Fire us with the spirit of our fathers! — fire us with thy Own spirit! — and let the flame of our patriotism and our piety burn together, TILL OUR COUNTRY AND THY GLORY ARE SAFE!

# PART VII
# SPEECH FOR CONNECTICUT

Being an Historical Estimate of the State, delivered before the legislature and other invited guests, at theNormal School in New Britain, June 4, 1851.

Note. The festival, in connection with which this discourse was delivered, celebrated the opening of the new building for the Normal School of Connecticut; a fine spacious structure, erected by the munificence of the citizens of New Britain, and presented, on this occasion, to the State.

# SPEECH

FRIENDS AND FELLOW CITIZENS:

THE occasion which has brought us together celebrates another stage of advance in the cause of public education in our commonwealth. When I accepted the call to address you on this occasion, I designed to prepare a theme immediately related to the subject of popular education itself. But on more mature consideration, taking counsel also of others, I have concluded that, as the occasion belongs to the state, and as I am to speak to the Legislature of the state, I cannot do better than to make the state itself — its character and wants and prospects — the subject of my address. And I do it the more readily, because of the conviction I feel, and hope also to produce, that, if there be any state in the world, whose history itself is specially appropriate to a festival of popular education, that state is Connecticut.

IT IS a fact often remarked by the students of history, that all the states or nations, that have most impressed the world by their high civilization and their genius, have been small in territorial extent. If we ask for the reason, it is probably because society is sufficiently concentrated only in small communities, to produce the intensest development of mind and character. Hence it is not in the ancient Roman or Persian empires, but in little sterile Attica, territorially small in comparison even with Connecticut, that the chief lawgivers, philosophers, orators, poets of antiquity have their spring; sending out their unarmed thoughts to subdue and occupy the mind of the world, in the distant ages of time. So again, and probably for a similar reason, it is not in the great kingdoms or empires of Western Europe, that the quickening powers of modern history have their birth; but in the Florentine Republic, in Flanders, and the free commercial cities, in Saxony, Holland, and England. Here is the birth place of modern art. Here it is that manufactures originate and flourish. Here it is that, having no territory at home, commerce builds its ships and sends them out to claim the seas for a territory. Here is the cradle of the Reformation. Here the free principles of government, that are running but not yet glorified, took their spring.

In view of facts like these, it is a great excellence of our confederated form of government, that it combines the advantages both of great and small communities. We have a common country, and yet we have many small countries; a vast` republic that embosoms many small republics, each possessing a qualified sovereignty, each to have a character and make a history of its own. There is brought into play, in this manner, without infringing at all on the general unity of the republic, a more special and homelike feeling in the several states (sharpened by mutual comparison) which, as a tonic power in society, is necessary to the highest developments of character and civilization. Spreading out, in a vast republican empire that spans a continent, we are thus to be condensed into small communities, each distinctly and completely conscious of itself, and all acting as mutual stimulants to each other. Nor is any thing more to be desired, in this view, than that we preserve our distinct position as states, and embody as much of a state feeling as possible, about our several centers of public life and action. Let Virginia have her "cavaliers" and her "old dominion." Let Massachusetts be conscious always of Massachusetts, and let every man of her sons, in every grade and party, exult in the honors that crown her history. Let the Vermonter speak of his "Green Mountain state," with the sturdy pride of a mountaineer. Let the sons of Rhode Island exult in the history and spirit of their little fiery republic. This state feeling has an immense value, and the want of it is a want much to be deplored. I would even prefer to have this feeling developed so strongly as to create some friction between the citizens of the different states, rather than to have it deficient.

Pardon me if I suggest the conviction, that this feeling is not as decided and distinct, in our state, as it may be and ought to be. It is our misfortune that we hold a position midway between two capital cities; that of New England on one side, and the commercial capital of the nation on the other. To these we go as our market places. From these we get our fashions, our news, and too often our prejudices and opinions; or, what is worse, just that neutral state of both, which is created by the very incongruous mixture they produce. Meantime, it is a great misfortune that we have no capital of our own, or if any, a migratory capital. For public sentiment, in order to get firmness and become distinctly conscious, must have fixed objects about which it may embody itself. A capital which is here and there is neither here nor there. It is no capital, but a symbol rather of vagrancy, and probably of what is worse, of local jealousies which are too contemptible to be inspiring. Besides we are too little aware of our own noble history as a state. The historical writers of Massachusetts have been more numerous and better qualified than ours, and they have naturally seen the events of New England history, with the eyes of metropolitans. We have, as yet, nothing that can be called a just and spirited history of our state, and the mass of our citizens seem to suppose that we have no history worthy attention. It is only a dry record, they fancy, of puritanical severities, destitute of incident and too unheroic to support any generous emotions. Our sense of it is expressed in the single epithet "the blue law state." Never were any people more miserably defrauded. Meantime we are continually sinking in relative power, as a member of the confederacy. Our public men no longer represent the fourth state in the Union, as in the Revolution, but the little, comparatively declining state of Connecticut. And the danger is that, as we sink, in the relative scale of numbers, the little enthusiasm left us will die out, as a spark on our altars, and we shall become as insignificant in the scale of moral, as of territorial consequence.

Accordingly it becomes a very interesting question to the people of our state, what shall we do to maintain a position of respect and power? — how shall we kindle and feed the true fire of public feeling necessary to our character and our standing in the republic? If there be a citizen present, of any sect or party, who can see no interest in such a problem, to him I have nothing to say. The man who does not wish to love and honor the state, in which he and his children are born, has no heart in his bosom, and it is not in any words or arguments of mine, certainly, to give him what the sterility of his nature denies.

It will occur to you at once, in the problem raised, that what any people can be and ought to be, depends, in a principal degree, on what they have been. And so much is there in this principle, that scarcely any thing is necessary, as it seems to me, to exalt our public consciousness and set us forward in the path of honor, but simply to receive the true idea of our history and be kindled with a genuine inspiration derived from a just recollection of the past.

In this view it is, that I now propose to give you a sketch, or outline of our history; or perhaps I should rather say, an historic estimate of our standing as a member of the republic. In giving this outline, or estimate, I must deal, of course, with facts that are familiar to many; but we have a history of such transcendent beauty, freshened by so many inspiring and heroic incidents, that we should not easily tire under the recital, however familiar. Nothing should tire us but the mortifying fact, that as a people, we have not yet attained to the sense of our own public honors. Mr. Bancroft, the historian, thoroughly acquainted with the relative character and merit of the American States, not long ago said, — "There is no state in the Union, and I know not any in the world, in whose early history, if I were a citizen, I could find more of which to be proud, and less that I should wish to blot." My own conviction is that this early history, though not the most prominent, is really the most beautiful that was ever permitted to any state or people in the world.

In tracing its outline, I shall be obliged to make some reference to that of other states, but I will endeavor not to make the comparison odious. I must infringe, a little, in particular, on some of the claims of Massachusetts, and therefore I ought to say beforehand, that no one is more sensible than I to the historic merit, or rejoices more heartily, in the proud eminence of that state, as one of the members of the republic — a member without which, indeed, the republic would want a necessary support of its character and felicity. It can the better afford to yield us, therefore, what is our own; or rather can the less afford to diminish our just honors, by claiming to itself what is quite unnecessary to its true pre-eminence of name and its metropolitan position as a state.


IT MAY WELL BE a subject of pride to our state that the original settlement of the Connecticut and New Haven colonies, afterwards called Connecticut, comprised an amount of character and talent so very remarkable.

There was Ludlow, said to have been the first lawyer of the colonies, assisting at the construction of the first written constitution originated in the new world; one that was the type of all that came after, even that of the Republic itself. Whether it was that he was too much of a lawyer to be a hearty Puritan, or had too much of the unhappy and refractory element in his temper to be comfortable any where, it is somewhat difficult to judge. But he became dissatisfied, removed to the Fairfield settlement, and afterwards to Virginia. The casual hints and traditions, left us of his character, impress the feeling that he was a very remarkable man, and excite in us the wish that a more adequate account of his somewhat irregular history had been preserved to us.

There was Haynes, also, the first Governor, a man of higher moral qualities, and different, though not perhaps inferior accomplishments. He was a gentleman of fortune, holding an elegant seat in Essex. But the American wilderness, with a right to his own religious convictions, he could easily prefer to the charms of affluence and refinement. Turning his back upon these, he came over to Boston. And it is a sufficient proof of his character and ability that, during his short stay there, he was elected Governor of the Massachusetts colony. In the new colony that came out afterwards to settle on the banks of the Connecticut, he was leader and father from the beginning. He was a man of great practical wisdom and personal address; liberal in his opinions, firm in his piety, a man every way fit to lay republican foundations.

Governor Hopkins, a rich Turkey merchant of London, was another of the founders; a man of less gravity though not inferior in the qualities of fortune, or personal excellence, and superior to all in his great munificence. By his bequest the Grammar schools of Hartford and New Haven, and the Professorship of Divinity in Harvard College, were founded. His talents are sufficiently evinced by the fact that, returning on a visit to his estate and his friends in England, he was detained there by an unexpected promotion from Cromwell to be Commissioner of the Navy and Admiralty.

Governor Winthrop, or as he is commonly called, the younger Winthrop, was the most accomplished scholar and gentleman of New England. Educated to society, liberalized in his views by foreign travel, which in that day was a more remarkable distinction than it is at present, he was qualified by his manners and address thus cultivated, to shine as a courtier in the highest circles of influence. A sufficient proof of his power in this way, may be found in the fact that the Connecticut charter was obtained by him; an instrument so republican, so singularly liberal in its terms, that it has greatly puzzled the historians to guess by what means any king could have been induced to give it, and especially to give it to a Puritan.

John Mason, the soldier, I will speak of in another place, only observing here that he was trained to arms under Lord Fairfax, in Holland, and gave so high a proof of his valor and capacity, both there and here, that he was solicited by Cromwell to return to England, and occupy the high post of Major General in his army.

Thomas Hooker, another of the founders, and first minister of the Hartford colony, was distinguished as a graduate and fellow of Cambridge University, and more as a minister and preacher of the established church. He was called the Luther of New England, for the reason, I suppose, that the sturdy emphasis and thunder tone of his style resembled him to the great Reformer. Whenever he visited Boston, after his removal to Connecticut, crowds rushed to hear him as the great preacher of the colonies. As a specimen of physical humanity, if we may trust the descriptions given of his person, he was one of the most remarkable of men; uniting the greatest beauty of countenance with a heighth and breadth of frame almost gigantic. The works he has left, more voluminous and various than those of any other of the New England founders, are his monument.

John Davenport, of the New Haven colony, was a different, though by no means, inferior man. He was a son of the mayor of Coventry, a student and afterwards Bachelor of Divinity at Oxford University. Settled as the incumbent of St. Stephen's Church, in London, he exerted great influence and power among the clergy of the metropolis. His effect lay more exclusively than Hooker's, in the rigid, argumentative vigor of his opinions. Probably no other, unless perhaps we except John Cotton, impressed himself more deeply on the churches of New England.

Governor Eaton, of the New Haven colony, had become rich by his great and judicious operations, as a merchant in the trade of the

Baltic. Attracting, in this way, the attention of the court, he was honored as the King's Ambassador at the court of Denmark; evidence sufficiently clear of the high estimation in which he was held, and also of his talents and character-a character not diminished by the noble virtues and the high capacities, revealed in his long and beautifully paternal administration, as a Christian ruler here.

Desborough, the New Haven colony soldier, afterwards returned to England and held the office of Major General in Cromwell's army, a fact which sufficiently exhibits him.

Such were nine of the original founders of Connecticut. What one of them has left a blot on his character, or that of the state? What one of them ever failed to fill his place? And that, if I am right, is the truest evidence of merit; not the renown which place and circumstance may give to a far inferior merit, or which vain ambition, rioting for place, may be able to achieve. Is it not a most singular felicity, that our little state, planted in a remote wilderness, should have had, among its founders, nine master spirits and leaders, so highly accomplished, so worthy to be revered for their talents and their virtues?

I have spoken of the civil constitution of the Hartford or Connecticut colony. Virginia began her experiment under martial law. The emigrants in the Mayflower are sometimes spoken of as having adopted a civil constitution before the landing at Plymouth; but it will be found that the brief document called by that name, is only a "covenant to be a body politic," not a proper constitution. The Massachusetts or Boston colony had the charter of a trading company, under cover of which, transferred to the emigrants, they maintained a civil organization. It was reserved to the infant colony on the Connecticut, only three years after the settlement, to model the first properly American constitution — a work in which the framers were permitted to give body and shape, for the first time, to the genuine republican idea, that dwelt as an actuating force, or inmost sense, in all the New England colonies. The trading-company governor and assistants of the Massachusetts colony, having emigrated bodily, and brought over the company charter with them, had been constrained to allow some modifications, by which their relation as directors of a stock subscription were transformed into a more properly civil and popular relation. In this manner, the government was gradually becoming a genuine elective republic, according to our sense of the term. The progress made was wholly in the direction taken by the framers of the Connecticut constitution; though, as yet, they had matured no such result. At the very time when our constitution was framed, they were endeavoring, in Massachusetts, to comfort the "hereditary gentlemen" by erecting them into a kind of American House of Lords, called the "Standing Council for Life." The deputies might be chosen from the colony at large, and were not required to be inhabitants of the town by which they were chosen. The freemen were required to be members of the church, and all the officers stood on the theocratic, or church basis, in the same way. They were also debating, at this time, the civil admissibility or propriety of dropping one governor and choosing another; Cotton and many of the principal men insisting that the office was a virtual freehold, or vested right. Holding these points in view, how evident is the distinctness and the proper originality of the Connecticut constitution. It organizes a government elective, annually, in all the departments. It ordains that no person shall be chosen governor for two successive years. It requires the deputies to be inhabitants and representatives of the towns where they are chosen. The elective franchise is not limited to members of the church, but conditioned simply on admission to the rights of an elector by a major vote of the town. In short, this constitution, the first one written out, as a complete frame of civil order, in the new world, embodies all the essential features of the constitutions of our states, and of the Republic itself, as they exist at the present day. It is the free representative plan, which now distinguishes our country in the eyes of the world.

"Nearly two centuries have elapsed," says Mr. Bancroft, "the world has been made wiser by various experience, political institutions have become the theme on which the most powerful and cultivated minds have been employed, dynasties of kings have been dethroned, recalled, dethroned again, and so many constitutions have been framed or reformed, stifled or subverted, that memory may despair of a complete catalogue; but the people of Connecticut have found no reason to deviate essentially from the government established by their fathers. History has ever celebrated the commanders of armies, on which victory has been entailed, the heroes who have won laurels in scenes of carnage and rapine. Has it no place for the founders of states — the wise legislators who struck the rock in the wilderness, and the waters of liberty gushed forth in copious and perennial fountains? They who judge of men, by their influence on public happiness, and by the services they render to the human race, will never cease to honor the memory of Hooker and Haynes."

Had Mr. Bancroft included, with the names of Hooker and Haynes, that also of Ludlow, placing it first in the list, I suspect that his very handsome and just tribute of honor would have found its mark more exactly. We know that Mr. Ludlow on two several occasions after this, was appointed by the Legislature to draft a code of laws for the state, and there is much reason, in that fact, to suppose that he drew the Constitution. itself. His impracticable, refractory temper set him on, farther as many suppose, in the direction of democracy, than any other of the distinguished men of the emigration; and they very naturally imagine, for this reason, that they see his hand, in particular, in the new Constitution framed.

I must not omit to mention, what is specially remarkable in this document, that no mention whatever is made in it, either of king or Parliament, or the least intimation given of allegiance to the mother country. On the contrary, an oath of allegiance is required directly to the state. And it is expressly declared that in the "General Court," as organized, shall exist "the SUPREME POWER of the Commonwealth."

The precedence we had thus gained, in the matter of constitutional history, I am happy to add, was honorably maintained afterwards, in the formation of the Constitution of the Republic itself; for it is a fact, which those who are wont to sneer at the blueness and legislative incapacity of our state, may be challenged also to remember, that Connecticut took the lead in proposing and, by the high abilities and the strenuous exertions of Ellsworth and Sherman, finally carried that distinction of the Constitution of the United States, which is most fundamental and peculiar to it as a frame of civil government, and which now is just beginning, as never before, to fix the attention and attract the admiration of the world. I speak here of the federative element, by which so many sovereign states are kept in distinct activity, while included under a higher sovereignty. When the Convention were assembled that framed the Constitution of the Republic, they were met, at the threshold, by a very important question, viz: — Whether the Constitution to be framed should be the Constitution of a 'Nation' or of a 'Confederacy of states.' Mr. Calhoun gave the true history of the struggle, in his speech before the Senate of the United States, Feb. 12th, 1847. "The three states, Massachusetts, Pennsylvania, and Virginia," he said, "were the largest and were actively and strenuously in favor of a 'National' government. The two leading spirits were Mr. Hamilton of New York, probably the author of the resolution, and Mr. Madison of Virginia. In the early stages of the Convention, there was a majority in favor of a 'National' government. But in this stage there were but eleven states in the Convention. In process of time, New Hampshire came in, a very great addition to the federal side, which now became predominant. It is owing mainly to the states of Connecticut and New Jersey that we have a 'Federal' instead of a 'National' government — the best government instead of the worst and most intolerable on earth. Who are the men of these states to whom we are indebted for this admirable government? I will name them — their names ought to be engraven on brass and live forever. They were Chief Justice

Ellsworth, Roger Sherman, and Judge Patterson of New Jersey. The other states farther South were blind — they did not see the future. But to the coolness and sagacity of these three men, aided by a few others, not so prominent, we owe the present Constitution."

Such is the tribute paid to Connecticut by one of the greatest of American statesmen. To have claimed this honor to ourselves might have been offensive. To receive it, when it is tendered, is no more than a duty. Here then we are in 1850, thirty-one states, skirting two oceans, still one republic, under one tribunal of justice, under one federal Constitution, which we boast as a frame of order that will some time shelter the rights and accommodate the manifold interests of 200,000,000 of people — the greatest achievement of legislative wisdom in the modern history of the world — and for Connecticut, who came as near being the author of these noble appointments as she could, and do it by the votes of other states — for her the principal honor and reward of many is a shrug of derision, and the sneer that calls her the blue law state!

SINCE I AM SPEAKING HERE of our agency in the matter of laws and constitutions, let me go a little farther, and show you with what justice our laws can be made, as they so commonly are, a subject of derision. The derisive epithet, by which we are so often distinguished, was given us by the tory renegade, Peters, who, while better men were fighting the battles of their country, was skulking in London, and getting his bread there, by the lies he could produce against Connecticut. The mendacity of his character and writings has been a thousand times. exposed, and the very laws that he published, as the "blue," shown to be forgeries invented by himself; and yet there are many, I am sorry to say, who do not soberly believe that wooden nutmegs were ever manufactured in Connecticut, who nevertheless accept the blue law fiction as the real fact of history. They do not understand, as they properly might, that the two greatest dishonors that ever befell Connecticut, are the giving birth to Benedict Arnold and the Reverend Samuel Peters — unless it be a third that she has given birth to so many who, denouncing one, are yet ready to believe and follow the other.

There is no state in the civilized world whose laws, headed by the noble Constitution of the Hartford Colony, are more simple and righteous; none where the redress of wrongs is less expensive, or less cumbered by tedious and useless technicalities. It is even doubtful whether the new code of practice in New York, which is just now attracting so much attention abroad, requires to be named as an exception. The first law Reports, published in the United States, were Kirby's Connecticut Reports. The first law school of the nation was the celebrated school of Judge Reeve, at Litchfield, a school which gave the first impulse to law as a science in our country. Chief Justice Ellsworth, Judges Smith, Gould, Kent, Walworth, and I know not how many others most distinguished in legal science in our country, were sons of Connecticut. Judge Ellsworth was chairman of the committee of Congress that prepared the Judiciary Act, by which the Supreme Court of the Nation was organized; and it will be found that some of the provisions of that Act that are most peculiar, are copied verbatim from the statutes of Connecticut. The practice of the Supreme Court is often said to resemble the practice of Connecticut more than that of any other state. And, what is more, the form of the Supreme Court itself, as a tribunal of law, chancery, admiralty and criminal jurisdiction, comprised in one, is copied from the laws of Massachusetts and Connecticut.

It is true indeed, reverting to the earlier laws of the commonwealth, that we find severities enacted against the Baptists and Quakers, precisely as in Virginia, New York, and Massachusetts. How far these laws were executed in Connecticut, or under what conditions, I will not undertake to say, but they seem to have been aimed only at a class of fanatics, who made it a point of duty to violate the religious convictions of everybody else; bringing their logs of wood to chop on the church steps on Sunday, and their spinning wheels to spin by the door, and walking the streets in the questionable grace of nudity, to testify against the sins of the people. In 1708, the English Quakers petitioned the government against these laws, when Governor Saltonstall wrote over in reply, to Sir Henry Ashurst, as follows, — "I may observe, from the matter of their objections, that they have a further reach than to obtain liberty for their own persuasion, as they pretend; (for many of the laws they object against concern them no more than if they were Turks or Jews,) for as there never was, that I know of, for this twenty years that I have resided in this government, any one Quaker, or other person, that suffered upon the account of his different persuasion, in religious matters, from the body of this people, so neither is there any of the society of Quakers any where in this government, unless one family or two, on the line between us and New York; which yet I am not certain of."

Episcopacy was tolerated here by a public act, when, as yet, there were not seventy families in the state of that denomination — at the very time too, when there were two Presbyterian clergymen lying in prison, at New York, for the crime of preaching a sermon and baptizing a child. After several months they obtained their release, by paying a fine of £500 sterling. Forty years later, Dr. Rogers, a Presbyterian clergyman, was deterred, by threats of a similar penalty, from preaching in Virginia. The whole system of tithes was there in force, as stiff as in Ireland now. Fees for marrying, churching and burying were established by law. In 1618, a law was passed in Virginia, requiring every person to attend church on Sundays and church holidays, on penalty of "lying neck and heels," as it was called, for one night, and being held to labor as a slave, by the colony, for the week following. Eleven years after, this penalty was changed, to a fine of one pound of tobacco, "to be paid to the minister." These facts I cite, not to bring reproach on other states, but simply to show that religious intolerance was the manner of the times. If, in the New Haven colony, it is a reproach that only members of the church were permitted to vote, the same was true, under the English constitution, even down to within our memory. There is no sufficient evidence that any person was ever executed for witchcraft in this state, though there were several trials, and one or two convictions; which the Governor and Council contrived, I believe, in one way or another, to release. Governor Winthrop professed sincere scruples about the crime itself. How it was in Massachusetts is sufficiently known to us all. An execution for this crime took place in Switzerland, in 1760; at Wurtzberg in Germany, in 1749; also, in Scotland, in 1722. And, as late as 1716, a poor woman, and her daughter only nine years old, were publicly hanged in England, for selling their souls to the devil, and for raising a storm by the conjuration of pulling off their stockings. The English statute against witchcraft stood unrepealed, even down to 1736.

I confess I was never able to see why so heavy a share of the odium of this kind of legislation should fall on the state of Connecticut; whose only reproach, in the matter, is that she was not farther in advance of the civilized world, by another half century. If the citizens of other states are able sometimes to amuse themselves at our expense, we certainly are not required to add to their amusement by an over sensitive resentment. But if any son or citizen of Connecticut is willing to accept and appropriate as characteristic of its history, the slang epithet which perpetuates a tory lie and forgery, then I have only to say that we have just so much reason to be ashamed of the state — on his account. He is either raw enough to be taken by a very low imposture, or base enough in feeling to enjoy a sneer at his mother's honor.

WE HAVE SOME RIGHT, I think, to another kind of distinction, which we have never asserted; that namely of being the colony most distinctively independent in our character and proceedings, in the times of the colonial history, previous to the revolution. We were able to be so, in part, from our more retired and sheltered position, and partly also because of the very peculiar terms of our charter.

Massachusetts, Virginia, New York, Pennsylvania, all the other states, with the exception of Rhode Island, were obliged by their charters, or the vacation of their charters, to accept a chief executive, or governor, appointed by the crown. These royal governors had a negative upon the laws. They personated the king, maintaining a kind of court pomp and majesty, overawing the people, thwarting their legislation, wielding a legal control, in right of the king, over the whole military force, much as at the present day in Canada. But the charter obtained for Connecticut, by the singular address of Winthrop, allowed us to choose our own governor and exercise all the functions of civil order. And so we grew up, as a people, unawed by the trappings of royalty, a race of simple, self-governing republicans.

For three little towns, on the Connecticut, to declare independence of the mother country, we can easily see would have been the part of madness — probably they had not so much as a thought of it — and yet they had a something, a wish, an instinct, call it what you will, which could write itself properly out, in their constitution, only in the words, "Supreme Power." And I see not how these words, formally asserting the sovereignty of their General Court, escaped chastisement; unless it was that they found a shelter for the crime, in their remoteness, and the obscurity of their position. In this view, there was a kind of sublimity in the sturdy growth of their sheltered and silent state. They had no theories of democracy to assert. They put on no brave airs for liberty. But they loved their conscience and their religion, and in just the same degree, loved not to be meddled with. In this habit their children grew up. Their very intelligence became an eye of jealousy, and they acknowledged the right of the king, much as when we acknowledge the lightning — by lifting a rod to carry it off! But when the king came down upon them, in some act of authority or royal interference that touched the security of their principles or their position, then it was as if the Great Being, who had "ordained whatsoever comes to pass," had ordained that some things should not come to pass.

On as many as four several occasions, during the colonial history, they set themselves in open conflict with the king's authority, and triumphed by their determination. First in the case of the regicide Judges, secreted at New Haven; when Davenport took for his text — "Make thy shadow as night in the midst of noon, hide the outcasts, bewray not him that wandereth." The king's officers were active in the search; but, for some reason, the noon was as the night, and their victims could not be found. Massachusetts expostulated with the refractory people of New Haven, representing how much they would endanger all the colonies, if they did not hasten to address His Majesty in some proper excuse, to which they replied that they were ignorant of the form!

Again, by rallying a force at New London, when Sir Edmund Andross landed there, to proclaim the new patent of the Duke of York, and take possession of the town — silencing him in the act, and compelling him to return to his ships.

A third time, when this same officer came on to Hartford, to vacate the charter — a passage of history commemorated by the noble oak, whose gnarled trunk and limbs still remain, to represent the crabbed independence of the men, who would not yield their rights to the royal mandate. May the old oak live forever!

And yet a fourth time, by asserting and vindicating, what is the essential attribute of political independence, viz. the control and sovereignty of their own military force. Governor Fletcher came on to Hartford, from New York, to demand the control of the militia in the king's name; and when he insisted on reading the proclamation, he was drummed into silence by command of Wadsworth, the chief officer. When the drummer slacked, the word was, "Drum I say;" and to the Governor, "Stop, Sir, or I will make the sun shine through you in an instant." He withdrew, — the point was carried, and the control of the military was retained. After that, when Pitt, at the height of his power, wanted troops from Connecticut, he sent the request of a levy to the Legislature, not a military order.

It is not my design, as you have seen, to represent, in these facts of history, that we had consciously and purposely set up for independence; but only that we had so much of the selfgoverning spirit in us, nourished by the scope of our charter, and sheltered by our more retired position, that we took our independence before we knew it, and had the reality before we made the claim.

In Massachusetts, the metropolitan colony, which had a more open relation to the mother country, the spirit of independence was checked continually by considerations of prudence and, at Boston especially, by the presence of the king and a kind of court influence maintained by the royal governors. Accordingly the Rev. Daniel Barber, who went on with the Connecticut troops to Boston, at the first outbreak of the Revolution, says, — "In our march through Connecticut, the inhabitants seemed to view us with joy and gladness, but when we came into Massachusetts and advanced nearer to Boston, the inhabitants, where we stopped, seemed to have no better opinion of us than if we had been a banditti of rogues and thieves; which mortified our feelings, and drew from us expressions of angry resentment" — a fact in which we see, what could not be otherwise, that the people nearest to the court influence in the metropolis, were many of them infected with a spirit opposite to the cause of the colonies. But here in the rear ground, and a little removed from observation, it was far otherwise. Here the sturdy spirit found room to grow and embody itself, unrestrained by authority, uncorrupted by mixtures of opposing influence. How necessary this sound rear-work of independence and homogenous feeling, in Connecticut, may have been to the confidence and the finally decisive action of the men, who immediately confronted the royal supremacy in Massachusetts, we may never know. Suffice it to say that the causes of public events most prominent, are not always the most real and effective.

It is noticeable, also, that we went into the revolution under peculiar advantages. We were not obliged to fall into civil disorganization by ejecting a royal governor, in the manner of other colonies. Our state was full organized, under a chief magistracy of her own, having command of her own military force, ready to move, without loosing a pin in her political fabric. One of the royal governors ejected was even sent to Connecticut for safe keeping. We had kept up our fire in the rear, making every hamlet and village ring with defiance, and erecting our poles of liberty on every hill, during the very important interval between the passage of the Boston port bill and the stamp act. And so fierce and universal was the spirit of resistance here, that, while the stamps were carried into all the other states, no officer of the crown dared undertake the sale of them in Connecticut.

The forwardness of our state in the matter of independence, is sufficiently evinced by the fact that our Legislature passed a bill, on the 14th of June previous to the memorable 4th of July, instructing her delegates to urge an immediate declaration of independence. Nor did she sign that declaration by the hands only of her own delegates. Two of her descendants in New Jersey and one in Georgia, are among the names enrolled in that honored instrument. Georgia withheld herself, at first, from the Revolution. But there was a little Puritan settlement at Midway, in that state, in which, as a physician and a man of public influence, resided Doctor Hall, a native of Wallingford, and a graduate of Yale College. These Midway Puritans were resolved to have their part in the Revolution, at all hazards. They made choice of Doctor Hall and sent him on to the Congress as their delegate. He signed the declaration and, the next year, Georgia came forward and took her place, led into the Revolution by the hand of Connecticut. Is it then too much to affirm, in view of all these facts, that if any state in the union deserves to be called the Independent State, Connecticut may safely challenge that honor.

I MUST ALSO SPEAK of the military honors of our history. Martial distinctions are not the highest, and yet there is a kind of military glory that can never fade; that, I mean, which is gained in the defence of justice and liberty, as distinguished from the idle bravery of chivalry, and the rapacious violence of conquest.

It is abundantly clear, as a fact of history, that our two colonies meant, in their public relations with the Indian tribes, to fulfil the exactest terms of justice and good neighborhood. Still it happened, doubtless, as it always will in such cases, that individuals, instigated by a spirit of mischief or insolence, or by the cupidity of gain, trepassed on their rights, not seldom, in acts of bitter outrage. Such wrongs could not be absolutely prevented, and, by reason of a diversity of language and the separate, wild habit of the Indians, could not be effectually investigated or redressed. Exasperated, in this manner, they of course would take their revenge in acts of violence and blood; and then it would be necessary to arm the public force against them, for the public protection. It is very easy to theorize in this matter, and say how it should be, but this issue, much as we deplore it, could not well be avoided.

It is affirmed and, by many, believed that the Pequods had been instigated in this manner, to the thirty murders perpetrated in their incursions on the river settlements, during the winter and spring of 1637. Be it so, the colony must still be defended. Every settlement is filled with consternation. They set their watch by night, and tend their signal flag by day to give notice of enemies. The Pequods have been described to them as one of the most numerous and powerful of the Indian tribes. They imagine them dwelling in the deep woods, guessing how powerful they may be, and at what hour the foe may burst upon their settlement, here or there, in the fury of savage war. What they dread, in the power of their enemy, so long and wearily, they, of course, magnify. It is no time now for such points of casuistry as entertain us. The hour has come, a decisive blow must be struck; for the danger and the dread are no longer supportable.

It had also been ascertained that the Pequods were endeavoring to enlist all the other tribes, in a common cause against the colonies. Massachusetts, accordingly, had agreed to join the expedition against them, but at what point the junction would be made could not be settled beforehand. With his ninety men, a full half the able bodied men of the colony, Capt. Mason descended the river to Saybrook, passed round to the Narragansett Bay, and, falling in there with a small party of Massachusetts men returning from Block Island, made his landing. His inferior officers, when he opened his plan, proposing to march directly into the Pequod country, waiting for no junction with the Massachusetts troops, strenuously opposed him. They were to pierce an unknown country and meet an unknown enemy. What could assure this little band of men against extermination, fighting in the woods with a fierce nation of savages? But the chaplain led them to God for direction, and they yielded their dissent. And here, in the stand of Mason, is, in fact, the battle and the victory; for they came upon the great fort of the enemy, after a rapid march, and took it so completely by surprise, that what was to be a battle became only a conflagration and a massacre. The glory is not here, but in the celerity of movement and the peremptory military decision that brought them here. They are too few in number to make prisoners of their enemy, and another body of the tribe, whose number is unknown, are near at hand. Accordingly their work must be short and decisive — a work they make it of extermination. We look on the scene with sadness and with mixtures of revolted feeling; but we are none the less able to see, in this exploit of Mason, with his ninety men, why Cromwell wanted him for a Major General in his army. He understands, we perceive, as thoroughly as Napoleon, that celerity and decision are sometimes necessary elements of success, and even of safety. This kind of generalship too requires a great deal more of nerve and military courage often, than the fighting of a hard contested battle.

This reduction of the Pequods is remarkable as being the first proper military expedition, or trial of arms in New England. If they had been wronged, we pity them. If not, still we pity them. In any view, the colony has done what it could not avoid, and the long agony of their fear is over. Their wives and children can sleep in peace.

Mason returned with his little Puritan legion to Hartford, having lost in the encounter but a single man, the guns of the fort at Saybrook booming out through the forests, in a salute of victory, as he passed, and was immediately complimented, by the Legislature, in the appointment of general-in-chief to the colony. Hooker was designated to deliver him his commission, in presence of the assembled people.

Here is a scene for the painter of some future day — I see it even now before me. In the distance and behind the huts of Hartford, waves the signal flag by which the town watch is to give notice of enemies. In the foreground, stands the tall, swart form of the soldier in his armor; and before him, in sacred apostolic beauty, the majestic Hooker. Haynes and Hopkins, with the Legislature and the hardy, toil-worn settlers and their wives and daughters, are gathered round them in close order, gazing, with moistened eyes, at the hand which lifts the open commission to God, and listening to the fervent prayer that the God of Israel will endue his servant, as heretofore, with courage and counsel to lead them in the days of their future peril. True there is nothing classic in this scene. This is no crown bestowed at the Olympic games, or at a Roman triumph, and yet there is a severe, primitive sublimity in the picture, that will sometime be invested with feelings of the deepest reverence. Has not the time already come, when the people of Connecticut will gladly testify that reverence, by a monument that shall make the beautiful valley of the Yantic, where Mason sleeps, as beautifully historic, and be a mark to the eye from one of the most ancient and loveliest, as well as most populous, towns of our ancient commonwealth?

The conduct of our state, in two other chapters of history of a later date, displays a moral dignity, as well as military firmness, of which we have the highest reason to be proud. The Dutch governor of New York, it was ascertained, had entered into an alliance with the savages, to make war upon the English colonies. The commissioners of these colonies, already united in a federal compact with each other, had voted a levy of troops for the defence, and assessed the number to be raised by each. The Hartford and New Haven colonies were prompt and indefatigable in their exertions, as their own more immediate exposure required. Plymouth was ready and kept her faith, but Massachusetts tempted, for once, to an act of perfidy, most sadly contrasted with her noble history, refused; leaving the Connecticut colonies cruelly exposed to the whole force of the enemy. The condition of our people was one of distressing excitement. Every hour, for a whole half year, it was expected that the invasion would begin. Forts were erected, a frigate was manned, night and day were spent in watching; till, at length, the victory of the English over the Dutch fleet at sea put an end to the danger; only leaving the two colonies of Connecticut overwhelmed by enormous expenses incurred for their defence. The indignation was universal. And when the commissioners were assembled again, at their annual meeting, our commissioners magnanimously refused to sit with those from Massachusetts, without some atonement for their ignominious breach of faith and duty.

Then came the turn of Massachusetts. King Philip, as he was called, had rallied all the savage tribes of New England, for a last, desperate effort to expel and exterminate the colonies, The havoc was dreadful — whole towns swept away by the nightly incursions of the savages, wives and children massacred, companies of troops surprised and butchered, all the frontier settlements of Massachusetts smoking in blood and conflagration. It was the dark day of the colonies, and, for a time, it really seemed that they must be exterminated. Then it was that Connecticut proved her fidelity, sending out five companies of troops to the aid of Massachusetts. And the combined troops marched together, in a cold snowy day, fifteen miles through the forests, fought in the deep snow one of the bloodiest battles on record, and then marched back, carrying their wounded with them, to encamp in the open air. The attack was upon the great fort of the Narragansets, and was led by the Massachusetts troops, in a spirit of valor worthy of success. Unable, however, to force the entrance, they were obliged, after suffering greatly from the enemy, to fall back. The Connecticut troops were then brought up, and we may judge of their determination by the fact, that nearly one-third of their number fell in the assault, and that, out of their five captains, three were killed on the spot, and a fourth died of his wounds afterwards. The assault was carried. The second winter, four companies of rangers, raised in New London county, were sent out, by turns, to scour the Narragansett country, and harrass the enemy by a continual desultory warfare. Finally, the tide was turned, and the capture of Philip ended the struggle. Thus nobly did Connecticut repay the injustice and wrong of her sister colony.

We can hardly imagine it, but there was seldom a year in the early history of our state, now so quiet and remote from the turmoils of war, when she was not marching her troops, one way or another, to defend her own, or more commonly some neighboring settlement — to Albany, to Brookfield, to Springfield, to the Narragansett country, to Schenectady, to Crown Point, to Louisburg, to Canada — issuing bills of credit, levying, all the while, enormous taxes, and maintaining a warlike activity scarcely surpassed by Lacedemon itself. There was never a spark of chivalry in her leaders, and yet there was never a coward among them. Their courage had the Christian stamp, it was practical and related to duty; always exerted for some object of defence and safety. They knew nothing of fighting without an object, and when they had one, they went to the work bravely, simply because it was sound economy to fight well! We are accustomed to speak of the wars of the revolution, but these earlier wars, so little remembered, were far more adventurous and required a much stouter endurance.

When combined with the British forces, our troops were, of course, commanded in chief by British leaders, and these were generally incompetent to the kind of warfare necessary in this country. Scarcely ever did they lose a battle or suffer a defeat in these wars, in which our provincial captains did not first protest against their plan. Sometimes the Parliament were constrained to compliment our troops, but more generally, if some exploit was carried by the prowess of a colonial captain, as in the case of Lyman, the hero of Crown Point, his superior was knighted and he forgotten. In the last French war, under Pitt, when a large part of her little territory was yet a wilderness, Connecticut raised and kept in the field, at her own expense, for three successive years, 5,000 men; so great was her endurance and her zeal against the common enemy. It was here that Putnam and Worcester took their lessons of exercise in the military art, and practiced their courage for a more serious and eventful struggle.

This eventful struggle came; finding no state readier to act a worthy and heroic part in it. As early as September, 1774, the false rumor of an outbreak in Boston had set the whole military force of the colony in motion — a sign, before the time, of what was to be done when the time arrived. In April of 1775, before the battle of Lexington and before the Revolution could be generally regarded as an ascertained fact, a circle o f sagacious, patriotic men, assembled in Hartford, perceiving the immense advantage that would accrue to the cause, from the capture and possession of the Northern fortresses that commanded Lake Champlain, Ticonderoga and Crown Point, embarked in a scheme, to seize them, by a surprise of the British garrisons. They had a secret understanding with Governor Trumbull, and drew their funds from the public treasury, by a note under the joint signature of their names, eleven in number. The enterprise was committed to Ethan Allen and Seth Warner, both natives of Roxbury, now residing in Vermont. A few men were sent on from Connecticut, forty or fifty more were collected in Berkshire county, in Massachusetts, and the remainder were enlisted in Vermont. The enterprise was successful. More than two hundred cannon were captured — the same that were afterwards dragged across the mountains to Boston, and employed by Washington in the seige and final expulsion of Lord Howe. When the commander, of Ticonderoga, inquired by what authority the surrender was demanded, Allen's reply was — "In the name of the Great Jehovah and the Continental Congress." That he had no authority from the Continental Congress, save what had come to him through the Great Jehovah, is certainly very clear; hence, I suppose, the form of his answer.

It appears that Benedict Arnold, who was in Boston about this time, obtained a commission from the committee of safety there, authorizing him to conduct, in their behalf, a similar undertaking. But finding himself anticipated, when he reached Vermont, he was obliged to waive his right of command and took his place, as a volunteer, under Allen. Some of the Massachusetts historians, who have claimed the credit of this exploit, in behalf of their state, are clearly seen, therefore, to have trespassed on the honors of Connecticut. Connecticut projected and executed the movement. The treasury of Connecticut footed the bills. The prisoners were brought to Connecticut and quartered at West Hartford.

The surrender of these fortresses took place on the 10th of May. Meantime, on the 18th of April, and before the capture was consummated, the news of the battles of Concord and Lexington had arrived, and resistance to the mother country was seen to be openly begun. Putnam left his plow in the furrow, not remaining, it is even said, to unyoke his oxen, and flew to the field of action. The troops of the state poured after him, to be gathered under his command. The battle of Bunker Hill soon followed.

It is remarkable that the question, who commanded in this very celebrated battle, has never yet been settled. The Massachusetts historians have generally maintained that Prescott was the commander; and some of them have even gone so far as not to recognize the presence of Putnam in it. The more candid and moderate have generally admitted his presence in the field and the valuable service rendered, by his inspiriting and heroic conduct. Prescott, they say, commanded in the trenches, and Putnam was engaged outside of the trenches, in the open field and about the other hill by which the redoubt was overlooked or commanded;

doing what he could for the success of the day, but only in virtue of the commission he had from his own personal enthusiasm. As regards any chief command over the whole field of operations, they suppose there probably was none, alleging that the army was really not organized, and no scale of proper military precedence established.

As respects this latter point, which at first view might seem to be true, they are certainly in a mistake. For Putnam had been expressly ordered, by our Legislature, to put himself under the chief command of Massachusetts; as the conditions of the case evidently required. He was serving, therefore, as an integral part of the military force of Massachusetts. Neither was he or Prescott, or Warren, the general-in-chief of the army, so raw in the practice of arms as not to know that, being on the ground as a general of brigade, the scale of military precedence made him, *ipso facto*, principal in command over the colonel of a regiment.

To the same conclusion we are brought, by a careful review of all the facts pertaining to the battle itself. There appears to be sufficient evidence that General Putnam, after his successful encounter sometimes called the battle of Chelsea, which took place on the 27th of May previous, and by which he had produced some stir of sensation in the army, became more impatient of a state of inaction than ever, and proposed himself, in the council of war, that they should take up this advanced position on Bunker Hill. Prescott was in favor of the movement, but, Gen. Ward and others, including even Gen. Warren a member of the Council of Safety, were opposed; regarding the attempt as being too hazardous in itself, and one that would endanger the main position at Cambridge. Besides, what probably had quite as much influence, they distrusted the spirit of the troops, still raw in discipline; doubting whether they would come to the point of an open, pitched battle with the king and stand their ground. They had the same feeling that Washington had, when he enquired, after the battle — "Could they stand fire?" and when the answer was given, replied — "the cause is safe!" Putnam believed they would stand fire before hand, urging the necessity of action to bring out the spirit that was in them and confirm it. Give them a good breast-work on the hill, he said, laughingly, and they will hold it. "They are not afraid of their heads, though very much afraid of their legs; if you cover these they will fight forever." Warren, who was pacing the room, paused over a chair, and said, "Almost thou persuadest me, Putnam. Still, I think the project rash; but if you undertake it, ['*you*,' observe] you will not be surprised to find me at your side." Finally, ascertaining that Gen. Gage was about to do the very thing proposed, their hesitation was brought to an end.

It was supposed, in the council, that "two thousand men" would be required to effect and maintain the proposed occupation. Accordingly we are to understand that, when only a thousand were detailed, under Col. Prescott, to occupy the hill and open the entrenchments on the night of the 16th, it was expected that other troops were to be sent forward under a more general command, when they were wanted. And beyond a question this command was to be in Putnam, the chief mover of the enterprise. Accordingly we see that Putnam went over with the detachment, under Prescott, and assisted in directing where the entrenchment should be opened, viz: on the lower summit, or part of Bunker Hill, nearest to the city, afterwards called Breed's Hill; in the understanding that the higher eminence should be taken afterward, when required, and entrenchments opened there. Putnam returned that night to Cambridge, and was back in the early dawn of the morning, as a responsible officer should be, to see the condition of the works. At ten o'clock, he was in the field again. And as soon as it became evident that there was to be an assault upon the works, he ordered on the Connecticut troops, by the consent of General Ward, and was there, on the field, at the beginning of the engagement. Leaving Prescott, of course, to his position, which he had simply to maintain, we see him directing the detachments to their places; beginning entrenchments on the other summit; rebuking and rallying the timid; seizing on a cannon, which it was said, could not be loaded, and loading and firing it himself; maintaining the left wing which Lord Howe was constantly endeavoring to carry, and the yielding of which would, at any moment, have ended the struggle of Prescott on the hill; saving also, by his firmness here, the retreat of Prescott from being only a slaughter or a capture; last in the retreat himself, trying to rally for a stand upon the other hill, and only not endeavoring to maintain the post alone; then withdrawing and, of his own counsel, mounting Prospect Hill with the Connecticut forces, opening his entrenchments there in the night, and holding it as a position between the enemy and Cambridge; a movement by which he probably saved the town and the public stores of the army; for when the enemy saw his works there the next morning, they had no courage left to try a second day, against a position so admirably chosen — a position in which he was afterwards installed, by Washington, to maintain the honors of the centre of the army.

There was little reason, as we have seen, for Putnam to be multiplying orders to Prescott; the only thing to be done was to enable Prescott, if possible, to hold his position. But it is in evidence that he did order away the entrenching tools, against the judgment of Prescott; also that, when Warren came upon the ground, he went to Putnam, as the officer of direction, to ask where he should go to serve as a volunteer, and that Putnam sent him to the redoubt, to the aid of Prescott; also that the same order, in regard to firing, occasioned by the shortness of their ammunition, was given every where on the field, as well out of the redoubt as in it, and that Putnam said himself that he gave the order.

It is very easy to see, regarding this statement of facts, how Prescott should often have been spoken of as being the chief in command in this battle, and even how he should have thought himself to be; for he had the redoubt in charge at the beginning, and maintained the internal command of it. He came under a higher command, only by silent rules of military precedence, when other forces were upon the ground; of which he would hardly take note himself, so little was he interfered with. Putnam had work enough without, in the open field, and was very sure that Prescott would do his part within. It is only a little remarkable that Col. Prescott, when questioned by Mr. Adams, at Philadelphia, in regard to the battle, does not even name Gen. Putnam, as having been upon the ground at all; and apparently had not ascertained, two months after the battle, whether the Connecticut militia, sent out by himself, under Knowlton, to hold a position against the enemy's right, had obeyed his orders or had run away. And it is even the more remarkable, that this body of men, assisted by the brave Capt. Chester of Wethersfield, and others whom Putnam was rallying to their support during the whole engagement, had been able, by raising an extempore breast work of fence and new-mown grass, and defending it with Spartan fidelity, to save him all the while from being flanked and cut to pieces. For upon just this point Lord Howe was rolling his columns, with the greatest emphasis of assault, resting his main hope of success on turning the position so gallantly defended, and gaining, in this manner, the other summit of the hill, which, if he had been able to do, Prescott and his regiment would have been, from that moment, prisoners of war. In this view, it is a total mistake to look upon the defence of the redoubt, brilliant as it was and prominent to the eye, as the battle of Bunker Hill. The place of extempore counsel and varying fortune, the hinge of the day, was really, not there, but in the open field; and especially in moving, there, raw bodies of troops, with any such effect as to maintain the critical point of the engagement.

The testimony of authorities, in respect to the question of the chief command, you will understand is various and contradictory, as it naturally would be. And yet the contradiction is rather verbal than real; for as Prescott held the redoubt, in the manner described, it would be very natural, taking a more restricted view of the field, to speak of him as chief in command; though the facts already recited, show most clearly, that Col. Sweet gave the true testimony, when he said that Col. Prescott "was ordered to proceed to Charlestown, Gen. Putnam having the principal direction and superintendence of the expedition concerning it." This too was the testimony of Putnam himself, as Rev. Josiah Whitney testifies, in a note to the funeral sermon preached at Putnam's death. He says, "The detachment was first put under the command of Gen. Putnam. With it he took possession of the hill, and ordered the battle from the beginning to the end." Does any one imagine that Gen. Putnam was a man to assert claims of honor that belonged to others? Far more likely was he, in the generosity of his nature, to give up such as were properly his own.

The testimony of the old Courant, commenting on the battle, shortly after, corresponds. "In the list of heroes it is needless to expatiate on the character and bravery of Major Gen. Putnam, whose capacity to *form and execute* great designs, is known through Europe, and whose undaunted courage and martial abilities have raised him to an incredible height, in the esteem and friendship of his American brethren; it is sufficient to say, that he seems to be inspired by God Almighty with a military genius." Col. Humphrey, writing his Life of Putnam at Mount Vernon, under the eye of Washington, and Botta, who derives his facts from original sources, agree in representing Putnam as the chief in command.

Moreover, Washington, when he came upon the field only a few days after the battle, with commissions from the Congress appointing four Major Generals, immediately delivered Putnam his commission, placing him second in command to himself, and reserved the three others for the further consideration of Congress; though Putnam's commission, placing him above two very talented officers of the state, superior in rank to himself, had created more complaint than either of the others. Why this remarkable deference to Putnam, unless he has been the chief actuating spirit in some great success? Why this signal hónor on Gen. Putnam, when the eyes of the army and of the public at large, in the flush of enthusiasm that follows the late battle, are centered on another — who, I believe, was never afterwards promoted?

I have seen too, within a very few days, an original engraving of

Gen. Putnam, published in England three months after the battle, which has at the foot these words, — "Major Gen. Putnam, of the Connecticut forces, and Commander in Chief of the engagement on Buncker's Hill, near Boston. Published, as the Act directs, by C. Shepherd, 9th Sept. 1775." That he had the chief command here assigned him I firmly believe; which if he has lost, it has been at least three months subsequent to the battle; and by means that often discolor the truth of history. The occupation of the hill, I believe, was emphatically Putnam's measure; and one that truly represents the man. How can we think otherwise? See him in the council, the march, the beginning of the entrenchment, the fight itself; present every where, directing, cheering on the men, *rallying all the force he can to keep the difficult point of the field;* last in the retreat, issuing grimmed with smoke and gunpowder, and seizing, with his force, another hill, there to entrench again and wait the fortune of another day. Do this, I say, and there is but one conclusion for us to receive. Our conviction will be clear that, if the monument on Bunker Hill is a worthy testimony for Massachusetts, it testifies as much also for Connecticut; and I hope our Connecticut eyes will be pardoned, if we see it tapering off into a top-stone, that represents the little town of Pomfret!

I have dwelt the more at length on this question, because we seem to have lost our rights here, in a transaction that in one view stands at the head of our American history; and yet more because of the good it will do us to reclaim our rights. I suppose it may well enough be doubted whether Putnam was the ablest of all great commanders; whether, in fact, he was the general to head what would be called, in history, a great military campaign. He was a man of action, inspiration, adventure, and he made men feel as he felt. "You seem to have the faculty, Sir," said Washington, "of infusing your own spirit." Nothing was more truly distinctive of the man. His value lay in the immense volume of impulse or martial enthusiasm there was in him, and in the fact that his time was always now. And the country wanted impulse to break silence, and make its first trial with the British arms. He was the man, above all others in the colonies, to give that impulse. A more cautious man, probably would not have advised to such an attempt; possibly a wise man would not; but Putnam, whose impetuous soul had only a feeble connection with prudence, or with mere science, was the man to say, "let us have the fight first, and settle the wisdom of it afterwards." Possibly there is a higher kind of generalship; but, I know not how it is, when I see how much depended for our country, at that time, on a real beginning of action, I am ready for once, to accept impulse as the truest counsel, and the fire of martial passion as being only the inspired form of prudence.

I cannot give you the details of our military transactions in the Revolution. I can only name a few facts, that will suffice to indicate the spirit and devotion of our people. Connecticut was the second state in the Union as regards the amount of military force contributed to the common cause. She had twenty-five regiments of militia and of these, it is said, that twenty-two full regiments were in actual service, out of the state, at one and the same time, and that the most busy and pressing season of the year; leaving the women at home to hoe their fields and assist the boys and old men in gathering the harvests. And such a class of material has seldom been gathered into an army. When Trumbull sent on fourteen regiments to Washington, at New York, he described them as "regiments of substantial farmers." And General Root, as a friend of mine remembers, declared that, in his brigade alone, there came out seven ministers, as captains of their own congregations. Among their leaders was Colonel Knowlton, than whom there was not a more gallant officer, or one more respected by the commander-in-chief in the army of the Revolution. And when he fell, in the disastrous day at Harlaem, with so many hundreds of the sons of Connecticut, Washington evinced his affliction for the loss of this favorite officer, as being the loss most deplorable of all that befell the cause, on that losing day. Among the leaders, too, were Parsons, and Spencer, and Wooster, and Wolcott, and Ledyard, and, last of all, but not least worthy to be named, though to name him should never be necessary before a Connecticut audience, that mournful flower of patriotism, the young scholar of Coventry; he whom no service could daunt that Washington desired, and who, when he was called to die an ignominious death, nobly said to his enemies and executioners, that "his only regret was that he had but one life to give for his country."

But I must not omit to speak of our venerable Governor, the patriotic Trumbull, under whom we acted our part in this eventful struggle. He was one of those patient, true-minded men, that hold an even hand of authority in stormy times, and suffer nothing to fall out of place either by excess or defect of service to whom Washington could say, "I cannot sufficiently express my thanks, not only for your constant and ready compliance with every request of mine, but for your prudent forecast, in ordering matters, so that your force has been collected and put in motion as soon as it has been demanded." And yet there like to have been a fatal breach between them, at the beginning of the war. The British ships in the sound were threatening to land on our coast, and Trumbull requested that a part of the troops he was raising might remain to guard our own soil. No request, apparently, could be more reasonable. Washington refused and ordered them all to Boston. Trumbull wrote him a most pungent letter; adding, however, like a true patriot, who sees the necessity of subordination to all power and effect, that he will comply; "for it is plain that such jealousies indulged, however just, will destroy the cause." Noble answer! worthy to be recorded, as a rebuke to faction, while the republic lasts! Washington immediately explained, the misunderstanding was healed, and from that time forth he leaned upon Trumbull as one of his chief supports; confident always of this, that he could calculate on marching the whole state bodily just where he pleased.

Neither let us forget, in this connection, what appears to be sufficiently authenticated, that our Trumbull is no other than the world-renowned Brother Jonathan, accepted as the soubriquet of the United States of America. Our Connecticut Jonathan was to

Washington what the scripture Jonathan was to David, a true friend, a counsellor and stay of confidence — Washington's brother. When he wanted honest counsel and wise, he would say, "let us consult brother Jonathan;" and then afterwards, partly from habit and partly in playfulness of phrase, he would say the same when referring any matter to the Congress, — "let us consult Brother Jonathan." And so it fell out rightly, that as Washington was called the Father of his Country, so he named the fine boy, the nation, after his brother Jonathan — a good, solid, scripture name, which as our sons and daughters of the coming time may speak it, any where between the two oceans, let them remember honest, old Connecticut and the faithful and true brother she gave to Washington!

CONSIDERING the very intimate historic connection of our Revolution with the influence of the clergy, their active instigation to it and their constant, powerful cooperation in it, the transition we make in passing from our military history to that of the pulpit, is by no means violent. Only in speaking of our great men here and our theologic standing generally, I must speak in the briefest manner. No mean distinction is it to say that the renowned theologian, preacher and philosopher, Jonathan Edwards, was a native of Connecticut, and a graduate of Yale College. And though the more active part of his life was spent in Massachusetts, he retained his affinities, more especially, with the churches and ministers of Connecticut. I need not say that there is no American name of higher repute, not only among the divines, but also among the metaphysicians both of this country and of Europe. Dr. Dwight was born in Massachusetts but educated here, and here was the scene of his life. Besides these, having our Hooker, and Davenport, and Bellamy, and Smalley, and by a less exclusive property, our Hopkins and Emmons, and Griffin, all sons of Connecticut, we have abundant reason, I think, to be satisfied with our high eminence in the department of theological literature and pulpit effect.

AS REGARDS our poets I will only detain you to say that, while I am far from thinking that every thing which beats time in verse is poetry, it is yet something that we have our Trumbull, and Hillhouse, and Brainard, and Percival, and Pierpont, and Halleck, who, not to speak of others closer to our acquaintance, have written what can never perish, while wit may enliven men's hearts, or music and the sense of beauty remain.

INCLUDING, next, in our inventory, mechanical inventions, I may say that the great improvements in cotton machinery, by Gilbert Brewster, justify the title sometimes given him of the Arkwright of our country.

The cotton gin of Whitney, is a machine that, by itself, has doubled the productive power, and so the value of the Southern half of our country. If the inventor had been paid for his invention, and not defrauded of his rights by a conspiracy too strong for the laws, the interest of his money would redeem all the fugitives that cross the line of free labor, as long as there is such a line to cross.

The first two printing presses patented in the United States, were from Hartford.

Joshua Fitch of Connecticut, has the distinguished honor of producing the first steam boat that ever moved upon the waters of the world. He was unfortunate in his character, though a man of genius and high enthusiasm. Failing of the means necessary to complete his experiments, and universally derided by the public, he persisted in the confidence that steam was to be the great agent of river navigation in the world, and gave it, as a last request, that "his body might be buried on the banks of the Ohio, where his rest would be soothed by the blowing of the steam and the splash of the waters."

It is not as generally known, I believe, that the first steam locomotive, ever constructed, was run in the streets of Hartford. The inventor was Doctor Kinsley, a man whose history was strikingly similar to that of Fitch. The late Theodore Dwight, known to many in this audience, lent him the money with which he made his experiments. He succeeded in part, but fell through into bankruptcy, at the end, still persisting that steam was to be the agent of the land travel of the world. His experiments were made between the years '97 and '9, previous to the introduction of rails as the guides and supports of motion.

It now remains to speak of the rank we have held, in the matter of education, and the power we have exerted by that means, in the republic. It is remarkable that a very large share of the colleges in our nation draw their lineage, not from Harvard, most distinguished in the fruits of elegant literature, but from Yale. This is true of Dartmouth, Princeton, Williams, Middlebury, Hamilton, Western Reserve, Jacksonville, and Athens University in Georgia. These institutions were some of them planned in Connecticut, others of them moved, or in some principal degree manned, by the graduates of Yale College and sons of Connecticut. Dr. Johnson of Stratford, a graduate of Yale and afterwards of Oxford, was the principal originator and first President also of Columbia College, New York. I find in the office of our Secretary of State, a petition to our Legislature from the Trustees of Princeton College, asking leave to draw a lottery here for the benefit of their institution, such leave being denied them by their own state. They aver in their petition, that "it would be a happy means of establishing and perpetuating a desirable harmony between the two institutions, Yale and Princeton, which it will be the care of your petitioners to promote and preserve." Leave was granted; for it was the manner of our state to seize every opportunity in every place, for the assistance of learning. I may also add that Mr. Crary, to whose active exertions in behalf of education the school system and the State University of Michigan are mainly due, is a son of Connecticut and a graduate of Trinity College.

Our system of common schools, originated by a public statute, which is one of the very first statutes passed by the colonial Legislature and faithfully maintained, down to within the past twenty years, was till then acknowledged to be far in advance of that of any other state. The founding of our school fund, too, was an act generally regarded and spoken of with admiration every where, as characteristic of the state.

And now, if you will see what force there is in education, what precedence it gives and preponderance of weight, even to a small and otherwise insignificant state, you have only to see what Connecticut has effected through the medium of her older college and her once comparatively vigorous system of common schools.

I have spoken of the numerous colleges dotting the map of the republic, which are seen to be more or less directly offshoots of Yale. If you ask what parts of the republic were settled principally by emigrations from Connecticut, they are the Eastern part of Long Island, the Northern half of New Jersey, the Western sections of Massachusetts and Vermont, Middle and Western New York, the Susquehanna valley in Pennsylvania, and the Western Reserve territory in Ohio — just those portions of our country, more recently settled, as you will perceive, that are most distinguished for industry, thrift, intelligence, good morals and character.

Again, if you enter into the legislative bodies of other states. west of us, and ask who are the members, you will find the sons of Connecticut among them in a large proportion of numbers compared with those of any other state. In the convention, for example, that revised the Constitution of New York in 1821, it was found that, out of one hundred and twenty-six members, thirty-two were natives of Connecticut, not including those who were born of a Connecticut parentage in that state. Of the sons of Massachusetts, which according to the ratio of population, ought to had about seventy, there were only nine. If you add to the thirty-two natives of Connecticut, in that body, her descendants born in New York, and those who came in through Vermont, New Jersey, and other states, it is altogether probable that they would be found to compose a majority of the body; presenting the very interesting fact that Connecticut is found sitting there, to make a Constitution for the great state of New York. I found on inquiry, four or five winters ago, that the New York Legislature contained fifteen natives of Connecticut, while of Massachusetts there were only nine; though, according to her ratio of numbers, there should have been about forty. So also in the Ohio Legislature of 1838-9, there were found in the lower house of seventy-four members, twelve from Connecticut, two from Massachusetts, two from Vermont.

If we repair to the Halls of the American Congress, we shall there discover what Connecticut is doing on a still larger scale of comparison. The late Hon. James Hillhouse, when he was in Congress, ascertained that forty-seven of the members, or about one-fifth of the whole number in both Houses, were native born sons of Connecticut. Mr. Calhoun assured one of our Representatives, when upon the floor of the House with him, that he had seen the time, when the natives of Connecticut, together with all the graduates of Yale College there collected, wanted only five of being a majority of that body. I took some

pains in the winter, I think, of '43, to ascertain how the composition of the Congress stood at that time. There could not, of course be as many native citizens of Connecticut among the members, as in the days of Mr. Hillhouse; but including native citizens and descendants born out of the state, I found exactly his number, forty-seven. Of the New York representation, sixteen or two-fifths were sons or descendants, in the male line, of Connecticut.

Saying nothing of descendants born out of the state, there were at that time, eighteen native born sons of Connecticut in the

Congress. According to the Blue Book, Massachusetts had seventeen; when taken in the proportion of numbers she should have had forty-two. New Hampshire should have had eighteen also, but had only seven; Vermont eighteen, but had only four; Louisiana eighteen, but had only two; New Jersey twenty-one, but had only nine. I see no way to account for these facts, especially when the comparison is taken between Connecticut and Massachusetts, unless it be that, prior to a time quite recent, our school system was farther advanced and the education imparted to our youth more universal and more perfect.

How beautiful is the attitude of our little state, when seen through the medium of facts like these. Unable to carry weight by numbers, she is seen marching out her sons to conquer other posts of influence and represent her honor in other fields of action. Which, if she continues to do, if she takes the past simply as a beginning and returns to that beginning with a fixed determination to make it simply the germ of a higher and more perfect culture, there need scarcely be a limit to the power she may exert, as a member of the republic. The smallness of our territory is an advantage even, as regards the highest form of social development and the most abundant fruits of genius. Our state under a skillful and sufficient agriculture with a proper improvement of our water falls, is capable of sustaining a million of people, in a condition of competence and social ornament; and that is a number as large as any state government can manage with the highest effect. No part of our country between the two oceans is susceptible of greater external beauty. What now looks rough and forbidding in our jagged hill-sides and our raw beginnings of culture, will be softened, in the future landscape, to an ornamental rock-work, skirted by fertility; pressing out in the cheeks of the green dells, where the farm-houses are nested; bursting up through the waving slopes of the meadows, and walling the horizon about with wooded hills of rock and pastured summits. We have pure transparent waters, a clear bell-toned atmosphere and, with all, a robust, healthy minded stock of people; uncorrupted by luxury, unhumiliated by superstition, sharpened by good necessities, industrious in their habits, simple in their manners and tastes, rigid in their morals and principles; combining, in short, all the higher possibilities of character and genius, in a degree that will seldom be exceeded in any people of the world. These are the mines, the golden *placers* of Connecticut. Turning now to these as our principal hope for the future, let us endeavor, with a fixed and resolute concentration of our public aim, to keep the creative school-house in action, and raise our institutions of learning to the highest pitch of excellence.

I am far from thinking that our schools have ever been as low, or inefficient as many have supposed; the facts I have recited clearly show the contrary. And yet they certainly are not worthy of our high advantages, or the age of improvement in which we live. Therefore I rejoice that our lethargy is now finally broken, and that we are fairly embarked in an organized plan for the raising of our schools to a pitch of culture and perfection, worthy of our former precedence.

I remember with fresh interest, to-day, how my talented friend, who has most reason of all to rejoice in the festivities of this occasion, consulted with me, as many as thirteen years ago, in regard to his plans of life; raising, in particular, the question whether he should give himself wholly and finally up to the cause of public schools. I knew his motives, the growing distaste he had for political life, in which he was already embarked with prospects of success, and the desire he felt to occupy some field more immediately and simply beneficent. He made his choice; and now, after encountering years of untoward hindrance here, winning golden opinions meantime from every other state in the republic, and from ministers of education in almost every nation of the old world, by his thoroughly practical understanding of all that pertains to the subject; after raising also into vigorous action the school system of another state, and setting it forward in a tide of progress, he returns to the scene of his beginnings and permits us here to congratulate both him and ourselves, in the prospect that his original choice and purpose are finally to be fulfilled. He has our confidence; we are to have his ripe experience; and the work now fairly begun is to go on, I trust, by the common consent of us all, till the schools of our state are placed on a footing of the highest possible energy and perfection.

To exhibit the kind of expectation we are to set before Connecticut as a state, let me give you the picture of a little obscure parish in Litchfield county; and I hope you will pardon me if I do it, as I must, with a degree of personal satisfaction; for it is not any very bad vice in a son to be satisfied with his parentage. This little parish is made up of the corners of three towns, and the ragged ends and corners of twice as many mountains and stony sided hills. But this rough, wild region, bears a race of healthy minded, healthy bodied, industrious and religious people, They love to educate their sons and God gives them their reward. Out of this little, obscure nook among the mountains have come forth two presidents of colleges, the two that a few years ago presided, at the same time, over the two institutions, Yale and Washington, or Trinity. Besides these they have furnished a secretary of state for the commonwealth, during a quarter of a century or more. Also a member of congress. Also a distinguished professor. And besides these a greater number of lawyers, physicians, preachers and teachers, both male and female, than I am now able to enumerate. Probably some of you have never so much as heard the name of this little bye-place on the map of Connecticut, generally it is not on the maps at all, but how many cities are there of 20,000 inhabitants in our country, that have not exerted one-half the influence on mankind. The power of this little parish, it is not too much to say, is felt in every part of our great nation. Recognized, of course, it is not; but still it is felt.

This, now, is the kind of power in which Connecticut is to have her name and greatness. This, in small, is what Connecticut should be. She is to find her first and noblest interest, apart from religion, in the full and perfect education of her sons and daughters. And so she is to be sending out her youth, empowered in capacity and fortified by virtue, to take their posts of honor and influence in the other states; in her behalf to be their physicians and ministers of religion, their professors and lawyers, their wise senators, their great orators and incorruptible judges, bulwarks of virtue, truth and order to the republic, in all coming time. And then, when the vast area of our country between the two oceans is filled with a teeming population, when the delegates of sixty or a hundred states, from the granite shores of the East, and the alluvial plains of the South, and the golden mountains of the West, are assembled in the Halls of our Congress, and little Connecticut is there represented in her own behalf, by her one delegate, it will still and always be found that she is numerously represented also by her sons from other states, and her one delegate shall be himself regarded in his person, as the symbol of that true Brother Jonathan, whose name still designates the great republic of the world.

Meantime, if any son of Connecticut will indulge in the degraded sneer, by which ignorant and malicious custom, has learned to insult her name, let him be looked upon as the man who is able to please himself in defiling the ashes of his mother. Let me testify my hearty joy too, in the presence of this assembly, that a citizen of Connecticut has at last been heard in the Senate of this great nation, doing honor to its noble history, by a fit chastisement of the insult, which a volunteer malice, emboldened by former impunity, was tempted again to offer to our commonwealth.

Fellow citizens, I have endeavored, this evening, to show you Connecticut, what she has been, and so what she is and ought to be. I undertook this subject, simply because of the chilling and depressing influence I have so often experienced from the want of any sufficient public feeling in our state. I am not a historian, and I may have fallen into some mistakes, which a critic in American history will detect. I knew but imperfectly when I began, how great a wealth of character and incident our history contains. I supposed it might be more defective than I could wish, as regards the kind of material most fitted to inspire a public enthusiasm. But, as I proceeded patiently in my questions, gathering, stage by stage, this inventory, which

I have condensed even to dryness, I began to be mortified by the discovery that the age of Connecticut history most defective and least worthy of respect is the present — that we are most to be honored in that which we have forgot, and least because we have forgotten it.

Such, I say, is Connecticut! There is no outburst of splendor in her history, no glaring or obtrusive prominence to attract the applause of the multitude. Her true merit and position are discovered only by search, she is seen only through the sacred veil of modesty — great only, in the silent energy of worth and beneficence. But when she is brought forth out of her retirement, instead of the little, declining, undistinguished, scarcely distinguishable state of Connecticut, you behold, rising to view, a history of practical greatness and true honor; illustrious in its beginning; serious and faithful in its progress; dispensing intelligence, without the rewards of fame; heroic for the right, instigated by no hope of applause; independent, as not knowing how to be otherwise; adorned with names of wisdom and greatness fit to be revered, as long as true excellence may have a place in the reverence of mankind.

# PART VIII

# CALIFORNIA: ITS CHARACTERISTICS AND PROSPECTS

WRITTEN BY REV. HORACE BUSHNELL, D.D., AND PUBLISHED ORIGINALLY IN THE "NEW ENGLANDER." [PAMPHLET PUBLISHED 1858.]

# PAMPHLET

WHOEVER wishes, for health's sake or for any other reason, to change the sceneries or the objects and associations of his life, should set off, not for Europe, but for California. And this the more certainly, if he is a loving and sharp observer of nature; for nature meets us here in moods entirely new; so that we have even to make her acquaintance over again; going back, as it were, to be started in a fresh childhood. All our common, or previously formed impressions, calculations and weather-wisdoms are at fault. We find that we really understand nothing and have everything to learn. We begin to imagine, for example, that her way is to be thus, or thus; or that her operations are to be solved in this, or that manner, but we very soon discover that it will not hold. Our guess must be given up and we must try again. A person who is at all curious in the study of natural phenomena, will be held in a puzzle thus for whole months, and will nearly complete the cycle of the year, before he seems to himself to have come into any real understanding with the new world he is in; just as if he were sent on a visit to Jupiter, and wanted to sail round the sun with him, for at least once, and feel out his year, before he can be sure that he understands a single day.

California being to this extent a new world, having its own combinations, characters, and colors, it is not to be supposed that we can make any reader acquainted with it by words of description. The most we can hope to accomplish is, that by giving some notes on its physical and social characteristics, we may excite a a more curious and possibly a more intelligent interest in California life, and the certainly great scenes preparing to be revealed in that far off, outside, isolated state of the Republic. It is not to be supposed that every particular representation or suggestion we may offer will be verified by the experiments and exact observations of science, or by the tests of moral and economical statistics; we only look on with our mere eyes, giving our impressions, and venturing what guesses and possible applications may occur to us.

The first and most difficult thing to apprehend respecting California is the climate, upon which, of course, depend the advantages of health and physical development, the growths and their conditions and kinds, and the *modus operandi,* or general cast, of the seasons. But this, again, is scarcely possible, without dismissing, first of all, the word climate, and substituting the plural climates. For it cannot be said of California, as of New England, or the Middle States, that it has a climate. On the contrary, it has a great multitude of them, curiously pitched together, at short distances, one from another, defying too, not seldom, our most accepted notions of the effects of latitude and altitude and the defences of mountain ranges. The only way, therefore, is to dismiss generalities, cease to look for a climate, and find, if we can, by what process the combinations and varieties are made; for when we get hold of the manner and going on of cause, all the varieties are easily reducible.

To make this matter intelligible, conceive that middle California, the region of which we now speak, lying between the head waters of the two great rivers, and about four hundred and fifty or five hundred miles long from north to south, is divided lengthwise, parallel to the coast, into three strips, or ribands of about equal width. First, the coast-wise region, comprising two, three, and sometimes four parallel tiers of mountains, from five hundred to four thousand, five thousand, or even ten thousand feet high. Next, advancing inward, we have a middle strip, from fifty to seventy miles wide, of almost dead plain, which is called the great valley; down the scarcely perceptible slopes of which, from south, to north, run the two great rivers, the Sacramento and the San Joaquin, to join their waters at the middle of the basin and pass off to the sea. The third long strip or riband, is the slope of the Sierra Nevada chain, which bounds the great valley on the east, and contains in its foot-hills, or rather in its lower half, all the gold mines. The upper half is, to a great extent, bare granite rock, and is crowned at the summit with snow, about eight months of the year.

Now the climate of these parallel strips will be different almost of course, and subordinate, local differences, quite as remarkable, will result from subordinate features in the local configurations, particularly of the seaward strip or portion. For all the varieties of climate, distinct as they become, are made by variations wrought in the rates of motion, the courses, the temperature, and the dryness of a single wind, viz, the trade wind of the summer months, which blows directly inward all the time, only with much greater power during that part of the day when the rarefaction of the great central valley comes to its aid; that is from ten o'clock in the morning until the setting of the sun. Conceive such a wind, chilled by the cold waters which have come down from the Northern Pacific, perhaps from Behring Straits, combing the tops and wheeling through the valleys of the coast-wise mountains, crossing the great valley at a much retarded rate, and growing hot and dry, fanning gently the foot-hills and sides of the Sierra, still more retarded by the piling necessary to break over into Utah, and the conditions of the California climate, or climates, will be understood with general accuracy. Greater simplicity in the matter of climate is impossible, and greater variety is hardly to be imagined.

For the whole dry season, viz, from May to November, this wind is in full blast, day by day, only sometimes approaching a little more nearly to a tempest than at others. It never brings a drop of rain, however thick and rain-like the clouds it sometimes drives before it. The cloud element, indeed, is always in it. Sometimes it is floated above, in the manner commonly designated by the term cloud. Sometimes, as in the early morning, when the wind is most quiet, it may be seen as a kind of fog bank resting on the sea-wall mountains, or rolling down landward through the interstices of their summits. When the wind begins to hurry and take on less composedly, the fog becomes blown fog, a kind of lead dust driven through the air, reducing it from a transparent to a semi-transparent or merely translucent state, so that if any one looks up the bay, from a point twenty or thirty miles south of San Francisco, in the afternoon, he will commonly see, directly abreast of the Golden Gate, where the wind drives in with its greatest power, a pencil of the lead dust shooting upward at an angle of thirty or forty degrees, (which is the aim of the wind preparing to leap the second chain of mountains, the other side of the bay,) and finally tapering off and vanishing, at a mid-air point eight or ten miles inland, where the increased heat of the atmosphere has taken up the moisture, and restored its complete transparency. The wind is so cold, that one who will sit upon the deck of the afternoon steamer passing up the Bay, will even require his heaviest winter clothing. And so rough are the waters of the Bay, land-locked and narrow as it is, that sea-sickness is a kind of regular experience, with such as are candidates for that kind of felicity.

We return now to the middle strip of the great valley, where the engine or rather boiler power, that operates the coast wind in a great part of its velocity, is located. Here the heat, reverberated as in a forge or oven, whence *Cali-fornia* (*Caleo* and *fornan*) becomes, even in the early spring, so much raised that the ground is no longer able, by any remaining cold there is in it, to condense the clouds, and rain ceases. A little further on in the season, there is not cooling influence enough left to allow even the phenomena of a cloud, and for weeks together not a cloud will be seen, unless, by chance, the skirt of one may appear now and then, hanging over the summit of the western mountains. The sun rises, fixing his hot stare on the world, and stares through the day. Then he returns as in an orrery, and stares through another, in exactly the same way. The thermometer will go up, not seldom, to 100 or even 110 deg., and judging by what we know of effects here in New England, we should suppose that life would scarcely be supportable. And yet there is much less suffering from heat in this valley than with us, for the reason probably that the nights are uniformly cool. The thermometer goes down regularly with the sun, and one or two blankets are wanted for the comfort of the night. This cooling of the night is probably determined by the fact that the cool sea-wind, sweeping through the upper air of the valley, from the coast mountains on one side, over the mountains and mountain passes of the Sierra on the other, is not able to get down to the ground of the valley during the day, because of the powerfully steaming column of heat that rises from it; but as soon as the sun goes down, it drops immediately to the level of the plain, bathing it for the night with a kind of perpendicular sea breeze, that has lost for the time a great part of its lateral motion. The consequence is, that no one is greatly debilitated by the heat. On the contrary, it is the general testimony, that a man can do as much of mental or bodily labor in this climate, as in any other. And it is good confirmation of this opinion, that horses will here maintain a wonderful energy, traveling greater distances, complaining far less of heat, and sustaining their spirit a great deal better than with us. It is also noted that there is no special tendency to fevers in this hot region, except in what is called the *tule* bottom, a kind of giant bulrush region, along the most depressed. and marshiest portions of the rivers.

Passing now to the eastern strip or portion, the slope of the Nevada, the heat, except in those deep cañons where the reverberation makes it sometimes even insupportable, is qualified in degree, according to the altitude. A gentle west wind, heated in the lower part of the foothills by the heat of the valley, fans it all day. At points which are higher, the wind is cooler. Here also, on the slope of the Nevada, the nights are always cool in summer; so cool that the late and early frosts leave too short a space for the ordinary summer crop to mature, even where the altitude is not more than 3,000 or 4,000 feet. Meantime, at the top of the Sierra, where the west wind piling up from below, breaks over into Utah, travellers undertake to say that, in some passes it blows with such stress as even to polish the rocks, by the gravel and sand which it drives before it. The day is cloudless on the slope of the Sierra, as in the valley, but on the top there is now and then, or once in a year or two, a moderate thunder shower. With this exception, as referring to a part uninhabitable, thunder is scarcely ever heard in California. The principal thunders of California are under ground.

We return now to the coast-wise mountain region, where the multiplicity and confusion of climates is most remarkable. Their variety we shall find depends on the courses of the wind currents, turned hither and thither by the mountains; partly also on the side any given place occupies of its valley or mountain; and partly on the proximity of the sea. Sprinkled in among these mountains, and more or less enclosed by them, are valleys, large and small, of the highest beauty. But a valley in California means something more than a scoop, or depression. It means a rich land-lake, leveled between the mountains, with a sharply defined, picturesque shore, where it meets the sides and runs into the indentations of the mountains. What is called the Bay of San Francisco, is a large salt water lake in the middle of a much larger land-lake, sometimes called the San José valley. It extends south of the city forty miles, and northward among islands and mountains twenty-five more, if we include what is called the San Pablo Bay. Three beautiful valleys of agricultural country, the Petaluma, Sonoma, and Napa valleys, open into this larger valley of the Bay on the north end of it, between four mountain barriers, having each a short navigable creek or inlet. Still farther north is the Russian River valley, opening towards the sea, and the Clear Lake valley and region, which is the

Switzerland of California. East of the San José valley, too, at the foot of Diabolo, and up among the mountains, are the large Amador and San Ramon valleys, also the little gem of the Suñole. Now these valleys, which if we except the great valley of the two rivers, comprise the plow-land of middle California, have each a climate of their own, and productions that correspond. We have only to observe further, that the east side of any valley will commonly be much warmer than the west; for the very paradoxical reason that the cold coast-wind always blows much harder on the side or steep slope even, of a mountain, opposite or away from the wind, than it does on the side towards it, reversing all our notions of the sheltering effects of mountain ridges.

Nothing will so fatally puzzle a stranger as the observing of this fact; for he will doubt for a long time, first, whether it be a fact, and then, what possible account to make of it. Crossing the Golden Gate in a small steamer, for example, to Saucelito, whence the water is brought for the city, he will look for a quiet shelter to the little craft, apparently in danger of foundering, when it comes under the lee of that grand mountain wall that overhangs the water on the west. But he is surprised when he arrives, to find the wind blowing straight down the face of it, harder even than elsewhere, gouging into the water by a visible depression, and actually raising caps of white within a rod of the shore. In San Francisco itself, he will find the cold coastwind pouring down over the western barrier with uncomfortable rawness, when returning from a ride at Point Lobos, on the very beach of the sea, where the air was comparatively soft and quiet. So, crossing the Sonoma valley, he will come out into it from the west, through a cold windy gorge, to find orange trees growing in Gen. Vallejo's garden, close under the eastern valley wall, as finely as in Cuba. In multitudes of places too on the eastern slopes of the mountains, he will notice that the trees, which have all their growth in the coast-wind season, have their tops thrown over, like cock's tails turned away from the wind. After he has been sufficiently perplexed, and stumbled by these facts, he will finally strike upon the reason, viz, that this cold, trade wind, being once lifted or driven over the sea-wall mountains, and being specifically heavier than the atmosphere into which it is going, no sooner reaches the summit than it pitches down as a cold cataract, with the uniformly accelerated motion of falling bodies. Then as confirmation, it will occur to him, perhaps, that he has been seeing it demonstrated all summer long, from his residence on the opposite or eastern side of the Bay; where, during all the fore part of the day, and sometimes for the whole afternoon, he has noticed a fog cap, or cloud rolling over the distant top of the western mountain, and driving more than half-way down the hither side of it, before it has caught sun enough or heat enough to become transparent.

Having gotten the understanding of this fact, many things are made plain. For example, in travelling down the western side of the Bay from San Francisco to San José, and passing directly under the mountain range just referred to, he has found himself passing through as many as four or five distinct climates; for, when abreast of some gap or depression in the western wall, the heavy wind has poured down with a chilling coldness, making even an overcoat desirable, though it be a clear, summer day; and then, when he is abreast of some high summit, which the fog-wind sweeps by, and therefore need not pass over, a sweltering and burning heat is felt, in which the lightest summer clothing is more than enough. He has also observed that directly opposite the Golden Gate, at Oakland, and the Alameda point, where the central column of this wind might be supposed to press most uncomfortably, the land is covered with growths of evergreen oak, standing fresh and erect, while north and south, on either side, scarcely a tree is to be seen for many miles; a mystery that is now explained by the fact that the wind, driving here square against the Contra Costa or second range, is piled and gets no current, till it slides off north and south from the point of quiet here made; which also is confirmed by the fact, that, in riding down from San Pablo on the north, he has the wind in his face, finds it slacken as he approaches Oakland, and passing on, till southward to San Leandro, has it blowing at his back.

The varieties, and even what appeared to be the incredible anomalies of the California climates, begin at last to be intelligible. The remarkable contrast, for example, between the climates of Benicia and Martinez, is clearly accounted for. These two places, only a mile and a half apart, on opposite sides of the straits of Carquinez, and connected by a ferry, like two points on a river, are yet more strikingly contrasted, in their summer climates, than Charleston and Quebec. Thus the Golden Gate column, wheeling upon Oakland, and just now described, sweeps along the face of the Contra Costa chain in its northward course, setting the few tree tops of San Pablo aslant, as weather vanes stuck fast by rust, and drives its cold sea-dust full in the face of Benicia. Meantime, at Martinez, close under the end of the mountain which has turned the wind directly by, and is itself cloven down here to let the straits of Carquinez pass through, the sun shines hot and with an almost dazzling clearness, and all the characters of the climate belong rather to the great valley cauldron, whose rim it may be said is here.

Equally plain now is the solution of those apparent inversions of latitude, which at first perplex the stranger. In the region about Marysville, for example, he is overtaken by a fierce sweltering heat in April, and scarcely hears, perhaps, in the travel of a day, a single bird sing as if meaning it for a song. He descends by steamer to San Francisco, and thence to San José, making a distance in all of more than two hundred miles, where he finds a cool, spring-like freshness in the air, and hears the birds screaming with song even more vehement than in New England. It is as if he had passed out of a tropical into a temperate climate, when, in fact, he is due south of Marysville by the whole distance passed over. But the mystery is all removed by the discovery, that instead of keeping in the great valley, he broke out of it through the straits of Carquinez into the Bay valley, and the cold bath atmosphere of the coast-wise mountains; that now he is in fact within twenty miles of the sea, separated from it only by a single wall, while at Marysville, he was more than a hundred miles from the sea, with four or five high mountain tiers between them.

Thus much for the summer climate of California. The winter cliImate is the trade wind reversed. The Sierra is covered with snows of incredible depth at the top, and they extend even down to its foot, whitening also, not seldom, the great valley, which is much colder, at this season, than the coast-mountain region. Temperature, in short, is inverted, just as the winds are. The temperature in San Francisco, for example, ranges generally between 60 and 70 deg., as in the summer between 65 and 80 deg.; though the cold of experience will be scarcely greater in the winter than in the summer, because, in winter the air is comparatively still, and in summer adds a cooling effect by its motion. Probably there is not a more even climate in the world. Now and then the thermometer will sink low enough, at night, to produce a thin scale of ice; but geraniums will be seen in full blossom, on the terraces of the gardens, throughout the winter.

It is hardly necessary to say that this westward return of the trade winds brings the rainy season. All the rain of the year is from it. It sometimes blows too with terrific violence, and pours even cascades of rain for whole days together, producing immense floods; though generally the whole amount of rain which it brings is much too small for the supply of the springs and due moistening of the soil for the year. It is not to be understood that what is called the rainy season is a season of continual rain. It is scarcely more rainy, if at all, than our three autumnal months. And at about the mid-point of the season, or in the month of February, there is commonly a suspension, which separates what may be called the early from the latter rain, as in Palestine. This month of February is, in fact, the most lovely, and in many respects, the most beautiful month of the year. The green of the landscape is then freshest, the air is soft, the sky clear, the roads neither wet nor dusty — all the conditions of comfort and beauty meet, to crown it as the June of the Pacific.

If now it should appear that we have spent too much time on the winds.and meteorological phenomena of California, it is sufficient to answer, that while such an impression would be right if New England were the subject, it is not right when the subject is California. The winds of our eastern shore are a confused mixture, of which nothing can be predicated with certainty, except the uncertainty of the weather. The Pacific winds, on the other hand, are very nearly calculable quantities; and by them are determined, to a great degree, the temperature of places, the rains, the seasons, the almost uniform salubrity of the country, (for with all its varieties there is probably no healthier region on the globe,) the growths also, as respects both their rates and kinds, and further still, the immense commercial advantages; for California, as we shall by and by see, is elected for the great metropolitan centre of the commerce of the Pacific, quite as much by its winds, as by the magnificent harbor, whose Gate is here set open to let the ships fly in, as doves to their windows, from all the seas of the world. The gold of California, taken as a determining cause and physical endowment of its future, is not once to be compared with its winds. They are more necessary, by a thousand times, to the greatness of California than the mines. If any one judges from our description, that they are too cold, or too strong, or too much laden with moisture, he will greatly mistake. If they were warmer, softer and more dry on the coast, even by a few degrees, it would greatly injure the country and might even be a fatal blight on its prospects. Indeed, if California has any prospects, it is just because the light baffling winds, or rather no winds of the coast below, are here displaced by such blasts as have power to drive across its whole width and fan it with their cooling breath. Otherwise its rich valleys and lowlands would be arid deserts, its shores and rivers reeking places of disease, and even in its mining region too hot to be worked or even inhabited, in the summer months.

Having gotten our advantage therefore, in a due understanding of the winds and climate of California, our description may now proceed more rapidly. The scenery of California depends partly on the surfaces and partly on the seasons. It differs from our eastern shore, in the fact that it is made up of concave or scooped surfaces, flowing into convex summits or rounded surfaces only to a very limited extent; all the valleys being plains, or land-lakes, with definite indented shores, like shores of water. It differs also from the western prairies and the plains of the south, where the horizon is sunk and the sky becomes a small inverted bowl, in the fact that every spot, even in the widest of the valleys, has a mountain wall and horizon visible in the distance, which props the sky and lifts the vault of it, giving a look of airiness and expansion, and connecting impressions even of grandeur and beauty. Mountain and plain, plain and mountain, stretching generally coastwise in their figure, make up the rough calico of the surface. Sometimes the mountains are bare, or nearly so, showing a mottled look in the distance, where the sun, glancing down their sides, burnishes the points and casts a shade on the hollows. Here the cattle on a thousand hills are no figure; for the hills are pastures, covered many of them with a rich growth of grass and wild oats even to the top, and the cattle paths, beaten like shelf rows in their steep sides, just save them apparently from sliding off into the abysses, making every rod of pasture accessible and permitting them finally to emerge, as the triumph of their engineering instinct, on summits two thousand, or even three thousand feet high, where they are seen from below in clean relief of the sky. Sometimes again the montain sides are covered with a dense chapparal, appearing in the distance just as they would if darkened by a forest; save that, now and then, the chapparal is of a most intense, transparently green color, showing a summit that emerges into the sun, when surrounded by the driving clouds below, like a huge pile of emerald. Sometimes the distant summits are seen to be covered with a growth of redwoods, that stand posted there as giant sentinels, every trunk distinctly visible, and altogether, two hundred or three hundred feet high, combing the sky in dark relief upon it, giving to the horizon thus a most peculiar look of spirit and majesty. The lower half of the Sierra Nevada, comprising the foot hills and the whole mining region, is covered extensively with a timber growth of pines, cedars and other evergreens. The upper half is bald, ragged granite, the highest peaks of which are covered a great part of the year with snow. All the mountains differ from those of the east, in the fact that they are seamed or furrowed from the tops downwards, every few rods, by a ravine or water course. These ravines are many of them dry in the summer, though generally, or at least frequently, displaying a green line of shrubbery and trees in their course, which makes them very conspicuous from a distance; especially when the mountains are bare on their general surface. These ravines, too, are often cut miles deep into the hills, becoming immense chasms, cañons or gorges, out of which all the earth has been swept, to fill the rich valley bottom and make up the land-lake. deposit of the plain. All the mountains accordingly are flanked by spurs with intervening gorges, and these again by spurs, and these again by the same; so that, standing on the side of some grand amphitheater, the spectator may sometimes see that he is on the spur of a spur even in the fifth degree; all of which spurs run together, like pig iron castings in a furnace, only with a more disorderly complication. Hence, too, the impossibility in California, as we may here remark in passing, that any railroad should ever get over a mountain, as with us, by skirting along its sides till it has made the ascent; for such a line would be cut by the side cañons, or gorges, from a hundred to a thousand or even two thousand feet deep, every half mile. There is no way but to follow up the bottom of some great cañon, or river gorge, until it becomes too steep, and escape by a tunnel; or else to find some spur whose back can be ascended, and keep it to the top.

From these general descriptions of the surface it will be naturally inferred that there is a great deal, both of beautiful and of grand scenery, in California. Few countries are richer in their varieties, and none more peculiar in all. Here sleeps in quiet, earthly beauty the rich vale of Sonoma, backed in rough grandeur by the towering Diabolo, a picture in a frame. Here in the deep chasm or angle that foots the Yo Hamite Falls, a river is beheld pitching off a summit twenty-four hundred feet high, and by two leaps, reaching the bottom; type, as it were, of heaven's mercy pouring from the sky. Here on the other hand, at the Geysers, in the cracking, cannonading, whistling and roaring of steam, and spouting of hot mud, and the brimstone fumes of the place, we look on a field, under which we may well enough imagine the infernals, sweltering and tearing, as it were, diabolically, to break loose. At the Big Trees, we enter a dell quietly lapped in the mountains, where the domestic vegetable minarets are crowded, as in some city of pilgrimage; there to look up, for the first time, in silent awe of the mere life principle.

The scene of the city and bay, from the high background of the city, is one that any lover of nature might travel far to see. The same reversed, from the east side of the bay, at Clinton, is more remarkable. In the unalterable green foreground, are the oaks of Oakland and Alameda; here and there flows a strip or armlet of water; next comes the Bay, in the middle, with its picturesque islands; beyond are the City, and the open Gate, showing the Farralone Islands far off to sea; right and left each side of the Gate, the grand sea-wall of mountains stretches north and south, for a background, at least fifty miles — it is not the bay of Naples, the dreamy softness and quiet luxury are not here — but with more severity, the scene unites a higher spirit and beauty as much more impressive and brilliant. The Gate itself, cleaving down the mountains to let the commerce of the Great Ocean of the world pass in, has a look of destiny in it strong enough to be sublime.

There is a little valley owned by a wealthy and respectable Spanish Californian, Mr. Suñole, which is commonly called by his name, and is occupied as a pasture ground or ranch for his herds. It lies over among the Contra Costa, or second range of mountains east of Mission San José, and is entered by a pass some four hundred feet above the valley bottom, which comprises about a thousand acres. Through this valley bottom runs a clear, rapid stream, which in the spring would be called a river, and which, wheeling round to the northwest, cuts the mountain to its base, dashing through one of the wildest gorges that can be conceived, fifteen hundred feet deep, and hurrying off into the Bay. On the north rises a huge bare summit two thousand feet high. On the southwest the Mission Peak, twenty-five hundred feet high. On the southwest, across the narrow wooded gorge through which the river breaks into the valley, other fantastic peaks three thousand feet high. On the east the enclosure is made by a low, steep range of naked hills showing others higher and still higher behind them. A stranger, fresh arrived in May, at the Mission, takes his horse, for example, the next morning, and finding a road that turns into the narrow gorge or opening of the hills near by, goes in to explore a little and find whither it leads. The steep, smooth-faced hills, or rather mountains, pile in with rounding fronts on either side, just leaving a passage between; and they are so lighted up by the sun brushing down their translucent surfaces of green, and tuned to such wild harmony by their many-colored flowers, that sight overflows, and he begins unwittingly to listen; as if there must be something audible, some hymn or note of Memnon in the scene. Passing a low summit, the beautiful valley opens to view, and such a combination of colors no eastern man or European has ever seen or conceived. The green is not what we call a grass green. Neither is it the pale bluish green of England, but a soft yellow green, covering the whole landscape — the steeps even to the summits, all the roundings and hollows, as well as a rich floor of the valley bottom — like an immense carpet of plush spread over the scene; which carpet is so matted with flowers in all the highest colors, sprinkled sometimes in groups, that we call it by this name without any effort of fancy — we can think of nothing else. No painter, practised in our common styles of scenery, could manage at such a picture, without much study, assisted probably by many failures.

Descending next into the valley, he finishes out the picturesque of the morning, in looking on a scene quite as new and peculiar as the scenery. In the extreme southern angle of the plain, just where the river issues from the gorge of the mountains, he observes a cloud of dust rising, and horsemen rushing wildly through it in all directions. Something brisk is evidently going on here, and he must needs learn what it is. Approaching the spot he discovers an immense herd of cattle brought together from the hills, which the owners and their herdsmen are either sorting by their marks, or which else they are sorting out, in sale of a part, for the market — they are Spanish, native Californians all, and do not answer English questions. This at least is plain, that they are gathering out of the great herd of a thousand or more, to make up another and separate herd a short distance off, and the lasso practice is the power. Riding into the herd and through it, they chase out one, turning him towards the new herd. But he runs by, and back into the herd, or he strikes out into the plain, in some other direction. But the pursuer is after him. Round and round swings the fatal loop or noose above his head as he goes, till he gets in reach, at three or four rods distance, when he lets it fly, and it drops with a kind of astronomic certainty round the poor animal's horns. Feeling it fast upon him, the animal now turns upon his persecutor, and it is convenient for him also to fly in his turn — only keeping the cord still fast to the horn of his saddle. Another horseman follows immediately, and another lasso drops and is drawn fast. Now the animal, in a line between the two pursuers, strikes off, throwing his whole momentum, if he can, upon the straight line, at right angles to it, which gives him advantage enough to unhorse both of them, if they let him come to the blow. All three, therefore, now are in a race together, and as soon as this is seen, a third horseman is in pursuit, and throwing his lasso, he picks up a hind leg of the ox as he runs, doing it as easily as a knitter might take up a fallen stitch. This done, while the two others are spreading right and left, he darts off sideways at a prick of the spur, and jerks the refractory beast flat upon the ground; where he lies bellowing in fright and despair, held fast by three cords, at three angles, as little able to escape as a fly in a spider's web. Next a huge, fiery bull is seen rushing out of the herd, pursued by a small, sharp looking herdsman, who says, by a certain look of his eye, that he will show the green stranger a trick. Bolting into the plain, the mettlesome, tall animal, leads off in a race which puts the horse to his best speed. But as the pursuer comes up with him, he seizes the tail of the renegade, streaming level behind him, winds it by a quick turn round the horn of his saddle, and darting off suddenly by a spring, as if it were done by some concussion of gunpowder, he jerks the bull flat down and rolls him clean over! Whereupon there is a shout from all — but the bull; who gets up, as it were, in an effort of self-recollection, and walks off meekly where they show him the way.

We only add, as regards the scenery in California, that everything is here inverted which we commonly assume in respect to the effects of culture. Culture improves nothing. California was finished as a world of beauty, before civilization appeared. The magnificent valleys opened wide and clean. The scattered oaks stood in majesty, here and there, and took away the nakedness. Civilization comes, cuts down the oaks for firewood, fences off the plains into squares, covers them with grain or stubble, scatters wild mustard over them, it may be, and converts them into a weedy desolation. The only attractive looking surface ever to be seen in California, is the native original surface; for there is never to be a lawn, or a neat grassy slope, as with us, because there is no proper turf. Shrubbery itself can never be made ornamental in California, except where there is irrigation to maintain it. Where there is irrigation, a garden or house lot may be covered in with trees and set off with flowers, so as to be really fresh in beauty at all times; but this is not the kind of beauty that makes a landscape. In the mining country, the natural beauty of the scenery is defaced by another process. Here a thin but stately growth of evergreens is sprinkled over the generally graceful slopes and rounds of the hills, and a pure crystal leaps along down the trough of the hills, over cliffs of rock and pebbly beds. But the miner comes. Finding gold that will "pay" in the soil, he rents a head of water from the ditch company, whose ditch bringing on the water from some level far up in the Sierra, flows it along from hill top down to hill top, and across from one hill to another, leaping hollows and ravines on wooden tresselwork, sometimes even two hundred feet high, till it reaches a point abreast of his placer, and directly above it. Bringing it down the hill in immense cotton hose, with a nozzle pipe like that of a fire engine, he plays it into the side of the hill, with a pressure perhaps of one hundred and fifty feet fall; tears down the hill, acre by acre, and floats it off, rolling the loose stones with it down his wooden trunk or sluice, in which the gold is arrested, and so continues, till he has carried off a large section of the hill-side, even a hundred feet deep. His neighbors are doing the same thing right and left. Pits are also sunk downward, and tunnels bored in level into the sides of the hills, and the earth from so many burrows, is piled at their mouths.

The trees are cut down for timber and firewood. The stream of the valley runs thick with creamy richness, and the cliffs and pebbly beds are covered fifty feet deep with stones and mudwashings. The result is a most horrid desolation, of which every line of the natural beauty is gone forever. If some camp of demons had been pitched here for a year, tearing the earth by their fury, and converting it to the model of their own bad thought, they could hardly make it look worse. The whole mining region is finally to become a desolation in just this manner. There is no possibility of a process more delicate for extracting the gold. Indeed there seems to be a kind of prior necessity, which nature must needs recognize, that gold and desolation go together. What we see then, at the mines, only represents too faithfully what holds good historically in the moral desolations of plunder, fraud, and avarice, instigated by this treasure of the mountains. The only part of California, in short, that will not be damaged in its scenery by the arrival of culture, is the broken country of the coast region, or the region of natural pasturage; except that possibly the artesian wells may be carried so far as to irrigate a considerable part of the valley surfaces. Thus while there is almost no stream running through a valley bottom in the summer, because every issue from the mountains sinks immediately into the gravel beds of the plains, and runs under, it may turn out generally, in the narrow valleys, as in that of San José, that artesian wells, sunk two hundred or three hundred feet, will bring it up, spouting into liberty on the surface. Two or three of the wells in this town throw a column nine inches in diameter, ten or fifteen feet high, discharging water enough to turn a mill, and of course to irrigate a large surface.

It will doubtless occur to many, that the dry season of the year, which is the summer, must be a season of utter desolation as regards the scenery. What can be more desolate than a universal dry death? And if the water-runs, or ravines, are green; if the chapparal on some of the mountains, and occasionally trees in the plains, that have the faculty to bore deep for their water, show a semblance of life; if the gardens which are irrigated show a patch of luxuriance here and there, like an oasis in the yellow desert, what after all is the landscape but a desert? Suppose then it were to be covered with snows two or three feet deep, and every solitary thing stripped of its green, would the scenery be less desolate? But this is our winter. The wintry, or suspension time of California is in the summer, and the winter months of the almanac are dressed in the richest, freshest green. And yet the Californians speak of beautiful scenery in the summer, and any one who has been there a few months begins to sympathize with them. Trees and chapparal are stronger marks on the landscape than with us; green spots, such as watered fields and gardens, have a fascinating freshness. And even the dry surfaces, in certain lights, make a picture, by aid of the shadows on the hollow surfaces, and the occasional green of trees and chapparal and gardens, that is really beautiful. The little valley just described, for example, puts off its green and puts on a dress of drab, velvety and soft in the glancing strokes of light, and becomes for all the world a neat Quarker bonnet; only that the deep blue green of the gorges, and the lively green ribands that hang down the water courses are a little too dressy and fantastic, and suggest a case of sumptuary discipline. The most that can be said of the Pacific hybernation time is, that while our winter is absolute, unconquerable désolation, the Californian can go into his garden, turn on the water, make an outdoor green-house of it, filled with all richest fruits and singing birds, and there wait patiently till the months of green return.

The growths of California are as peculiar as their climate. To make this subject intelligible, let it be understood that where there is no irrigation, natural or artificial, nothing grows perennially in California, except trees that have a tap root, and shrubs and grasses that have some peculiar kind of root that enables them to get sufficient moisture, where only a little is given. There is a coarse perennial grass, for example, that is found, when dug, to grow out of perpendicular rootlets eight or ten inches long, which themselves grow out of large horizontal roots, that serve as water cisterns or sponges for the uses overhead. None of the common upland, or hay grasses, live through the summer, and therefore none make what can be called a turf. The grasses of every season are started in November, from the ripe seeds dropped into the chinks of the ground, in the dry season previous. It results accordingly, that no crop can be raised in California which does not ripen before the dry season commences, or by about the first of June. The only exceptions possible to this are made by irrigation, either where water is artificially supplied, or where, as will sometimes be the case, there is a supply from stores, or filterings underneath. It is only under these conditions that crop of Indian corn or potatoes can be raised; though an early crop of potatoes, ripening in June or July, can be raised anywhere; and where the ground is sufficiently moistened from below, two crops a year are frequently grown upon the same soil. Potatoes of the late crop are grown too in some places near the coast, where they get moisture enough from the atmosphere and the fog, to answer their purpose. A summer garden will commonly make but a poor figure, unless it is recruited by supplies of water not contained in the natural soil of the place. The dry season is, in fact, the wintering season of vegetation, though it is the summer. Whatever lives, hybernates, rests. The strawberry, for example, ripens its fruit in April, has its growth, ceases, begins to look rusty, and passes into the state of suspension, finally to die. Let on now a flow of water, and it wakes, blossoms again, bears another crop, and passes into another suspension, and then is ready to be wakened and bear a third crop. And so by alternating in times with different beds, a succession is kept up, and a bountiful supply is obtained from April to November.

The principle growths or products of California are, accordingly, the fruits and the cereals. Most of the fruits really want irrigation, though there are many tracts of soil in which they will flourish without, and will not ripen prematurely. The fruits are grapes, figs, olives, pomegranates, almonds, plums, apricots, pears, peaches and apples. Finer grapes are grown nowhere in the world. The apples are large and fair, and wonderfully precocious in bearing, but there is reason to suspect, from experiments made in the old mission gardens, that they may be short lived. Peaches, plums, and pears bear only too profusely. Indeed, there is a wonderous tendency to fructification in every kind of growth, animal and vegetable. As yet, the fruits sell at enormous prices, because of the shortness of supply. In a very few years they will be plenty and cheap. And even now there is no city on the earth, where the fruit shops make as fine a show as in San Francisco. Considering the size, the fairness, the varieties, and all that goes to make a show of richness and profusion, there is probably nothing in the world to match the displays of fruit in this new city of the Pacific.

But the great agricultural crops of California are the cereals, wheat, and barley, and oats. These are sown at any time, when it is both wet enough and dry enough to plow, between November and March; harvested any time between the ripening of June and the rain-falls of November; for they will stand uninjured, or lie, as left by the reaper, and without shelling, all that time; so that a small force suffices both to raise and to harvest a large crop. And the yield is from twenty to sixty bushels of wheat to the acre, subject to no contingencies but wet and premature drought, which latter only shortens the crop. Even one hundred and forty bushels of barley have been harvested on a single acre. Oats are said to degenerate in the seeding, but we have seen the stalk even twelve feet high. These crops again, will sow themselves for a second crop the next year, and that will yield more than any crop sown in the Western or Atlantic States. Sixty or eighty bushels have been gathered from the volunteer crop of barley. This, in fact, is one of the evils to be encountered by California agriculture, that every crop perpetuates itself as a weed; so that no good wheat crop, for example, can be raised on a field once sown with barley, till the barley is exterminated; and one barleysowing will sometimes yield three or four volunteer crops that are worth havesting. Even potatoes will perpetuate themselves in the same way. Change of crops, therefore, is difficult. When the problem accordingly is raised, how or by what process exhausted soils are to be restored in California, it is not easy now to answer; but some process will be doubtless discovered in due time. In many cases this exhaustion will come to pass slowly; for the good soil is not unfrequently two, and three, and sometimes eight feet deep. A piece of ground sown regularly with wheat for sixteen years, has been known to yield forty bushels and more to the acre. A single deep plowing, probably enough, would make it good for another sixteen years.

As regards the enormous growths of California, it should be understood that they are not ordinary. The ordinary fruits, for example, are not larger than ours, and where the trees are overloaded, are commonly small. The extraordinary growths appear to be easily accounted for. First, there is a soil too deep and rich for any kind of growth to measure it. Next, there is either a natural under-supply of water, or an artificial irrigation. Next, the settings of fruit are limited. And then, as no time is lost in cloudings and rain, and the sun drives on his work unimpeded, month by month, the growth is pushed to its utmost limit. So a pear will occasionally be produced weighing three and a half pounds, or an apple tree, or a cherry will grow a stem ten or twelve feet high in a season. The mammoth turnips, onions, beets and cabbages, depend on a like occurrence. But these are freaks, or extravagances of nature — only they are such as can be equalled nowhere else. The Big Trees depend, in part, on these same contingencies, and partly on the remarkable longevity of their species. A tree that is watered without rain, having a deep vegetable mold in which to stand, and not so much as one hour's umbrella of cloud to fence off the sun for the whole warm season, and a capacity to live withal for two thousand years or more, may as well grow three hundred and fifty or four hundred feet high and twentyfive feet in diameter, and show the very centre point or pith still sound, at the age of thirteen hundred years, as to make any smaller figure with conditions proportionally restricted.

The agricultural capacities of California, it will be seen, are very great as regards the rate and facility of production. The only drawback now experienced is in the want of a reliable and sufficient market. The mines and the cities are now the principal consumers. The result is, that if the product is a little short, the prices rise extravagantly, because there is no other supply. On the other hand, if it is a little over the demand, the prices fall as extravagantly. And then, as the producers are flying always towards that which yields the best reward, every kind of product is likely to be overgrown in its turn, and so the prices become even more capricious, for the reason that they are capricious. When markets are opened by an outside commerce, as they will be, and when all the whaling ships are fitted and sent from San Francisco and Puget Sound, the mischief will be repaired. At present, owing to this caprice of the market, agriculture is scarcely less of a venture than mining.

Accordingly the attention of land-owners is now being turned, more than before, to pasturage. The old Spanish breed of cattle is giving way to the new cultivated breeds most valued here, and large ranges of land are taken up in the hill regions, where immense herds of from one to ten thousand head of cattle are collected, which are yielding a rich revenue to their owners. These herds are kept sometimes wholly without fodder, and generally with very little. They fatten most in the summer, when the feed is dry, and only suffer when the falling rains have rotted the old growth, and have not yet sufficiently started the new. Hence it is common to burn over a considerable portion of the ranges, just before the rains, that the cattle may be able to get access to the first sprouting of the seeds, at the earliest moment possible. The air, accordingly, is filled with smoke for many days; the mountains are flaming round the horizon day and night, as if the last day had come, and horsemen are rushing hither and thither to fight off the fires from the wheat fields and the pastures of the plains. And then the result is, that the yellow, yellow, ever yellow hills that were, as soon as good rain has sprouted the seeds, come forth — green out of black — and the body of the high burnt hill or mountain, is turned to a beryl, without so much as a twig or a weed-stalk, to mar the color. This great interest of pasturage promises even to exceed the plowing interest in importance. The home market for it is equally reliable, and the salted and dried meats, the hides, the tallow, and wool, are products that can take the world for their market.

The culture of the grape, too, promises much. Whether it can be successfully prosecuted without irrigation is doubtful, though it is well known that old, deep rooted vines will bear a crop without. It is commonly believed that California is hereafter to become the great wine growing country of the Pacific.

With so many advantages, it is impossible that California should not become one of the richest countries in the world, on the score of its mere land interest and the products yielded by its soil. It has garnered up also, in the soil itself, treasures that no other can boast. It will take thousand years to wash over all the pay dirt of the gold mines. It is computed also to have, in a single quartz lead, more gold, five times over, than is owned by the whole world; and other veins are being opened, almost every month, which are ready to yield great revenues of profits as soon as they are worked. The quartz mills, once supposed to be a failure, are now so perfected as to yield immense profits, almost without exception. The waters too of the mountains are a great wealth, and the thirty or forty millions already invested in the ditches ought to be yielding a great revenue, as much of it already is. Besides, there are mines of quicksilver, such as make all other mines in the world comparatively worthless; deposits of borax, rocks of alum, hills of sulphur, quarries of marble, beds of coal and of iron — in short, there was never a country so underlaid with treasure of every kind.

The commercial advantages are not yet developed, and will not be, till the Pacific shores are lined with new nations, and the untold riches of their natural resources are brought into the circulations of trade. Even if a railroad were built across the continent, it is not likely that any very great amount of merchandise, or any but the most precious forms of merchandise, would pass that way. Probably there is a greater amount of expectation vested in such an improvement, than the actual experiment will justify. The distance is too great, the grades too heavy, (as heretofore reported,) the running expenses too enormous, to allow the freight of common articles of trade. And yet California is on the great water highway of the Pacific, and her Gate the certain goal of its travel. For it is remarkable that this Golden Gate is at the southmost limb of the variable trade winds, and that these, blowing in a little north of east, will drive a ship directly out to China, directly in from China — whichever way they blow — laying a straight course on one of the great circles of the earth; while immediately south of the Gate the winds begin to change character, and are much less available for sailing purposes, and continue to be so, even down as far in the south latitude as to Valparaiso. Thus to sail a ship up the western coast of the continent, from Panama to San Francisco, would probably require a whole summer, and even that might not suffice for the passage. No ship can ever approach that shore by sail without falling into a contest with currents, which the light baffling winds and doldrums make it difficult to maintain with success. To get in is difficult, to get away more difficult. And hence perhaps it is, at least in part, that one may pass down that whole stretch of coast, a distance of three thousand miles, in one of the California steamers, and actually not see on the passage so much as a rag of sail of any description. On the other hand, at Puget Sound, the only available harbor ground on the north, the winds blow off the coast with such violence that vessels after pounding there for weeks together, till the crews were quite worn out, have returned to San Francisco to fit for a new trial. Besides in the winter-trades, which are from the northeast, a vessel sailing from China for the Sound will have the whole distance to make with a wind directly against her; while she might lay her course for San Francisco and straight in, without once shifting her sails.

Nature, it will thus be seen, has set her seal on San Francisco, appointing it to be the great commercial centre of that coast and ocean. Here rests the future axis of motion. Indeed it is hardly extravagant to imagine that, in some distant age, when the enterprise and resources of that ocean, with its islands and coasts, are fully developed, the Atlantic commerce will be a thing by the way, an affair of the outskirts.

All such expectation, it is obvious, must depend, in a great degree, on the political and moral condition of California. And here one very great danger happily is already past, viz.; the introduction of human slavery. There is no State in the Union where slavery could be worked to greater advantage than in California. Connected with this fact, we have also the concomitant fact, that the office holders and political operators of the State have very generally been men from the south. To understand, therefore, even after the fact, how it is that slavery is excluded, is what any stranger will accomplish with the greatest difficulty. No inquiries he can make will quite solve the riddle. Some have spoken of the known weight of laboring and money making classes being always opposed to slavery, and silently constraining the politicians, who were not, to respect their position. Some have ascribed much to the personal influence of Colonel Fremont. Others have given the credit of the fact mainly to Captain Halleck, sometimes called the father of the constitution, a gentleman of weight and capacity, who is known to have been the draughtsman of many of its provisions, but has since that time given himself wholly to his profession as a lawyer, and withdrawn himself altogether from the game of political life. Be it as it may, slavery is forever excluded from California, and so from that whole coast; and that without even so much as a word of debate; for this article of the constitution was simply read and passed by consent, in absolute silence. What a fact of history, this, to be the child of silence!

California unites in its population great elements of diversity. The fifty thousand or sixty thousand of Chinese simply stay as foreigners. The native Californian or Spanish race, comprises gentlemen of real respectability, wealth, and character; but the inferior class of herdsmen and retainers that were, are more wild and vicious, and really more hopeless, than before the change of masters. They live on horseback, without contracting any friendship with their horses, which might raise them a little. They are cruel to animals of all kinds, cowardly to superiors, ignorant, superstitious, frivolous, with little prospect of being advanced to anything better hereafter.

A considerable part of the emigration to California since we took possession, is made up of persons from the extreme west, who crossed over by the plains — the class who are called Border Ruffians with us, and which there are called, more or less derisively, Pikes, from Pike county in Missouri. They are by no means any such desperate or ruffian class of people as they are just now commonly regarded here. They are, for the most part, uncultivated and rough, crude in their notions of religion, and like all such people, coarse in their prejudices; but they have great honesty and frankness, their impulses are strong, and generally magnanimous. They really contain the staple qualities or possibilities of a high character. They have true manhood, which is not to be said of every people.

Another element of the emigration is from the southern and southwestern States, comprising many gentlemen with their families, who are a great accession to the society and manners of the cities, and particularly of San Francisco; and with these a much larger, or at least noisier class of broken down politicians, who have fled, as it were, to California, to farm the voters and offices of a new world, where their stock of capital has not yet been exhausted. The former class comprise men who appear, like Mr. Stanly, to have emigrated rather to get away from political life, and to apply themselves to other pursuits. The latter, trained to public speaking and the management of assemblies, and having this for their trade, have hitherto been able to obtain almost all the offices of the State, and have distributed the rewards of office to themselves, in a scale of unexampled liberality. Happily there was an end to the credit of the State, and that limit has been finally reached. The bankrupt people, too, are beginning to ask questions they had no time to ask before; competitors also are coming into the field, whose morality and trustworthiness in other relations have been already proved. The dynasty of plunder, therefore, is rapidly coming to an end.

Another large class of the emigration is from New England, New York and the middle and north-western States. And these again are in two classes. First, the merchants, bankers, lawyers, engineers, surveyors, and many of the head miners — men who have come to California as to a field of enterprise, and who bend all their energies to the particular personal calling that engages them. Secondly, a class of reprobates in all styles and degrees, who find their way to California just because they are not wanted anywhere. These are the fugitives from justice, the absconding bigamists, the felons and prisonbirds who want a new field where they are not known, defalcators, pimps, shoulder-strikers and prize fighters, drunkards, sons that could not be endured at home, and vagabond gentlemen whose friends have been willing to escape the burden of their support, by giving them an outfit for some very distant region. These and such like characters were turned for a time, in shoals, upon California. But the pistol, the knife, the halter, bad liquors, and the Vigilance Committees are scattering them rapidly and killing them off. They flourished for a time, as the under-fighters and ballot-box operators of the politician class just referred to; assuming the alliance to be one of natural good-fellowship, inasmuch as they too use the tools of honor themselves. But their trade is gone; they cannot even be drunk in the streets, or draw a knife out of their pocket, without a painfully certain prospect of appearing in the chain gang the next morning. Meantime, the former and better class above named, with many of the better class from the South, are building churches, organizing institutions, looking after charities, and showing more and more distinctly that the great hope of California is in them. They will even consent to serve on juries, and some of them also to be named for public offices of trust and power, which formerly they would not. Time is giving them the controlling position, as by a kind of necessary process, and even compelling them to assume it.

The composition, or the combined elements of the emigration, it will be seen, are not favorable to the immediate coalescence of the new state, in terms of order and public virtue. Besides a good many hostile influences of a more special character, it will be easy to perceive, concur in detaining or holding back the new community, from the kind of civil administration necessary to its good name and social comfort.

Thus, in the mining towns, are gathered large bodies of men, without wives or children, living as cenobites in their dens, and no one needs to be informed that men, living separately from women, are sure to make a large stride towards barbarism. The occupation of mining is also more adventurous in itself, than consists with the best habits of application; for if the digging is a venture, why should there not be a venture at the gaming table, without the digging? It is not unfrequent that the placer mining gives out, and it is known to be always more or less precarious. Hence many of the towns are mere encampments, and are called "camps." And some that assumed to be more are already given up and nearly forsaken. Hence the miners become more or less migratory themselves, and their towns are too nearly so, many of them, to be much cared for, either in the building, or in the establishment of social and religious institutions. A stranger, too, will see a very distinct and significant character in the names given to places; such as Yankee Jim, Fiddletown, Jackass' Gulch, Whisky Bar, and a whole hundred names, of which these are the choicer specimens. It appears to be the general opinion, that there is a decided moral and social improvement in the mining population. But one who has attended church for two Sundays, in a mining town of the very first order, finding about forty persons present to hear a good Christian sermon, and passing in the street when returning from church, in both cases full five hundred men, who had rushed together as spectators of a street fight, will hardly think it possible that there should have been a very great moral improvement there.

Agriculture, too, has been connected in California with unwonted and even wholly peculiar causes of moral deterioration. The titles to land have many of them been so uncertain, or so far unsettled by frauds and charges of fraud, that there has been a natural reluctance in emigrants to incur the risk of a loss, in purchasing the soil. Hence, also in part, the very peculiar kind of squatting that has come into vogue in California and probably a full half of the agriculture of the State, either now or at some former time, has been carried on as an operation of squatting in this manner, viz., by taking possession of lands generally known to be vested in private owners by title derived from the Mexican government, and not in the United States as in other new territories, where the laws of Congress authorize the occupation and make it a legitimate act. An American purchaser, for example, buys one of the old Mission properties, comprising a tract seven or eight miles square, of the very best land in California, and everybody knows the title to be perfect, because the land has been held and occupied by the Mission for more than fifty years. He expends over $100,000 in fencing it, and the property rises in value so rapidly, that he begins to be rated and to rate himself as being worth, at least a million dollars. But behold, a cloud of squatters suddenly appears pouring in upon his lands, squatting inside of his fences and among his wheat, erecting their tents or huts, and leaving him to pay the taxes, while they reap the harvests. He is now the bankrupt purchaser, and they are the occupants, till at least six or eight years of litigation, terminated at Washington, have established the title to his creditors, which everybody knew was in himself. Meantime they have gotten the use of the rent for so many years, which is to them a handsome outfit. The old native Californians are treated in the same way. No chapter of wrong and oppression, in which our countrymen have had their part, is more sad or revolting. Even between the old ranchero's house and wall, the squatter has taken his post and set up his hut. Then, assuming also that the cattle are wild, as that the lands are public, the squatter wanting a steak has taken his rifle and killed an ox. And so the poor herdsman has been stripped both of lands and herds, by the remorseless Sabeans, and that with airs of indignity and low-bred consequence more difficult to bear than the robberies themselves. The truculent savage spirit generated by these land-piracies, will be readily understood. The tragedy of young Suñole is happily an extreme instance. He was a gentleman, educated as we have heard in Paris, equal if not superior to most of the educated Americans. But he ventured to remonstrate very gently with a squatter for cutting down the trees of his father's exquisite valley, and selling them for wood, giving him liberty at the same time, to cut what he wanted for himself; but the next time he passed by, on his way over the ranch in company with a friend, the savage came out with his rifle, got him in range as he threw himself over the side of his horse, and drew him dead to the ground. Sheltered and secreted by others like himself, he could never be found. As the titles are now being settled by the decisions of the courts, the squatters are gradually yielding to the law and becoming purchasers. All these wrongs will gradually be a thing of the past.

By the very latest advices, it appears that the squatter combination is just beginning to yield some respect to the decisions of law. Heretofore the owners, in establishing their title, have commonly got possession, but only a right to pay the taxes. Indeed, this third estate of squatterdom had sufficient power in the legislature, two years ago, to get a law enacted requiring owners, when dislodging or ejecting them, to pay for the improvements according to the appraisal of a committee from the precinct; a plan by which they expected to get back the value of the land, for the appraisers would be squatters almost of course. Happily the courts would not execute the law. And but a year since, the venerable patriarch of the Napa valley, who came over from Missouri as a trapper more than forty years ago, having finally established his old homestead title, comprising eight or ten thousand acres of the best land in the State, was evidently beginning also to find a much harder question on his hands, viz., how to move the squatters without periling his life. And yet, among the land-pirates called squatters, are a great many persons from the East, and even from Massachusetts and Connecticut; and what is more, from our Christian churches; and some of them appear even now to be seriously minded and conscientious in their life. Because the same word, *squatter*, is used to designate this known act of robbery, (for it is often such and nothing else,) they really suppose that they are doing the same lawful and right thing, which is practiced under the acts of Congress, in the West.

As the mining and agriculture of California appear, thus far, to have been connected with unpropitious moral influences, so also it has been, even to a much greater degree, with the trade of politics. Composed of elements so various and repellant, it was not to be expected, for a time, that there would be much confidence in public men or proceedings. And the moral character of the political operators and office holders, was generally of a kind not to inspire confidence. They were gamblers, debauchees, drunkards, men who lined their bosoms not with virtue, but with knives and pistols. They were just such men, in short, as could never be in confidence, even if they violated no trust. The bullies they had in their employ, as inspectors of the ballot, could not swear to a true count and be believed. Juries were distrusted, because the panel was so easily made up, to include one whom the criminal on trial might "hang" to stand out for him in the verdict. The judges were such characters that they plainly ought to be bribed, if they were not. Administrators and trustees were suspected, as being appointed by the connivance of judges. Legislators and governors were distrusted also. This distrust became, in due time, a torment to the public peace, by its uncertainty; and none the less a torment that the worst rumors and suspicions were most likely to be true; till finally everything bad began to be true; and the public prints made it a point of heroism in dealing out their accusations with unsparing boldness. A stranger could hardly guess what it meant. Every print was for California. Nothing too laudatory could be said for it; meanwhile, as if a paradasaic whole could be made up of diabolical particulars, the sweeping denunciations of individuals appeared to leave no honest man in it. And what was more remarkable in all these accusations, was that every charge made against judges or others of bribery or of fraud was given circumstantially; names, dates, amounts, agents, all stated with exactness. Probably a very considerable share of these charges of bribery, and perjury, and fraud, were true. But the misery was, that no one could guess which. Society was dissolved and law was reduced to an instrument of suspicion. It was a state most bitter and even horrible. Whether their facts were only suspicions and rumors converted into facts by repetition, or real and veritable truths of history; whether it was the licentiousness of the press or its uncommon fidelity, or whether, possibly, it was not all the fatality which attends every community where confidence is gone, no one could know, or satisfactorily judge. Be it as it may, out of this general distrust and demoralization came the Vigilance Committee. It was raised by the torture that exasperates society when confidence is gone. So far not to sympathize with it is impossible, and the more that almost all the better citizens were in it.

Even Christian professors left the church and the communion to be in the outbreak, and to bear arms in that vast congregation, gathered as a thunder-cloud round the jail, on the distant hill side.

It is not our design to discuss the Committee. Suffice it to say that their intent was good, their proceedings honest and carefully deliberate, and their military conduct admirably decisive and efficient. Their great fault was that they did not see their point exactly, and offered reasons for their action a great deal worse than their action. If they had undertaken, not to administer the laws, or take them back into their own hands, but to restore the laws by plucking down the usurpers, who stood in no right of law, being elected only by the perjury of the inspectors, their question would have been greatly simplified. Then, because of the almost impossibility of convicting the perjured inspectors, by any ordinary proceedings of law, they would only have done it by extraordinary; and it would have been all the better if, to make a due impression of this crime, as the greatest of all crimes, they had sacked the whole tribe, be they many or few, and sunk them in the bottom of the Bay. Doing this, instead of resuming functions, the right of which strikes at the root of all constitutional government, they need only have insisted on some extraordinary means of restoring functions already taken away. The whole experiment was critical, more critical than our eastern communities know; for there was a time, a terrible twelve hours, just after the release of Judge Terry, when the question of a new Executive Committee, who should be more efficient and bolder, i. e., more bloody, was pending and apparently just ready to be carried by the whirlwind of passion outside, which new committee, if it had not been dexterously avoided, would have been like the new committee of Paris, and similar scenes would probably have followed. The escape was narrow; so narrow that if the leading gentlemen concerned had now the question of a new Vigilance Committee on hand, they would probably hesitate long. And yet it must be granted for the honor of this same questionable, perilous adventure of reform, that San Francisco is probably now the best governed city in the Union. The laws are now enforced, the economies are duly attended to, there is no plunder, and every evil doer stands in fear. It is the beginning, apparently, of a great moral reaction, which is felt by the whole State. Whatever may be true, therefore, of this great popular movement, whether it is right or wrong, wise or unwise, it will be impossible ever to turn it as a reproach on the certainly patriotic men who were foremost in it. They are much more likely to be celebrated hereafter, with Harmodius and Aristogiton, and other great leaders of mutiny that have been deliverers of their country.

We state these facts concerning the moral aspects of mining; the occupation by force of lands known to be held by legal right; and the usurpations, and perjuries, and briberies of political intriguers and demagogues, connected with the general destruction of confidence, and the necessary throes of violence by which they must inevitably be redressed, not as being, in themselves, any picture of California. We know they are not. They are only facts, without which any description is rose colored and without sound verity — such facts as will meet a stranger first, because they are most outstanding and impressive. And for this the reader will make due allowance, even as in reading history; for it is not the virtues, and the smooth and silent flowings of goodness that make up ever the staple of history, but the explosive wrongs and outrages rather, by which the evenness of good was disturbed. For ourselves, we regard these facts not with any feelings of despair or discouragement. On the contrary, we perceive a certain sublimity in the contest here begun, and the clearing process going forward, which creates appetite to us. We know the certain victory, we see it coming, and we envy especially those young heroic spirits who have set themselves, in the love of God and their newly adopted State, to such works of duty and sacrifice as are necessary to the sublime future they have in prospect.

Opposite to these facts we have stated others which awaken our respect and inspire our confidence. They have a good and able ministry, for example, such a ministry as will compare favorably, in all denominations, with any of the older States. They have churches in every denomination, not inferior to the churches here. The attendance is good, especially in the cities, and the order, the dress, the music, are only too much evened by the manner of the East.

The Sabbath also is becoming a more established institution, and to be without a Sabbath, as a day of rest, is more and more distinctly felt to be an oppression. And therefore the traders and shopkeepers, in most of the country villages, are petitioning the Legislature, more earnestly every year, for the establishment of a complete suspension of trade.

Education is not forgotten. The towns and cities are allowed by statute to tax themselves for this purpose, and many of them do it most liberally. The public schools of San Francisco are not inferior to those of our Eastern cities — many think them even superior.

There is no reason to apprehend any loss of natural vigor and tone from the climate on that shore. Some have taken it as a bad indication that the Digger Indians (the aboriginals of California) are the most spiritless and abject of all known tribes on the continent, and about the lowest specimens of humanity found upon the earth. But this may be sufficiently accounted for by the general softness of the climate and the fact that they have never been required to feed themselves by the manly exploits of a hunter life; having always at hand enough of bugs, and fish, and sugar pine bark, to serve their purpose. Sometimes also a degree of discouragement has been derived from the analogical or symbolical fact, that there is not a stick of smart, hard timber in all California; nothing out of which an axe-handle, or a spoke, or a felloe could be made; every hardest, soundest tree, being brittle to such a degree (*"brash,"* they say in California, and in New England *"spalt,"*) that the trunk will probably break asunder five or six times when it is felled, and lie as a pile of fragments on the ground, even though it is three feet in diameter. Is this a natural token, some have asked with a little feeling of superstition, that the future men of California are to be only a brittle or brash stock, and without any real timber of endurance in them? Why any more a token than the giant pines, and redwoods, and cedars, are a token of prodigiously tall men, a race at least twelve or fifteen feet high? Why any more than the often naked hills and plains are a token of no men at all? What other sign do we in fact require that all the future stock of California will be a stock of high capacity, than that the climate is healthy, the growths bountiful, and that we are capable ourselves of the greatest endurance there, both bodily and mental, and have, in fact, a sense of robustness that we have nowhere else?

At the same time it requires no gift of prophecy to perceive in the physical resources and commercial advantages of the country, that an immense wealth is, in due time, to be developed there; such wealth as will give vigor to all institutions and works that require expense, and put everything on a scale of breadth and magnificence. If there is any country in the world where the future men are not to be cramped and whittled by close restrictions, it is California. At present the Californians say that they are poor; they feel poor, because they are now at the dead point of retrocession, where their extravagant expectations are being shortened in for that second beginning which every new State and city has to make. And yet there is nothing more wonderful, with all this depression, than the amount of wealth already created on that shore. How many thousand years of day labor, has it taken simply to build so many houses, fences, shops, steamers, ditches, towns, and cities. Three of these cities, San Francisco, Sacramento, and Marysville, have so much of city life and character that we hardly recognize their newness. And yet only nine years have passed since all this immense wealth began to be created! — and that five thousand miles away, on the shore, as it were, of another continent.

There is good and cultivated society in California such as there never has been in any other State in the Union. The number of liberally educated men is greater by far than was ever found in any other State twice the same political age. Carpets, good beds, clean tables, bright knives and forks, courtesy, hospitality, public entertainments and pleasures on a footing of civilizotion — all these indications of comfort and society are widely diffused. One sign or token of this kind we cannot forbear to mention, because it signifies much. Passing hither and thither on the little steamers, up to Marysville, to Stockton, to the towns north of the bay, where often the number ef passengers did not exceed thirty, we have seen, again and again, a table most neatly set, the silver bright and clean, the meats well prepared and good, without any nonsense of show dishes, the servants tidy, quiet, and respectful — in short, the whole figure of the entertainment more rational and better than we have ever seen, either on the boats of the Mississippi or the Atlantic coast. Such facts indicate society, more than any most splendid entertainment gotten up by private opulence can.

One other consideration must be named, if California is to be well understood, viz: that with all the violence and savage wrongs, and dark vices that have heretofore abounded there, they seldom do a mean thing. They can perpetrate real atrocities, but they must be generous. A considerable part of their blameable profusions comes of their extreme jealousy of littleness, or meanness. Men really poor will often share their last dollar in helping a sick friend, or even a sick stranger. If a poor minister, whom they have only seen at their funerals, is known to be on short allowance, they will have a ticketed supper, not unlikely, to him; which, if it is not the best way of establishing religion, does at least show their generosity. If a preacher asks the privilege of addressing them in a gambling saloon, on Sunday, they are very likely to accede, to hear him respectfully, pass round a hat and make up a liberal purse for him, then put down their stakes and resume their play! The recent vote of the people to assume and pay the State debt was an act of pure magnanimity. Here was a debt of $5,000,000, the creation of which was expressly forbidden by the Constitution of the State. This provision of the Constitution was known, discussed, openly understood, and the loan was obtained directly in the face of it. The money, too, had gone for nothing but to feed the political vampires for whose plunder it was raised; and the State has not a vestige of property to show for it, but some old benches that belonged to the State House at Vallejo. If then a people have any right, by Constitution, to guard themselves against being plundered by their rulers, the people of California had a right to stand upon the restriction so prudently established in their Constitution, and were under no obligations, whether of right or of honor, to pay this debt — to refuse was no act of repudiation. But their instincts were too generous, they had too much pride of feeling to insist on their right. Where Mississippi raised a quibble to get off her honest debt, California took a gratuitous obligation to get it on, and to fasten it.

There remains a single topic to which, in the conclusion of our article, already too far extended, we must briefly refer, viz: to the effort now on foot to establish a College or University in California. The heaviest detraction, after all, from the future prospects of California, is in the fact that so many only go thither as adventurers, not meaning to stay, and that so many, often the most prosperous, are continually returning. And they do it, in great part, because they cannot educate their families there, as their means allow them to desire. In the first place, many never take out their families for this reason, and in the next place, when they have done it, and their sons are grown up to the age at which they begin to want the best advantages, they return with them, and are so lost to the State as a family; for the distance, and the moral perils of a separation from parents are so great, that there is no alternative but a reemigration. This begets an unsettled feeling in those who remain, which makes them careless often of the good of the State, and besides it carries off a large percentage of the wealth created; for the families that return are commonly such as have been most successful, and all which they have gained they carry with them. And the probability is, that if the contemplated railroad were built across the continent, (which it will not be for a long time to come,) it would scarcely help them at all, but might rather hasten them in this losing process.

What they want, therefore, at this time, above all things else, is a good College, or University. Such an institution would do more to consolidate and settle their State, and to settle the confidence of their future, than even the railroad itself. There are no five States together, in our western world, which, if they had none at all, would want an institution of this kind so much as California. For the supply of this want, some of their best and ablest men are preparing. They have had a charter for three years, organizing the "College of California." Their Board of Trustees contains a representation of all the Christian denominations, who are united in cordiality and good understanding. They are said lately to have fixed on their site — on the eastern side of the Bay, opposite San Francisco. They have had a preparatory school for three years past, under the tuition of Rev. Henry Durant, an accomplished scholar and a Christian, and the design is to organize a Freshman Class the coming autumn.

What then is now wanted is the endowment, and for this everything is ready. To obtain this endowment in California, except in part, will now be impossible. Much of the wealth is not in the right hands; and where it is not, where there is every disposition to aid, the possibility is very much reduced by the heavy loads of debt, which many who ought to be rich are required just now to carry. When money will bring three per cent. per month, year by year, on perfect security, the lending party is not likely to put much of it in a College, and the borrowing party still less. Are there no great men in the East, no millionaires or less in computation, who will be induced to look at such an opportunity? Had we the fortune of but half a million in our editorial hands, we are quite sure of this, that whoever might want to assume the endowment of such an institution would have to be very quick in his action, or he would lose the chance. What an opportunity for a man of fortune, who has no object in life, no family to provide for, or none but such as are already rich enough, and who would be greatly more ennobled, by his name and example, as the founder of such an institution, than by all his property without a name. How many such, too, are there, who are really meaning, when they die, to accomplish some great work with their money! Why not do it when they are living, and have a satisfaction of a consciousness enriched, and a heart enlarged by their beneficence? To have one's name on such an institution as this, connected with the great history, and with all the learning, and all the most forward influences of this New World on the Pacific, is a thought which might quicken the blood even of a man most sluggish and dull. For it is to win a greater honor, by many times, than the President of our great Republic. That is an honor, which, as the line grows longer, loses more and more its significance, till finally, it will signify as little to have been one of the Presidents as to have been one of the Doges of Venice. But the other, like the names of Harvard and Yale, will brighten and gather to itself a greater weight and power, as long as the tongue itself may exist. And the satisfaction one may have in this honor is sublimely justified in the fact, that he is not merely to be known, or mentioned in the future ages of the world — that might be a very common ambition, for who is there who does even naturally desire as much? — but is permitted to know that his name is to be a power, and to work for all the coming ages, growing brighter and doing more good than he himself while living. That is a legitimate and glorious ambition — the highest that a mortal can cherish. The Trustees, in the Appeal they published a year ago, placed the subject thus:

"Could some rich citizen, who can do it without injury to himself, step forward at this time of our beginning, and set his name upon the institution itself, by the side of a Harvard or a Yale, by subscribing a large part of the proposed endowment; giving us an opportunity, assisted by his beginning and example, to carry up the subscription even to the highest point we have named, he would be enriched by the sense of his munificence, as no man ever was or can be by the count of his money. We have no delicacy in respect to the customary honors conferred by universities, when they set the names of the benefactors on the halls, libraries and professorships endowed by their munificence; or when they drop the dry, impersonal name of their charter for one that represents the public spirit, and the living heart of a living man who could be more than rich, the patron of learning, the benefactor and father of coming ages. There are monuments that may well provoke a degree of ambition; not even an Egyptian pyramid raised over a man's ashes could so far ennoble him, as to have the learning and science of long ages and eternal realms of history superscribed to his name. And yet this better kind of monument is itself a power so beneficent, that he ought, even as duty, to desire it, and for no false modesty decline it. Such monuments are not like those of stone or brass, which simply stand doing nothing; they are monuments eternally fruitful, showing to men's eyes and ears what belongs to wealth, and what the founders of the times gone by have set as examples of beneficence."

www.ingramcontent.com/pod-product-compliance
Lightning Source LLC
Chambersburg PA
CBHW070442090526
44586CB00046B/1630